Clear Thinking

A Practical Introduction

Hy Ruchlis

with Sandra Oddo

Foreword by Isaac Asimov

Prometheus Books
Buffalo, New York

Illustrations by

ALBERT SARNEY: Figures 2.3, 2.4, 2.6, 3.2, 3.4, 3.5, 4.2, 5.1, 5.4, 5.6, 6.1, 6.2, 6.3, 7.2, 8.1, 8.2
ARNOLD LOBEL: Figures 3.1, 3.3, 4.7, 5.2, 5.5, 6.4, 8.3, 10.1, 10.3, 10.4
IRVING LAZARUS: Figures 4.1, 4.3, 4.4, 4.6, 6.5, 7.1, 7.3, 10.2
ALICE WENGROW: Figures 2.5, 4.5, 5.3

Published 1990 by Prometheus Books

Library of Congress Cataloging-in-Publication Data

Ruchlis, Hyman.
    Clear thinking : a practical introduction / by Hy Ruchlis, with Sandra Oddo.
        p.   cm.
    Includes bibliographical references.
    Includes index.
    Summary: Discusses reasoning and clear thinking, including such aspects as the nature of facts, language and reasoning, false analogies, and prejudice.
        ISBN 0-87975-594-6
        1. Thought and thinking—Young adult literature. [1. Thought and thinking. 2. Reasoning.] I. Oddo, Sandra. II. Title.
    LB1590.3.R82   1990
    370.15′2—dc20
                                                                        90-35711
                                                                        CIP

Printed in the United States of America on acid-free paper.

Foreword

There are at least two million species of organisms alive on Earth today. There have probably been twenty million species that lived in times past and are now extinct. Of all these millions, the human species, *Homo sapiens,* is the only one, as far as we can tell, that is capable of complex and even abstract reasoned thought. All of us, every one of us, if he or she approaches normality, can do it. It is part of our badge of humanity. Indeed, it is our only *true* badge of humanity since in no other characteristic are we truly unique and supreme among all species, living or extinct.

Why, then, is there a need for a book that will tell us how to think? Because although we all *can* think, we can't all think *clearly,* and the title of this book is not *Thinking* but is *Clear Thinking.*

Unfortunately, few human beings think clearly. And as a matter of fact, even those few who do may manage at times, for one reason or another, to fall into the trap of thinking foolishly. I need not point to others in this impeachment. I present you with—myself.

Every Tuesday I devote the time from 9 A.M. to 3 P.M. to seeing publishers and to attending a luncheon club of which I am president. It is a cherished routine with me. Now some Tuesdays are sunny and some are cloudy, rainy, sleety, or snowy. Some Tuesdays are mild and some are very cold or very hot.

When a Tuesday is reasonably pleasant, I pay no attention to it. It does not intrude on my notice. On the other hand, when it is unpleasant in any fashion, I am very aware of it, and my emotions vary from anger to misery. If there should be two bad Tuesdays in a row, I begin to feel very misused, and if there are three bad Tuesdays in five weeks, I begin to tell everyone that "it's always bad weather on Tuesdays." When a bright and pleasant Tuesday comes, I feel betrayed somehow: it's *supposed* to be nasty, and if it is pleasant, it is destroying my belief that "it is nasty every Tuesday."

Now I know as well as you do, or as anyone does, that the days of the week are purely artificial constructions invented by human beings and that the natural influences that govern the weather are not controlled by the weekday. I know as well as you do, or as anyone does, that if the weather forecasts were gone over for years past it would turn out that all days of the week experience just about the same types of distribution of weather in the long run. No one weekday is rainier or sunnier than any other—and can't be.

Then why do I insist that Tuesdays are always nasty? Because it makes me feel better to think that the universe is persecuting me; because it heightens my feeling of drama; because then when I wake up on Tuesdays and find the heavens dripping I can say triumphantly, "See!"

In other words, to be a devotee of clear thinking sometimes deprives you of pleasure.

Or, again, what if someone tries to interest you in a business deal? You don't know him and you don't know if he's to be trusted. In order to find out, the best way would be to consult people who have known him and dealt with him, to obtain bank references and other business information, to consult a lawyer on how best to defend your own interests, and so on. From all the evidence you obtain, you can reason out your wisest and safest course of action.

But why go to all that trouble, when all you have to do is to notice that his eyes are set close together and that this is an infallible sign that a man can't be trusted? Or else, it may be that it is his small, slick mustache that can't be trusted. Or, on the other hand, he may happen to look something like a movie star who always plays heroic roles, and so he just couldn't be mistrusted. It's a lot easier that way.

So you see, if you want to indulge in clear thinking, you have to be willing to go to a lot of trouble over such things as collecting and weighing evidence, reasoning correctly, and so on. It's so much easier to snatch at a generalization, even if you have to make one up yourself.

We even have New Age thinking, with that great philosopher Shirley MacLaine assuring everyone that truth is subjective, that some particular piece of nonsense is *your* truth and it doesn't have to match up with anyone else's truth. This instantly wipes out that one marvelous faculty humanity owns, renders thought worthless, and reduces us to the non-human level.

It is because so many people are in the habit of thinking muddily, thinking stereotypically, thinking emotionally, and of being cajoled into doing so by knaves, that there is so much trouble in the world today—so much hatred, cruelty, and misery.

Because fakers and charlatans offer people the lure of easy thinking, they are followed avidly by the public. Millions of people listen gullibly to the astrologers, the spoon-benders, the mindreaders, the spiritualists, the cultist, and all the other shoddy retailers of nonsense. And it is the habit of easy, emotional pseudo-thought that makes it so hard to wean people from this sort of folly.

Those who preach this nonsense make a great deal of money. Those who listen to them lose the money and gain nothing but illusion.

It may be argued that believing in nonsense—in astrology, for instance— gives you a greater feeling of assurance in your dealings with the world; that following some cultist's peculiar beliefs makes you feel that God loves you and all is well. What's wrong with doing what makes you feel good?

You might also argue that crack and heroin make you feel good. Does that justify the use of drugs?

False thought may make you feel good, but in the long run it contributes to the misery and anguish of the world, so that all of us will end by being part of an unhappy and, perhaps, dying society. It is a kind of drug more dangerous and insidious than any that primarily affect the physical body.

Clear thought is the only salvation, and here is Hy Ruchlis with an excellent book that, clearly and effectively, shows you what the rules are. It may well change your life. If everyone reads it, it might well change society. For the better, in both cases.

Isaac Asimov

Acknowledgments

Clear Thinking, originally published in 1962 by Harper and Row, had long been out of print when a letter from Richard Siegelman, a teacher at the Roosevelt School in Oyster Bay, New York, was forwarded to me by the publisher. How could he get a copy of the book to use as a source of ideas for lessons with his classes of gifted children?

Discussions with Mr. Siegelman about how he planned to use the book led me to revise *Clear Thinking* substantially and bring it up-to-date. I wish now to express my deep appreciation to Mr. Siegelman for initiating this revision.

My deep gratitude also goes to Sandra Oddo, who worked on the revision with me and made significant contributions to its approach and content.

It is customary for authors to acknowledge the sacrificial forbearance of a spouse during the difficult days of writing a book, or even rewriting one. But in my case, I really could not have completed the work without the absolutely essential assistance of Elsie Ruchlis, my wife and beloved companion for fifty-six years. I consider this book the result of a partnership, which included not only the easing of family responsibilities, but also vital editorial assistance and advice, as needed.

Steven L. Mitchell of Prometheus Books, who edited what I thought would be a final version of *Clear Thinking,* made many excellent suggestions for improvement, which I was happy to incorporate into the book.

And when that was done, my daughter Carol Ember, Professor of Anthropology at Hunter College in New York City, made a vital contribution by suggesting a number of sources of information that enhanced presentation of the concepts in the book.

All books are written in the hope that they might contribute to a "better world." These words are said so often that they become trite; nevertheless, they express the truth. I would not have undertaken to write and later revise *Clear Thinking* had I not believed that it might produce some small improvement in the ability of our society to cope with the many complex problems we confront. To express this hope, I dedicate this book to the generation that followed me, represented by Michael and Jan Ruchlis, Carol and Mel Ember, and to my granchildren, Annalisa Ruchlis and Julie and Kathy Ember. Along with the many good things in life my generation has bequeathed to them, we have also left them many difficult problems to solve.

My generation, now moving off the scene, did the best it could. But those who follow will have to do much better, and they need to think very clearly to meet that grave responsibility.

Hy Ruchlis
April 1990

Contents

1

The Importance of Clear Thinking

The sergeant at the nuclear missile base in the Arctic looked at the radar screen intently, then called to his captain in a quiet but tense voice. "Looks like a flock of missiles heading this way from the north."

The captain hurried over, glanced at the screen, then lifted the telephone and put through a call to his commanding officer. Meanwhile, a number of top officers had gathered around the screen.

Someone tried to put through a call to headquarters. His face blanched as he reported, "Can't get a call through, sir."

Was the phone call not getting through because nuclear bombs had already dropped on Washington? Did the moving dots on the screen mean that more nuclear bombs were on the way to wipe out their base and others?

Could these few men at a remote base take the terrible responsibility of pressing the buttons that would start our own nuclear bombs hurtling toward Soviet bases and cities?*

Suppose they guessed wrong and pressed the buttons. They would have started World War III and the extinction of hundreds of millions of people. For a moment the fate of the world depended on the ability of these men to think clearly.

Suddenly, the commanding officer uttered three simple words, which instantly supplied a missing fact that resolved the dilemma.

"Where is Khrushchev?" asked the commanding officer.

"In New York City, at the United Nations meeting," came the reply.

This one new fact saved the day, and perhaps the world. The Russians

---

*The account of this incident was pieced together from newspaper reports during 1961 and 1962. Details about the incident have been fictionalized for the purpose of this presentation, but there is little doubt that an incident of this kind occurred.

surely would not send off nuclear missiles to the United States while their head of state was within our borders.

This logical deduction was made by reasoning from facts stored in the human memory. The ability to reason logically enabled the officers at the base to conclude that the dots on the screen did not mean that missiles were coming. Something else was causing the dots to appear.

Later, an investigation of this incident indicated that the dots were probably caused by reflections of radar waves from the moon, then low in the sky. And the cut-off of communications with headquarters? That was due to a temporary breakdown of the communications system. As occasionally happens in real life, two uncommon events occurred at the same time.

This unusual incident illustrates the importance of clear thinking during a situation in which acting on a wrong judgment might have caused the outbreak of World War III and the destruction of civilization as we know it.

Few decisions humans make have such potentially drastic consequences, but each day we are called upon to make similar judgments. It is the purpose of this book to provide some basic principles of clear thinking and illustrate how they may be applied to avoid falling prey to many kinds of improper reasoning. Learning and using these principles may help improve reasoning ability, especially in solving the problems encountered in everyday situations.

HUMAN REASONING POWER

A panther can run much faster than a man on foot. Though lacking a gun or other such weapon, a lion can fight much better than a human. A bird possesses the extraordinary ability to fly. But there is one big advantage that humans have over all other creatures. We human beings have superior brain capacity.

With our superior "grey matter" we can combine sounds into meaningful speech to communicate complex ideas to others of our species. Then, using our nimble fingers, we can write and print these ideas on paper, or put them into computers, thereby quickly transmitting them to other people. Our ideas are recorded in books stored in libraries, and taught in schools so that each generation can build on the ideas of others who came before. In this way we amass immense bodies of knowledge far greater than the ability of any one person to master.

Finally, each of us can think about these ideas, put them together in different ways to generate new information, or even draw conclusions about things we cannot see or hear or touch. In this respect our reasoning power goes far beyond that of animals.

Human reasoning plus an ability to speak and the skillful use of our hands have made it possible for us to invent automobiles that travel faster than any panther. Airplanes leave the fastest birds far behind and cranes, derricks, and shovels lift hundreds of times more weight than any beast of burden ever could. Using our reasoning power, we have mastered the secrets of making many new foods; learned how to fashion clothes from newly created fibers; and developed ways of building bridges, skyscrapers, factories, homes, and many kinds of structures, each serving its own special purpose.

We have removed ore from the earth and changed it into iron, aluminum, lead, copper, tin, and other metals. We have learned to mine coal from the ground, retrieve oil and gas from wells, and burn these fuels in relatively safe ways to heat homes, produce electricity, and propel many kinds of machines and vehicles.

It once took months to cross an ocean or continent; today, many thousands of people do this in a matter of hours. And almost instantaneously we can deliver our messages personally anywhere in the world by just lifting up the telephone and dialing a number. On television we can see events around the globe the instant they occur. Our satellites can reach Neptune, two billion miles from Earth, on a twelve-year journey and send back detailed photographs for us to study and admire.

Reasoning power has made it possible to discover many biological principles that have enabled us to cure a host of deadly diseases. We have devised complex instruments to probe the secrets of invisible atoms, and have used the information gained to develop a new way of producing electricity.

Yet for all our complex reasoning ability and the many problems it has solved, our search for a better life often creates new problems. With the positive power of the atom came devastating nuclear weapons that could destroy civilization in a day. Our harvesting of the earth's resources has lead to pollution, scarce natural resources, endangered animal species, and many other environmental problems. Reasoning power will be essential if we are to find workable solutions to the problems created by our own technology.

The ability to reason is also essential to everyday living. We are constantly bombarded with advertisements to buy this soap, smoke that cigarette, or eat a certain brand of cereal. Our reasoning power is an important protection against spending money unwisely.

When it is time to vote, we need clear thinking to judge the statements of newpapers and politicians. Important questions of the day must be discussed, and correct reasoning will play an important part in arriving at sensible judgments. In order to be healthy, a democracy must have citizens with a foundation of knowledge of political issues and with the ability to think clearly.

There are many jobs in which reasoning ability is essential. Engineers, businessmen, teachers, doctors, mechanics, dentists, truck drivers—in fact, all people who work for a living—need reasoning power in their work. Science, mathematics, and other branches of learning require high levels of rational ability. In the decade of the 1990s and beyond, the proportion of our population engaged in jobs that require complex reasoning will increase dramatically.

The industrial revolution of the past four hundred years has completely transformed the world into what has been described as a "global village" in which every nation is increasingly dependent on other countries for raw materials, manufactured products, energy, transportation, and communication. Conflicts have also become global, making it necessary to apply even more brain power to figure out how to prevent future world conflicts.

A PRACTICAL CASE

In many everyday situations, clear thinking makes the difference between success or failure in performing a task. Sometimes it means the difference between life and death. For example, consider the case of ten-year-old Johnny Appleton who found that a fledgling robin had fallen into a narrow hole 30 inches deep in the cement-block wall of a building under construction. Workmen on the job had been stymied in their attempts to get the bird out, but Johnny thought of a good way to rescue it from a slow death.

Using sand from the construction site, he slowly poured it into the hole. After an hour the sand filled the hole, with the robin near the top, and Johnny was able to lift the bird out. By pouring the sand in slowly the bird had enough time to lift its feet out of the sand as the level rose, and constantly stayed on top of it.

Let us analyze the thoughts that might have passed though Johnny's mind as he sought a solution to the problem. Perhaps he began to search in his mind for all the different ways in which objects could be lifted. A rope or string attached to the bird could get it out. But how would he attach the rope? He may have thought about it a while and then rejected this approach because he could not think of a good way to get the rope around the bird. Note that if such thoughts occurred to Johnny, the process of "trying it out" took place, not by his actually doing it with a real rope, but by his *imagining* what would happen *if* he tried it. This is one fundamental aspect of reasoning. We say to ourselves, "*If* (something or other) *then* (this or that may happen)." The solution we choose may then be worked out in our minds without actually trying out every possibility. We can see that such *thought experiments* can save a lot of time. In some cases solutions to practical problems would be almost impossible without this wonderful time-saver.

But let's continue with Johnny. Having rejected the rope solution, he may then have thought of using a sticky material on the end of a rod. This could work if a coin were to be lifted. But Johnny could immediately imagine difficulties with this method. What sticky material could be used? Would he hurt the bird by pressing a stick against it? Would the bird struggle and tear itself loose? Although this method is not completely out of the question, it poses many problems. So it pays to explore some other method that might be easier.

Note how the mind *searches* for different facts that apply to the problem. As each fact is recalled it may be applied to the problem at hand with use of the "If . . . then . . ." method and tried out in the mind. This type of mental searching is one of the secrets of success of creative people such as artists, writers, scientists, mathematicians, inventors, and of successful business people and politicians. It would be wise to develop this kind of organized searching in the mind as one way to improve our ability to solve problems.

Now back to Johnny and his particular problem. The idea of using a magnet on a string may have flashed though his mind. But then Johnny probably knew from an experience with magnets that only certain kinds of materials are attracted, notably iron and steel. He may have toyed with the idea of getting some iron object under or around the bird. But he could quickly see that there were other serious problems to be solved here. So, on to another possible method.

Perhaps he could raise the bird by filling the hole with water. But would the water stay in the hole? And might not the bird drown?

Why use water? Maybe sand would do a better job. Johnny could imagine the sand coming into the hole and filling up the bottom. He could picture in his mind how the bird's feet would be slowly covered by sand. He could visualize the bird lifting its feet out of the sand and in so doing raising itself higher. He could also foresee that if he poured too much sand into the hole at one time, the bird might be buried and thus suffocate. So he made sure to pour the sand very slowly to give the bird a chance to get out of the sand and adjust its position on higher ground.

THE BASIC PATTERN OF PROBLEM SOLVING

Johnny's feat can serve as an example for us to follow in solving other problems. Let us note the basic features of this process:

1. The solution is based on past experience and facts that have been incorporated into the mind.

2. Those facts that apply to the problem are recalled by a *mental searching* process that digs into the huge fund of *memories* stored in the brain. Somehow, in a manner not fully understood, we are able to direct our minds to search out those facts that apply to the situation and thereby leave out the multitude of other facts that have nothing to do with the problem.

3. The facts that apply can then be juggled in our minds to evolve different possible solutions. This process of putting together the facts to try out *thought experiments,* reason correctly, and draw *conclusions* from them is the essence of clear thinking.

4. A chain of such reasoning activities, with the proposed solution to one problem leading to the creation of possible solutions, finally ends with an overall conclusion. We mentally evaluate each situation and render a *judgment.* We select one of several possible solutions as the one most likely to be successful.

5. Finally, we may take *action* to solve the problem. That is the basic purpose of "clear thinking" and the ultimate test of good reasoning. The best outcome, of course, is for the action to solve the problem. But if not, all is not lost. We put that outcome—whether a success or a failure—into our memory banks as an *experience.* The next time, in a similar situation, that experience may be drawn upon to speed up a proper decision.

Some problems are purely mental. For example, a mathematical problem perhaps ends in the mind without the need for doing anything more. So do most of our judgments about political matters and about people, although action in some cases may come later when we vote, speak out on an issue, or respond to another person.

But many problems involve situations outside our minds in a way that demands trying out our solution. Sometimes, as was the case with Johnny and the bird, the solution has to be applied quickly or it will not be of much use. At other times action is not so urgent and may be postponed. Such would be the case with a problem involving a method of building a structure, finding the best way of getting to work, or discerning the easiest way of transporting a heavy object.

In such instances it is important to apply the solution and check its correctness. Otherwise, we are left with a judgment that may be incorrect and possibly misapplied at some other time. Since judgments tend to be passed on to others—often down through many generations—it is important to check their accuracy as soon as possible.

In Johnny's case it would have been pointless to end his train of thought without actually trying out his solution. His thinking had practical significance because the solution actually worked when tried out. Now, because of the power of the printed word, his solution is being communicated to thousands of people who may be able to apply Johnny's thinking to solve a similar problem more quickly. The next time, a child may be saved, rather than a bird.

In this way a body of facts accumulates and makes it possible for people to solve many more problems than they could ever hope to handle successfully solely by their own thinking processes.

WHAT THIS BOOK IS ABOUT

This book will by no means enable us to solve every problem we confront. But if it succeeds in sharpening our wits, even a little, it will fulfill its purpose. Perhaps it may serve as an introduction to deeper study of ways of thinking and reasoning and thereby greatly affect our ability to solve many kinds of problems in life.

Chapter 2, "The Nature of Facts," will consider the tricky nature of most facts and how ignoring the many exceptions to most facts can seriously mislead us when we reason about problems.

In Chapter 3, "Superstition and Science," we will learn about the vital role that scientific thinking has played in improving our ability to reason, and the ways in which ancient superstition still clogs the thinking processes of many people, thus preventing them from solving many personal problems.

In Chapter 4, "The Reasoning Process," we will learn about the ways we reason: by the *inductive method* to derive generalized facts, and by the *deductive method,* which uses facts as the basis for logical reasoning.

Chapter 5, "Language and Reasoning," discusses the key role that language plays in reasoning and the many ways that clarity of thinking is disrupted by *semantic confusion:* failure to take into account the different meanings of words in diverse *contexts*.

Chapter 6, "Common Errors in Reasoning," describes the major types of reasoning errors that bedevil solutions to problems. We will learn how to avoid some of the common errors that are frequently made.

Chapter 7, "Astrology: A Case Study in Defective Reasoning," provides practice in analyzing a commonly held superstition that many people use as a guide to their lives.

Chapter 8, "Conflicting Opinions," discusses the role of "missing facts" in causing opinions to be less certain. Also discussed is the important role of opinion polls and the way they influence the public.

Chapter 9, "Stereotypes, Prejudice, and Discrimination," considers the harmful effects of prejudiced opinions in human relations, and suggests how they may be minimized.

Chapter 10, "How Opinions Are Influenced," alerts us to the many ways today's image-makers manipulate public opinion.

In Chapter 11, "Reasoning Errors in Advertising," we will learn about the many kinds of advertising tricks used to sell products of dubious merit or items at inflated prices.

Chapter 12, "The Big Picture," summarizes the main ideas in this book and suggests basic principles for clear thinking.

Throughout this book, at the end of each chapter, there are questions especially designed to sharpen the readers' wits. Improve your reasoning ability by answering these questions yourself first, rather than reading the sample answers at the back of the book.

Let's begin with an analysis of the nature of facts, the basis of all real-world problem solving. What is a fact? How do we know whether facts are true? What are the limits and exceptions to "fuzzy facts," which cause many errors in reasoning if ignored? The next chapter considers these important aspects of the reasoning process.

2

The Nature of Facts

In 1903 a new field of science seemed to have been opened with the "discovery" by the distinguished French physicist Rene Blondlot of what he called "N-rays" that seemed to be emitted by X-rays. Many French scientists began to explore this new phenomenon, and within a few years nearly 100 investigators, most of whom were French, had written more than 300 scientific papers.[1]

However, there was a problem with these N-rays. Their presence was supposed to be detected by a slight increase in brightness of an electric spark between two pointed wires.

> The increase in brightness had to be judged by eye, a notoriously subjective method of detection. But that seemed to matter little in view of the fact that other physicists were soon able to repeat and extend Blondlot's findings.
>
> A colleague at the University of Nancy discovered that N-rays were emitted not just by X-ray sources but also by the nervous system of the human body. A Sorbonne physicist noticed that the N-rays emanated from Broca's area, the part of the brain that governs speech while a person was talking. N-rays were discovered in gases, magnetic fields and chemicals. Soon the pursuit of N-rays had become a minor industry among French scientists.[2]

Blondlot received a major award from the French Academy of Sciences for initiating this new field of science. But it all began to come apart when an American physicist named R. W. Wood, while observing an N-ray experiment in the dark, removed a prism that Blondlot was using to show a presumed special property of N-rays. Removal of this key component of the experiment made no difference; Blondlot still observed the same results as though the prism had been in place. It was clear that Blondlot was "observing" effects of imaginary N-rays. Wood's report of the nonexistent N-rays eventually ended that "new field of science." But it took some time because of "national pride"; N-rays were viewed as an achievement of French science, which was otherwise being eclipsed by German science at that time. It seems that the eagerness of French scientists to have their own discovery equivalent to X-rays influenced many of them to see what was not there.

A similar event occurred in 1989 when two chemists, Stanley Pons and Martin Fleischmann, working at the University of Utah, reported an astonishing discovery of "cold fusion" in which nuclear energy by fusion of atoms of deuterium (heavy hydrogen) was supposedly produced merely by sending electric current through "heavy water" containing deuterium. If the scientists were right, their "discovery" implied the possibility of an almost limitless source of clean energy from water in the ocean.

Other scientists throughout the world immediately repeated the experiments, hoping to verify the "facts" reported by the two scientists, but were unable to confirm the results. As with the N-rays, the effects were slight, if any. It is likely that subjective factors, perhaps a strong desire to win a Nobel Prize, might have played a role in this matter. At any rate, the findings of the two scientists have not yet been accepted as "verified," and may never be.[3]

If the scientists in these two incidents (and there are many others) were not able to determine facts properly, what does that say to the rest of us? It tells us that reported facts are often not so, although people may believe that they are and act on them as though they were real facts. Similarly, many "facts" are only partly true, but people treat them as though they are true under all circumstances. Such completely false or partially true "facts" play havoc with our attempts to solve the many personal and societal problems of our complex civilization. It is of the utmost importance, therefore, to understand the nature of facts and how we may ensure that they are as true and as accurate as possible.

A word of caution is needed about the two incidents of poor observations by scientists, noted above. They should not be interpreted to mean that no facts can be trusted. In the case of N-rays the effect was very slight and scientists were relying on visual judgment of slight differences in brightness. This procedure was flawed because the results could be easily influenced by the observer's desire to get recognition or to contribute to the national honor.

In the case of cold fusion the measurement of heat is tricky and involves more than just measuring temperature. Mistakes are easy to make.

And nuclear fusion is also a complex process that requires expertise in measuring nuclear reactions, a skill that the two chemists making the "discovery" did not have.

The main point, then, is to be prudently cautious about accepting facts as true. We must be ready to listen to people who think our facts are wrong, and make an effort to check the facts we so often take for granted.

WHAT IS A FACT?

The key word defining a fact is *reality*. A fact can neither be based on fiction nor be a product of the imagination. "Reality" here means that the fact must be *observed* with our senses of sight, hearing, touch, smell, or taste, often with the use of instruments that aid us in detecting or measuring what might otherwise be difficult to observe.

Groups of facts may also be formed into *generalized* facts (discussed in chapter 4), giving us much greater power to solve problems. But such facts must be treated with caution because exceptions tend to appear when new circumstances arise. We will encounter many examples throughout this book.

Our minds cannot think in a vacuum. If facts are to be used to solve problems then the facts must be as correct as we can make them. There are times when we don't have really solid facts but find ourselves forced to make important judgments nonetheless. Then we just do the best we can, knowing that our "fuzzy interpretations of facts" need to be firmed up as quickly as possible.

That was certainly true about the "facts" in the dangerous nuclear missile incident at the Arctic base, described in chapter 1. It was a fact that there were dots on the screen. They were actually observed. But it was not a "fact" that missiles were coming our way, as these dots seemed to imply. That was an unwarranted "interpretation" of the dots on the screen.

MISSING FACTS

When the incident began at the Arctic radar base the facts were insufficient for making a clear-cut decision about what to do. It was a case of "missing facts" of the kind we confront in most problems that require solutions.

The basic difficulty stemmed from the nature of the radar equipment:

it does not actually "see" missiles. Like all instruments designed to produce facts, it serves as an extension of human senses. It does so by sending out radar waves and detecting any reflections from distant objects. What those objects are is often a matter of human interpretation, and that's where the trouble begins.

Consider the causes of most major accidents—the meltdown at the Three Mile Island nuclear power plant, the disaster at Chernobyl, the Challenger shuttle disaster, the gigantic oil spill off the Alaskan coast, the poisoning by chemicals of thousands of people in Bhopal, India—all are examples of human error in interpreting, handling, or designing equipment. Usually, instruments don't lie, although they sometimes might malfunction. Generally, they provide correct information if the data are read properly, but what people do with the information is quite another matter.

One of the big fears of our nuclear age is that World War III might accidentally start as a result of human error: e.g., using facts revealed by our senses or our instruments in a manner similar to the scenario at the Arctic missile base.

There are many historical examples in which fuzzy, wrong, or missing facts had very harmful consequences, sometimes lasting for centuries. For example, during the seventeenth and eighteenth centuries the practice of slavery developed in the American South and became a deeply embedded part of an economy that was based on farming cotton. This evil practice was justified by the widespread view that dark-skinned people from Africa were members of an inferior race of humans.

> The conception that certain people coming from the same general territory overseas and possessing similar physical traits were innately and immutably "different," enough to constitute a separate species, powerfully reinforced the position of slavery in America and especially in the South.[4]

This belief in a wrong "fact"—the racial superiority of whites, and the inferiority of blacks—had terrible consequences for the United States. It led to increasing social and political conflict that ultimately culminated in our Civil War, in which more than a million people were killed. Ironically, most of the victims had light-colored skin.

Today, more than two centuries after this wrong "fact" was embedded in the U.S. Constitution, our nation still suffers from the consequences of the deep-seated racial problems it generated, problems that are far from being completely solved.

Similarly, in the 1930s Adolf Hitler and his Nazi followers in Germany believed that they belonged to a superior "Aryan" race and that Jews,

Figure 2.1 A "missing facts" situation could result in an unjust attack on innocent bystanders—or even a world war with nuclear weapons. *(Reprinted by permission of the* Bulletin of the Atomic Scientists*)*

Gypsies, and other minorities were members of inferior, if not evil, races. This wrong belief, based on false "facts," was not only one of the causes of World War II, but it also led to the mass slaughter of millions during the horrible Holocaust (see chapter 9).

Missing facts are at the root of many difficulties in reaching arms-control agreements between the United States and the Soviet Union. Diplomats working on these problems spend much time devising systems to "verify" facts. How many missiles does each nation have and of what types? Where are they? How do we know designated missiles or warheads have really been destroyed? And on and on. . . .

There is also the danger that terrorists might explode a nuclear weapon, which might then precipitate a nuclear confrontation between the United States and the Soviet Union over what each might have thought was the other's unprovoked attack. All because of "missing facts." This frightening prospect is effectively portrayed in figure 2.1.

FACTS MUST BE OBJECTIVELY VERIFIED

There is usually no great difficulty verifying simple facts such as names, addresses, phone numbers, and social security numbers. They provide relatively few problems, unless there are errors in recording them, fraud, or two people with the same name. But more complex, generalized facts can be troublesome. For example, consider the statement "Planets are astronomical bodies that move in the sky against a background of fixed stars." Should this statement be accepted as true?

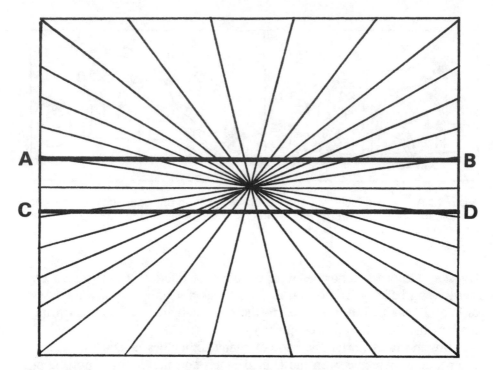

Figure 2.2 Our senses do not always provide correct facts. Lines AB and CD look curved. Place a ruler on the lines. What do you observe?

It is a fuzzy fact that is easily misinterpreted, as will be discussed in greater detail later in this chapter. Verifying such a fact and defining the limits under which it is or is not true can be a complex task.

At any rate, any statement claimed to be a fact cannot be accepted as true until it is *verified in some objective way*. The word *objective* refers to the attitude of the observer, who should remain unemotional, unbiased, and unprejudiced (impartial) when evaluating the truth or falsity of what are reported to be "facts." The validity of a fact must not be judged in advance (prejudged).

To be *subjective* is to be emotional, biased, and prejudiced (partial) in evaluating "facts." It is essentially the opposite of *objective*.

To *verify* implies that one gathers evidence, mainly through observations, which show a stated "fact" to be true. Quite often it turns out that facts are mostly true, but there are limits as to where, when, or how they apply in different circumstances. The idea of objective verification is a major contribution from science; it has proved to be very successful in gathering facts about the world. These concepts are now increasingly applied to social, economic, and political areas of knowledge, as well as to nature.

One of the main tools of fact gathering, learned from many successes in science, is the use of measurements. Our senses are often inadequate to judge dimensions of even simple things. We can greatly improve observations by using measuring instruments: rulers, scales, clocks, measuring cups, thermometers, barometers, speedometers, and other such devices. With the development of such fields of knowledge as psychology and anthropology, new methods of measurement have been devised in which human responses and judgments play an important role.

One of the basic problems that arises when using our senses for observation is that there are many kinds of *illusions* that distort our judgments. Figure 2.2 illustrates this point. Are the horizontal lines across the diagram straight or curved? They certainly do not appear to be parallel straight lines. Yet if we place a ruler on each line, it becomes abundantly clear that the lines are straight, as well as parallel to each other.

Dad: "*Please get me a piece of wood about this big.*"

Billy: "*Here it is. I made sure to measure it with my arms, just like you did.*"

Figure 2.3 Accurate measurements require standards that are the same for everyone. *(Drawing by Albert Sarney)*

Standards of measurement are also important. When someone measures a length of "5 centimeters" in one part of the world, or a time of "2 hours and 34 minutes," it is vital that anyone, anywhere, should be able to replicate (repeat) that measurement and do so accurately. Figure 2.3 illustrates the need for standards of measurement. Billy brings his father a much smaller piece of wood than needed because he incorrectly thinks that stretching his arms out the way Dad did is an adequate standard for measuring length.

Standards of measurement in the social sciences are more difficult to achieve because of the complexity of human responses. Nevertheless, progress has been made in these areas in recent years.

CHANGING FACTS

To illustrate the way we establish the truth or falsity of facts, consider the way our view of the solar system has changed over many centuries. If we had lived in the year 1300, there is little doubt that we would have agreed with two "obvious" facts: that the earth is flat and that the sun revolves around the earth. Why? Because it looks that way, and from logical reasoning, based on what was known in 1300, it seemed obvious that it must be so. The flatness of the earth seems to be verified by personal observation every time we walk around a town or city that has level streets. When rowing a boat on a quiet, windless, wave-free lake we verify by observation that the water is "perfectly" level, therefore "flat." We "know" from years of personal experience that if the water was not flat, it would flow "downhill" until it becomes "flat."

Logical reasoning based on experience would lead us believe that there is a limit to the extent of the ocean. How could it go on forever without an end? There had to be some kind of edge beyond which we would fall over, or be washed over into some mysterious chasm and oblivion, perhaps hell itself.

A round Earth was inconceivable. From personal experience we would "know" that people on the bottom of the earth would have to fall off. If anyone tried to tell us "Oh, but gravity keeps everyone glued to the earth," we might ask, "Who is he?" and then listen to the tortured explanations.

Try explaining the properties of gravity to someone who acts like a skeptic. How successful would we be answering these tough questions: "How does gravity pull us down to Earth? Where are the strings? Do you mean to say that it pulls me just as much with or without a ten-foot-thick slab of concrete between me and the earth? How does the stuff 4,000 miles down know how hard to pull me?"

Everyone in the United States sees the morning sun rise in the East and set in the West toward evening. We do not feel the enormous 1,000 m.p.h. motion of the earth required for our home planet to rotate once each day. We do see the sky as a kind of dome with fixed stars revolving around the earth once a day.

So, a thinking person in the 1300s would have said that these "facts" were "objectively verified" and therefore "true." Figure 2.4 illustrates how the "obvious" fact that the sun appears to move around the earth made it very difficult for people to accept the idea that the earth revolves around the sun. Our sense of sight seems to tell us otherwise.

The contemporary view of our solar system and the universe is the result of a gradual increase in knowledge gained by means of an interplay of observations, usually with the help of measuring instruments, and by logical reasoning, especially reasoning of a mathematical sort. The reasonable old "facts" were eventually replaced by more reasonable, complex new ones based on a diametrically opposing view.

Figure 2.4 "Don't you see that the sun is rising in the sky? Don't believe those crazy people who say it's the earth that's moving, not the sun." *(Drawing by Albert Sarney)*

This is basically the way most knowledge emerges. It implies that facts and views change over time.

EMOTION AND SUBJECTIVITY RUIN FACTS

It is not easy to remove the effect of emotion during an investigation. People who believe strongly in an idea often become so attached to it that they bend and twist any facts that cast doubt on the idea. This "mindset" or bias (prejudice that inhibits judgment) is often subconscious and so deeply embedded that most people are unaware of its influence on their reasoning (see chapter 6).

FRAUDULENT "FACTS"

Lying, cheating, hoaxes, and frauds are not new in this world. But we don't associate such chicanery with science, which, above all, values truth in its facts. Yet some cheating and even outright hoaxes do manage to get through the defenses, despite the barriers scientists take to minimize fraud.

Perhaps the most damaging case in science was the faked "discovery" in England of the "Piltdown Man," which threw a wrench into studies of human evolution for forty years. In 1912, Charles Dawson, a lawyer and amateur archaeologist, reported finding a human skull and near it a jaw at a depth in the earth that put their estimated age at 500,000 years. The skull and jaw were discolored, "confirming" that they had been buried for a long time.[5]

Anatomically, the modern-looking human skull and the ape-like jaw did not seem to belong together. On the other hand, the teeth in the jaw were not as sharp as those of apes, more like those of humans. Some experts thought that the skull and jaw were not from the same pre-human, but had somehow been buried in the same place. The possibility of an outright hoax was not seriously considered at that time.

However, the Piltdown Man gained acceptance and entered the textbooks as a "fact," a fossil of a pre-human that once existed, but it always seemed out of place in the evolutionary picture of early man that developed with other archeological finds. Forty years after its "discovery" a group of scientists decided to investigate the possibility of fraud. Tests immediately revealed that the skull and jaw had been treated with a chemical to make them appear discolored and therefore old. New methods of dating bone also indicated that the skull and jaw were both of recent origin. File marks on the teeth of the ape-like jaw showed that they had been altered to look more like those of a human. The jaw was then identified as that of an orangutan. The Piltdown Man was clearly a fake.

This hoax was very damaging to science, not only because it interfered with understanding human evolution, but also because it distracted many scientists from other research.

In another very destructive fraud, Cyril Burt, a British psychologist, knighted for his purported accomplishments and awarded the top prize of the American Psychological Association, was discovered to have consistently manufactured "data" over a period of nearly twenty years regarding the intelligence of identical twins. He imagined many nonexistent cases of identical twins, separated at birth and brought up in different homes. Then he gave them fictitious IQ tests, from which he imagined their scores. From this process of "garbage-in-garbage-out," he produced impressive tables and analyses based on faked figures. His sole purpose seems to have been to support his strongly held opinion that intelligence is mostly inherited. He even went so far as to invent two co-workers and write fictitious papers in their names, thereby providing impressive "independent" confirmation of his thesis.[6]

Although some people may have had suspicions about Burt's data, no one checked or challenged the "experiments" from which he concluded that intelligence was mostly inherited. Yet, in 1972, a year after Burt's death, it took Leon Kamin, a Princeton psychologist, only ten minutes to discover that one of Burt's papers was a fraud. Burt slipped up because he carelessly used the same figure of 0.771 as the "correlation coefficient" in three separate studies of IQ scores of identical twins separated at birth. Such precisely equal results for three different experiments is so improbable as to be considered virtually impossible.

It may be that Burt's opinion about the inheritability of intelligence is true, but then again it may not be. At this point all of Burt's work is absolutely worthless since no credible researcher can trust any of it. In effect, even if some of his research is correct, Burt destroyed his life's work with his pattern of deception.

All frauds do damage to the fabric of human knowledge. In addition to destroying trust, fraudulent "facts" are counterproductive. Problems are not likely to be correctly or even adequately resolved with lies.

Burt's fraud was especially destructive because his biased opinion, masquerading as "fact," became the basis for powerful "factual" arguments offered by some educational psychologists that compensatory education (in the form of extra help) for poor black and white children should be abandoned. Why spend extra money on teaching such children if they are thought to be genetically limited in their ability to learn?

Fortunately, the basic corrective mechanisms of science—checking and verifying facts—eventually did uncover the Burt and Piltdown frauds. However, serious defects in the system for checking research do obviously exist because Burt was able to get away with his deception for so many years. Improvements are being made, but humans being who they are, some cheating and deception in fact-gathering will probably be with us for a long time to come.

Honest errors will always occur as a natural part of any probing for new information. Every good researcher inevitably makes some mistakes. But deliberate deceit and fraud in a field of knowledge is such a serious offense that anyone caught in the act is thereafter barred from ever having an article published in a reputable journal. The person's career as a researcher is for all intent and purpose at an end. Then the long cleanup process begins in which each periodical lists all the articles written by the offender and asks readers not to give them any credence in their own work.

Fortunately, only an extremely small number of frauds are committed in the sciences (or so we hope). By and large, professional researchers try to be objective in their gathering of facts. If that were not so, there would be very serious consequences for those who develop the new knowledge upon which our world depends today.

HOW FACTUAL ERRORS ARE CORRECTED

Newspapers and magazines of the 1940s occasionally published articles comparing the speeds of humans and animals with those of airplanes and fast cars. One of the astonishing "facts" of the time was the speed of the "fastest living thing," a "deer fly" that was reported in various newspapers as flying at a speed of about 700 miles an hour—faster than any airplane of the time could travel.

A noted scientist, Irving Langmuir, wondered about this "fact" when he saw it in several newspapers. One day he read an article in the *Illustrated London News* of January 1, 1938, about the deer fly's great speed. The paper reported that the speed of the female deer fly was 614 miles an hour, while the male did somewhat better at 818 miles an hour. The newspaper also quoted the source of this "fact" as a Dr. Charles H. T. Townsend and quoted him as writing for the New York Entomological Society (no date given) that

On 12,000 feet summits in New Mexico I have seen pass me at an incredible velocity what were certainly the males of Cephenomyia (the deer fly). I could barely distinguish that something had passed—only a brownish blur in the air of about the right size for these flies and without a sense of form. As closely as I can estimate, their speed must have approximated 400 yards a second.[7]

A speed of 400 yards a second is the same as 818 miles per hour! And the only evidence Townsend had for his "estimate" was that he saw it as a "brownish blur." From that meager evidence, without even attempting to actually measure the speed, he jumped to the conclusion that the speed of the deer fly "must have approximated 400 yards a second"!

Langmuir did not think much of this "evidence" so he decided to check Townsend's conclusion. First, Langmuir made some calculations: How much power would a deer fly need to force its way through strongly resistant air at 818 miles per hour? His calculations indicated that the deer fly would have needed about one-half horsepower, about the same as that of four men! How much food would the deer fly have to eat to achieve such horsepower? About "1.5 times its own weight every second." Some glutton!

Then Langmuir did a simple experiment to measure the speed of the deer fly when it appears as a "brownish blur." He made an approximate model of a deer fly from a piece of brown-painted solder, tied it to a string, held it at arm's length and whirled it in a vertical circle while timing it to calculate the speed. At twenty-six miles per hour the imitation deer fly was "barely visible as a moving object," and at 43 miles per hour "it appeared as a very faint line." Langmuir concluded that "a speed of 25 miles per hour is a reasonable one for the deer fly, while 800 miles per hour is utterly impossible."

In this scientific way Langmuir demolished the exaggerated "fact" of the enormous speed attributed to the deer fly. Unfortunately, errors do not die that easily. For several more decades this wrong fact kept popping up in various newspapers and magazines, each taking it from some other incorrect source. However, after Langmuir wrote an article about this error of "fact" and had it published in a reputable science periodical, that was the end of it so far as scientists were concerned.

There is an important lesson in Langmuir's approach to doubtful facts: each must be checked with calculations and experiments that seek to verify it if true, or dispose of it if false. This is the only reliable way to ensure that the facts resting as the foundation of human knowledge remain as accurate as we can make them. Otherwise, the structure of knowledge crumbles, thereby rendering it worthless.

OBJECTIVITY IN A DEMOCRACY

The idea that facts must be objectively checked and verified is one of the scientific community's most important contributions to modern civilization. It serves as an extremely powerful tool—or perhaps an "engine"—for generating reliable facts in every field of human affairs.

For example, consider a democracy's basic procedure of voting for public officials by secret ballot. Historically, this was a great advance in the way people decided how they should be governed. The secret ballot together with impartial counting of the votes ensures that the electorate's decision does not succumb to the pressure and distortion of the public will, which often occurs under tyrannical governments. Our own system of elections is not totally free of distortion. The electoral college, for example, which was initially created as a compromise at the time our nation was established in 1787, has, on several occasions, served to elect a president with fewer popular votes than the losing candidate. But take away the right to vote by secret ballot and democracy is destroyed; dictatorship and loss of freedom become the only remaining alternatives.

Failure to vote weakens democracy. Many who are contemptuous of voting do not comprehend the simple relationship between the right to vote and democratic freedoms that that right symbolizes.

ANALYZING THE FUZZINESS IN FACTS

Leaves are green. True or false? Most people would probably answer, true. But with some time for reflection, doubt begins to erode this seemingly obvious answer. The green leaves of many trees turn orange, yellow, red, or brown during autumn. Some plants have leaves of mixed color, such as green and yellow. The green leaves of various grasses take on a straw color during dry periods. Some varieties of trees have copper-colored leaves. The leaves of some shrubs are tinged with violet.

So the simple statement "Leaves are green" is not completely correct. Although the overwhelming majority of leaves are green, most of the time, some are not completely green, and others are never green. Others are only green for a while.

A correct statement of fact is "Leaves are usually green." This statement makes us aware that there are exceptions. Most people would not worry about the variations, but there are times when exceptions can result in serious errors.

Consider another fact: "Ten dimes are worth one dollar." This kind of fact seems as certain as any can be because it comes directly from the definition of a dime. The U.S. government defines the dime as one tenth of a dollar. Can anybody reasonably argue that there might be nine or eleven dimes in a dollar?

But—there often are "buts" in apparently obvious facts—dimes contain silver, which has inherent value as a precious metal. Dollars are usually paper money, with the paper having no resale value of its own. This creates a situation in which ten dimes might have more value if sold for the value of its silver than in exchange for one paper dollar. (The price of silver would have to rise considerably, but it is possible.) In such a case people might be willing to take fewer than ten dimes for a dollar, illegally melt them down, and sell the silver at a profit.

Something like this actually occurred in 1981. The price of metals like gold, silver, and copper rose so much that some people began to accumulate coins, melt them, and sell the metal at a price greater than the government defined it. Pennies began to disappear from circulation and were sold as copper.

In 1982 the U.S. Treasury, which produces our money, changed the alloy from which pennies were made so that people could no longer profit from the copper in these coins. Although the Treasury did not change the silver alloys in dimes and quarters in 1982, it might do so in the future if the price of silver were ever to increase substantially.

So, even the statement "Ten dimes are worth one dollar" may not be absolutely true under all possible circumstances.

Consider this well-known fact, "The earth has a spherical shape." This fact has certainly been amply confirmed by photographs from outer space, so there is little doubt about its basic truth. Yet there is still a "Flat Earth Society" whose members have been known on radio talk shows to argue that the earth is really shaped like a flat pie.

Granted that the earth has been demonstrated to be "round," what kind of roundness does it have? Is it perfectly spherical? It's all a matter of how accurate we wish to be. Looking at it from outer space, no astronaut can visually detect variations from the spherical shape. But space scientists, who calculate the orbits of satellites, must take into account the small variations that do exist. These affect the amount of time a satellite takes to orbit the earth.

The earth's diameter is 27 miles less from the North Pole to the South Pole than at the equator, and it bulges slightly in places. Earth is a tiny bit pear-shaped; in some places there is a difference of little more than 50 feet between some dimensions of the northern and southern hemispheres.

But this is still not all there is to say about the earth, since it also has mountains, some of which are more than five miles high. To those who climb Mount Everest the earth doesn't seem round at all. And an ant, scrambling about in a meadow filled with lots of pebbles, doesn't see it that way either. So, the fact that the earth is spherical is really an approximation, not an absolute truth.

"Two plus two equals four," seems to be absolutely true. But suppose we try to apply the same concept to real life, not just to abstract numbers. What are two apples and two oranges?—two orange-apples? "Ah," you say, "they are four fruits." Yes, but that required some thinking about what new word to use, an exercise that takes us into a new realm of "semantics," the meaning of words, which will be discussed in more detail in chapter 5.

What happens if we say, "two pounds of force and two pounds of

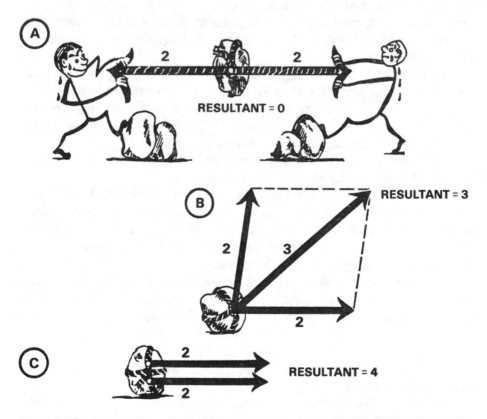

Figure 2.5 Two and two equals four? Yes, for abstract numbers, but not necessarily for forces. For example, two pounds of force and two pounds of force may not produce four pounds of force; they can produce any "resultant" from zero to four pounds, depending on the angle between them. *(Drawing by Alice Wengrow)*

force"? Does that produce four pounds of force? Yes, if they are pulling in the same direction, but not if they are pulling in opposite directions or tugging on something at an angle (see figure 2.5).

Let's look at an example from the realm of pure mathematics, something that we might think nobody could really argue about:

$$10 + 10 = 100$$

At first blush this is an obviously false statement. But wait. It all depends on our definition of zero. A mathematician may choose to develop a "binary number system" with only two digits, 1 and 0, instead of our more traditional decimal system rooted in the numbers 0, 1, 2, 3, 4, 5, 6, 7, 8, and 9. In a binary system 10 plus 10 *does* equal 100 and is equivalent to saying, "Two plus two are four." (This point is discussed further in question 3 at the end of this chapter.)

"Oh," you say, "that's just a mathematical abstraction, having nothing to do with reality." Don't tell that to those who program computers: the machines' internal workings are based on this binary mathematics!

Thus, most real-life "facts" are not necessarily absolutely true everywhere and for all time. There will be variations, and often significant exceptions, depending on how we look at facts and the purposes for which they are used. This is just another way of saying that "facts are fuzzy."

Some people have a hard time coping with such uncertainty. They like things absolutely "precise." They forget that we live in a real world in which facts approximate an ideal of precision to varying degrees. We accept life's uncertainties and do the best we can. Yet our struggle continues as we strive to develop the most accurate facts possible within a given set of circumstances. That's usually good enough, even if it's far from perfect.

DIFFERENT KINDS OF FACTS

The vast array of facts in our world can be categorized as follows:

1. Identification Facts

These include the names, addresses, phone numbers, social security numbers, and other naming or identifying information about *specific* people, animals, plants, businesses, nations, cities, rivers, oceans, prices, model numbers of equipment, and other products and things. Such facts are about as definite as we can get. If a person lives at a certain address and is known by a certain name, no one is likely to argue about *that* fact, unless, perhaps, he is a bigamist living under two different names at two different addresses, and the police are looking for him.

There are an enormous number of such *specific* identifying facts. They are essential to record keeping, especially computer records. Modern civilization could not function without such identifying facts.

2. Observations

This category of facts is the basis for most knowledge. Examples include: "This cat weighs 10 pounds," "This 12-gauge copper wire was stretched 1.2 millimeters by a 5 kilogram weight," "Sue Sutter had the highest grades in math," "George Moody is shy."

Any fuzziness that may intrude on such facts comes from the uncertainties inherent in all observations. We observe with our five basic senses aided by a host of instruments used for collecting and measuring information. Many kinds of observational errors are possible because of the limitations of both our senses and our instruments, as a result of the way we go about observing, or through improper use of instruments.

The word *data* means factual information gathered by observation and tabulated in a form suitable for analysis. If a *datum* (singular of data) is in numerical form, it is referred to as a *statistic*. Data and statistics are the foundation of many reasoning processes in research, such as those in the physical and biological sciences, social sciences, business, and accounting. Most information processing with computers requires data as its factual basis. The accuracy of such facts depends mainly on the care that observers take in noting and recording their observations.

Many kinds of devices are now available to assist in making observations and tabulating data, ranging from simple measuring instruments to telescopes, microscopes, computers, and a host of electrical instruments. The data or observational information may be recorded by means of photographs, charts, or tables of numbers, which could then be duplicated and studied later by other interested persons. Astronomers, for example, no longer visually observe planets and stars with their telescopes, but take photographs that provide permanent records of portions of space, frozen in time. These photographs may be duplicated and studied later by researchers who take measurements and record what the photographs show. Years later, the older photographs become increasingly valuable in detecting changes that occur over long periods of time. This type of observation is found in many fields. Biologists use photographs of microscopic organisms in a similar way. Detectives use photographs to establish factual records of the scene of a crime.

Watch the way groceries are checked out at the supermarket. As the clerk moves the barred symbol of a package over the red laser beam, a lens and an electronic device "read" the information it contains about the price and inventory number of the item. This information is recorded in the memory of a computer that processes it and prints out the list of items and the total of the bill. The computer also processes the information to provide the store manager with complete, automatic inventory of all products on the shelves.

Such automated devices, combined with computers, have transformed the way observations and data are made, processed, and recorded, and are the foundation for the "information revolution" now under way throughout the world.

The accuracy of such data is usually far superior to what may be obtained by direct human observation. However, instruments and computers occasionally make errors, and when they do, the mistakes can be serious. Occasionally, some wayward computer adds a string of zeros to a number like $10 and computes a check for a million dollars. Then, since the human operators have come to depend on the accuracy of computers and other automatic instruments, that check is likely to be mailed out to some startled customer.

3. Definitions

All reasoning requires words or mathematical terms that must be defined so that everyone uses them in the same way. Although definitions are generally based on observations, they serve as an especially important category of fundamental facts that serve as the starting point for much human reasoning.

Like all other facts, definitions generally have fuzzy boundaries. Ask five people about the meanings of words like *conservative* and *liberal* and you are likely to get substantially different answers. Dictionaries also differ somewhat in defining such words. The differences are usually greater if old dictionaries are consulted, since meanings change with time.

Even seemingly simple definitions can be quite complex. In 1790, for example, the length of a meter was defined as one ten-millionth of the distance from the equator to the North Pole, along the longitude line passing through Paris. By 1900, a more practical definition was based on the distance between two marks on a special metal bar located in Paris and kept at a constant temperature to avoid changes in length due to expansion by heat. In 1960, this definition was again changed to meet the needs of scientists for accurately measuring extremely small distances.

The meter is now defined as equal to 1,650,763.73 wavelengths in a vacuum of the orange-red radiation of krypton 86. As our knowledge increases, our ability to define sharpens.

Definitions are often modified as ideas change with time. In 1500, before Copernicus proposed his theory of the solar system, the word *planet* (based on the Latin word *planeta,* meaning "wanderer") meant any astronomical body that appeared to move against the background of the apparently fixed stars. That definition included the sun, the moon, and the planets Mercury, Venus, Mars, Jupiter and Saturn. The remaining planets were not yet known.

After the Copernican theory changed our view of the solar system, the word *planet* was redefined to mean only those astronomical bodies that revolve around the sun. So the sun is no longer considered a planet; nor is the moon, which is now viewed as a "satellite" that revolves around the earth. And the earth, formerly considered the center of the universe, is now classified as a planet even though it does not appear to "wander" in the sky. Most other definitions change in a similar way.

4. Descriptive Generalizations

Specific facts in the previous categories often accumulate to become *generalizations* (generalized facts) by means of *inductive reasoning* (to be discussed in chapter 4). The statement "Dogs bark" would be one such example, based on many observations of specific dogs barking. The statement "The surfaces of paved roads are made of either asphalt or concrete" is another example of such a generalization.

Generalized facts tend to develop, change, and evolve over time as new observations are made. For instance, somebody might one day breed a dog that tends to wheeze instead of bark. Perhaps some inventor might devise a way to use garbage instead of asphalt or concrete as a form of road-surfacing material.

5. Logical Reasoning

New facts may be obtained as *conclusions* by means of a kind of logical reasoning known as the *deductive method.* Conclusions are drawn from the given facts, or *premises,* as will be explained in chapter 4 on "The Reasoning Process."

Such new facts are often "fuzzy" because the premises—i.e., the facts on which they are based—may be faulty. However, in the field of mathematics, which is essentially deductive, if the logical reasoning is correct, fuzziness occurs only as a result of differences in the definitions and axioms upon which the mathematical system is based. This, too, is discussed in chapter 4.

The many facts of mathematics are derived by means of deductions. These mathematical relationships are of great value in research, engineering, and statistical analysis.

Logical reasoning is also utilized in every field of human endeavor to derive new factual information (see chapter 4).

6. Observed Relationships

Logical reasoning, operating on observations, may produce broad statements of "observed relationships" that link different qualities or quantities in unexpected but fruitful ways. These relationships, although often stated simply, are more complex and difficult to discover than "descriptive generalizations" such as "Dogs bark." For example, the Law of Supply and Demand states a basic observed relationship that generally determines the way prices of goods increase or decrease. It is a powerful tool for predicting economic activities.

The Law of Gravitation states an observed relationship that enables physicists to calculate the force of gravity between two known masses once the distance between them is established. Isaac Newton's discovery of this law required a high degree of creative logical reasoning, combined with many observations of the motion of the moon and calculations of its distance based on measurements of angles and distances on earth.

Let's take another example: Germs cause many diseases, such as smallpox, diphtheria, typhoid fever, and the like. But for the germ theory of disease to be considered a fact, one must often go through a long process of gathering observations under many different conditions until they are thoroughly checked, corroborated, and verified.

There is always some degree of fuzziness in even the most carefully checked facts. For instance, in 1900, Newtons's Laws of Motion and the Law of Gravitation were considered to be absolutely true because they had been checked and verified to a very high degree of accuracy. In fact, the planet Neptune had been discovered by predicting its position from slight deviations in the orbit of Uranus. Yet, in 1905, Einstein's Theory of Relativity began a process that led to basic corrections in Newton's Laws. Perhaps some day another Newton or Einstein will do the same to the Theory of Relativity.

HOW FACTS HELP SOLVE PROBLEMS

The main use for facts is to help solve the many problems encountered in every phase of life. The process by which problem solving occurs in the human brain is not known, but we do know that certain procedures are helpful, and often essential, for solving problems. These procedures have been greatly improved by scientists during the past few centuries.

The way scientists go about solving problems and making new discoveries is often called the *scientific method.* However, there is no one "method" for solving problems. Individuals generally develop their own way of going about it, but some general principles are important for everyone to know and utilize. Here are some of these general principles.

1. Define the Problem

All problem-solving actively begins with a problem whose true nature must first be recognized. For example, alcoholics often do not realize (or subconsciously do not want to realize) that they are addicted to alcohol. They may blame a nagging husband or wife, unfriendly co-workers, or a boss who bothers them about lateness or absence (see figure 2.6).

"My problem is I got a wife who bugs me about drinking. She ought to know I can control my liquor. I can stop any time I want to."

Figure 2.6 This alcoholic doesn't understand the true nature of his problem. *(Drawing by Albert Sarney)*

This is also true of societies and nations. Basic economic, social, and political problems are often camouflaged by complex circumstances. For example, the United States is plagued with a large budget deficit year after year. Simple reasoning tells us that this problem could be solved either by raising revenues through increased taxes (perhaps on those who can afford to pay), by cutting government spending, or a combination of the two. But our government seems paralyzed in the face of these options.

The deeper problem seems to be political. The various groups that form our society (workers, taxpayers, consumers, business people, etc.) are affected differently by the proposed solutions; each sees the problems and the solutions differently. Much of politics is like this. The struggle is often over who is to determine the nature of the problem, and therefore the direction of its solution.

In scientific research, problems often begin with human curiosity, or stem from the needs of an employer or the government. For example, a substantial worldwide effort is underway to produce energy by using nuclear fusion. The problem is clear—the need for more power to run factories and light our houses—and scientists are hired to work on it. But more often than not a research scientist is simply curious about some puzzling fact of nature: the problem is generated and off he goes to work on it without anyone telling him what to do. At one time, this was the way scientists worked. It is less common now, however, since scientific research has become so expensive and complex, often requiring large teams of specialists.

Consider the case of the British scientist James C. Maxwell, who, in the mid-1800s, began a five-year investigation centering on the question "What is light?" The outcome was his theory that light is an "electromagnetic wave." He also suggested that there might be other kinds of electromagnetic waves yet to be found.

Two decades later, the German scientist Heinrich Hertz decided to work on Maxwell's suggestion that new electromagnetic waves existed. He solved the problem by producing the first radio waves.

That early quest for the nature of light has since generated today's huge, indispensable, worldwide television and communications industries. It has transformed our world into a global community with many millions of people earning their living as a result of the clear thinking and masterful problem solving of Maxwell, Hertz, and many other scientists, engineers, inventors, and entrepreneurs.

2. Gather Facts to Solve the Problem

In our incident at the Arctic missile base, the fact that the missile station personnel could not get a telephone call through to headquarters left the officers at the base stranded with insufficient facts on which to make a decision. *They needed more facts.* Normally, the necessary facts would have been supplied by the call. Headquarters could have checked with other radar bases to either confirm or deny the fact that missiles were on the way.

3. Use Human Memory, Logical Reasoning, and
Reliable Information to Gather or Produce More Facts

The officers at the radar base dug into their mental memory banks to try to come up with any additional facts that might help solve the problem. The commanding officer hit the jackpot with his brilliant question regarding the whereabouts of the Soviet leader.

In most situations, with far less pressure than existed at the Arctic base, the process of gathering facts and using logical reasoning is one in which the human brain goes about solving problems in a "no holds barred" manner. We may talk to experts and get their advice, read books and technical periodicals in the library, keep thinking about the way all the information fits together, and even do experiments on our own. Eventually, the point is reached when we feel there is a sufficient body of facts upon which to base a decision.

4. Reach a Conclusion

With the help of the logical processes to be discussed in chapter 4, we can reach a conclusion, and perhaps even develop a decision for action to solve the problem.

In the incident at the Arctic missile base, steps 3 and 4 were telescoped into a fleeting moment because an extremely important logical deduction emerged from "Where is Khrushchev?" That is usually not the case in most problem-solving situations. More often than not it takes a lot of fact-gathering and thinking before a conclusion is reached.

In the next chapter, we will explore the ways in which imagination has been misinterpreted as fact to create many superstitions that hamper our efforts to solve real problems.

NOTES

1. William Broad and Nicholas Wade, *Betrayers of the Truth* (New York, Simon and Schuster, 1982), pp. 112–15.

2. Ibid.

3. Milton A. Rothman, "Cold Fusion: a Case History in Wishful Science," *Skeptical Inquirer* 14, No. 2 (Winter 1990): 161–70.

4. E. T. Thompson, *Plantation Societies, Race Relations, and the South* (Durham, N.C.: Duke University Press, 1975).

5. Stephen J. Gould, *Hen's Teeth and Horse's Toes* (New York, W. W. Norton Co., 1983), pp. 202–240.

6. William Broad and Nicholas Wade, *Betrayers of the Truth*, pp. 203–211.

7. Irving Langmuir, "The Speed of the Deer Fly," *Science* 87, No. 2254 (March 11, 1938): 233–34.

QUESTIONS (*Discussion of these Questions Begins on Page 237.*)

Evaluate the following statements. To what degree are they facts? Are they true under all circumstances? Are they probably true, but not always? If they are not true under all circumstances, can you modify them to eliminate the exceptions?

1. To see the sun at noon, face south.

2. One foot is 12 inches long.

3. 10 + 10 = 100 (This statement was discussed in the chapter.)

4. 14 + 14 = 33

5. Every living thing dies after a period of time.

6. The shadow of a telephone pole at noon points north.

7. An hour after we have looked at the moon in the sky it will appear to have moved to the right of where it was before.

8. Nobody can live in air that has reached a temperature of 150 degrees.

9. The roots of plants grow downward.

10. A bird is an animal that has wings and can fly.

11. Fish are confined to the water.

12. The use of computers greatly improves the operation of a business.

13. I exist.

3

Superstition and Science

In 480 B.C., the Persian King Xerxes sent a fleet of one thousand ships to attack the Greeks near Athens. Representatives of the Greek city-states met to consider what was to be done. Some thought they should surrender, while others insisted that they should fight, even against great odds. However, they could not agree upon a plan of action.

As was the custom of the time, the "Delphic oracle" was consulted. The priestess at the temple prepared herself by drinking water from a sacred spring, chewing laurel leaves, and shaking a laurel branch. After she had fallen into a trance, the problem was presented to her. She answered, supposedly giving advice from the god Apollo, that the people were to rely on "wooden walls."

But nothing was said as to where these walls were to be found. Some people thought they should build a wooden stockade on the old citadel of the town. Themistocles, the leader of the armed forces, who had a plan based upon a sea battle, insisted on the peculiar interpretation that "wooden walls" referred to wooden hulls of ships.

Utilizing a fleet of three hundred small ships in the narrow straits between the island of Salamis and the coast of Attica, he outmaneuvered the one thousand large ships of the Persian fleet and defeated them.

Since the "advice" supposedly given by the god Apollo had "proved" to be correct, faith in this way of solving problems was enhanced. But our admiration goes to Themistocles, who was able to put the proper interpretation on the oracle's "double talk" and mold it into an effective plan of action.

SUPERSTITION IN THE PAST

This incident illustrates a way of thinking that was typical of ancient peoples. They had little understanding of the forces of nature that affected them.

Storms arose for no apparent reason and smashed their huts. Lightning from the sky suddenly blasted trees and buildings with power beyond belief. Plagues invaded towns and killed many people. Drought might ruin crops one year, while good rains made them plentiful the next.

People sought the causes of such destructive events. If they knew the causes perhaps they could find ways to prevent or alleviate the damage. Over time, explanations were developed. People came to believe that there were many different gods or supernatural spirits who controlled natural events and who, like humans, were animated by their particular loves and hates.

It made sense to explain a bolt of lightning as a sign that Jove was angry at something the community, or one of its leaders, did (or did not) do. If someone fell down the steps and broke a leg, this might be because the victim had offended the ghost of a deceased person who formerly lived in the house. A disease might be caused by a witch, perhaps the reclusive old lady who lived in a ramshackle house down the street.

Until recent times such ways of thinking were all too frequent. As an example, consider our own "Salem witch trials" in Massachusetts during 1692 in which 150 innocent men and women were imprisoned for witchcraft, 19 of whom were tried by a special court, found guilty, and executed.

What was their crime? Beginning in December 1691, eight girls in Salem were observed behaving strangely, with disorganized speech, peculiar postures and body motions, and convulsions. Physicians could find no cause for this behavior, but one doctor suggested that it might be due to witchcraft. Several of the girls then accused one of their family's female house slaves of engaging in witchcraft, along with two elderly women who had "bad" reputations. All three were imprisoned.[1]

> Giles Corey had been pressed to death, an ordeal calulated to force him to enter a plea to the courts so that he could be tried. The evidence used to obtain the convictions was the "test of touch" and "spectral evidence." The afflicted girls were present at the examinations and trials, often creating such pandemonium that the proceedings were interrupted. The accused witches were, for the most part, persons of good reputation in the community; one was even a former minister in the village. . . .
>
> All the men and women who were hanged had maintained their innocence; not one confessor to the crime was executed. It had become obvious early in the course of the proceedings that those who confessed would not be executed.[2]

Two main kinds of evidence assured conviction. If any of the girls imagined they saw an apparition of the accused person, this initiated arrest and trial. In the "test of touch," if one of the girls who experienced a convulsive seizure was touched by the accused person and this caused the seizure to cease, then this "proved" that the accused was a witch.[3]

This kind of "test" for witchcraft was common and assumed many forms. In some cases the accused was bound and then thrown into water. If the person floated, this was proof of witchcraft; execution by hanging or burning quickly followed. On the other hand, if the accused drowned, this proved innocence! The fact that an innocent person died was irrelevant. It was more important that the authorities discover the "truth."

Were the eight girls afflicted with hysteria and vivid imaginations? Perhaps. But according to one proposed explanation, they may have been afflicted with "convulsive ergotism," a disease caused by "ergot," a fungus that grows on rye and some other grains during moist seasons. The bread made from such infected grains contains a substance similar to a drug popular in the 1960s known as LSD (lysergic acid diethylamide), which often produced hallucinations and seizures.[4]

Aren't we fortunate to be living today and not during a time when superstitions about witches, Satan, vindictive gods, and "black magic" were firmly believed by most people?

SUPERSTITION TODAY

Many vestiges of ancient ways of thinking still remain. People who "knock on wood" may not realize it, but this custom arose as an attempt to notify the forest elf or spirit—trapped in the wood when the tree was chopped down for lumber—that we know he is listening to our conversation. In effect, we are saying to him: "You just heard me say that I expect to inherit a fortune from my old uncle Ben. Don't you pull any of your dirty tricks and spoil it for me. I'm on to you. Watch out. I might send this table, your home, to the junk yard."

Someone who says "Uh, oh! Now I'll have some bad luck" when a black cat crosses his path, is buying into the notion that the feline is actually an old witch in disguise, out to make trouble for anyone in sight. However, a black cat means the opposite in England. According to the caption on a photograph of a theater, in an advertisement by British Airways, "To ensure good luck (and good 'notices'), most of London's theatres are home to at least one black cat."[5]

Similar peculiarities in beliefs among different regions and countries are observed for other superstitions. At any rate, these contradictory differences are just one more indication of the falsity of superstitious beliefs.

How can a black cat be "bad luck" in the United States, but "good luck" when one crosses the ocean?

Today, there are people in the United States who employ "black magic" or voodoo to punish their enemies: they stick pins into images or special paintings in the belief that discomfort will result. Others go to gypsies to have their fortunes told (figure 3.1). Some builders of skyscrapers still skip thirteen when they number the floors, because many people hesitate to work on the thirteenth floor. They think that the old superstition about thirteen being an unlucky number might just be true: "Why take a chance?" Those who are looking for office space may reject a building that has a thirteenth floor because, even though *they* are not superstitious, others are. So the custom persists (figure 3.2, p. 48).

Some superstitions have fatal consequences. In 1989, a jury convicted the mother of a four-year-old child for starving the youngster to death. The mother had followed the advice of the leader of her religious sect: he suggested that she "exorcise" the evil spirits from her child's body in this manner. In Mexico a gang of criminals periodically captured and executed young men in ritual murders to ward off bad luck.

"The crystal ball tells me that you may get a good job in the future."

Figure 3.1 Such "predictions" are so general that they apply to almost everybody. The job offer "may" (or may not) ever be made. *(Drawing by Arnold Lobel)*

"I'm not superstitious, but why take a chance by renting an office on the thirteenth floor? Besides, some people wouldn't want to work there."

Figure 3.2 Many people say they are not superstitious. The real test is the way they act. *(Drawing by Albert Sarney)*

BELIEF IN SUPERNATURAL MAGIC

The essence of superstition today is basically the same as in years past: belief in the supernatural; the magical power of mysterious, invisible, unknowable forces; and spirits, ghosts, or influences by planets and stars. Long ago, people "explained" many events by imagining an array of different agents with great powers: gods, elves, fairies, witches, ghosts, and goblins. These supernatural agents were invisible, could pass through solid walls, change their forms, dispense "bad luck" or "good luck," predict the future and even make those predictions come true.

Today, superstitious beliefs depend much less on the agents but more on abstract, magical manipulations and procedures. If someone "reads" the future by looking at cards, palms, tea leaves, crystal balls, or astrological charts and then says "I see good fortune coming your way," it is proper to ask "How do *you* know?" How does a card (or crystal ball or star) *know* anything? Do the tea leaves, or the spirits in the tea leaves, follow people around and then sometime later magically make money fall into their laps? How does the astrological chart, or a planet one hundred million miles away, or a star one hundred trillion miles distant, arrange to have people meet the partners of their dreams? How does the number thirteen on the door of an apartment manage to produce the "bad luck" that superstitious people associate with that number? Just asking such questions suggests the irrationality of superstitious beliefs.

Judging from the number of books published and the 1,200 newspaper columns on the subject, astrology seems to be the most widespread form of superstition today. For that reason chapter 7 analyzes in detail why astrology should be considered a superstition, despite the superficial veneer of "science" claimed for it as a result of its seemingly complex calculations of the positions of planets and stars.

There was a resurgence of superstitious beliefs during the 1960s, associated with disillusionment in "science" for creating nuclear weapons that threatened the globe with total destruction. It was also a time when an unpopular war in Vietnam was actively resisted by many young people. These events set many young minds against government, and authority in general. They also turned against "science," perceiving it to be an agent of government in creating destructive weaponry and therefore an enemy. These young people reacted to the rationality of science by turning to its opposite, superstitions like astrology. But in doing so, they also turned against the methods of science that had brought many benefits, including the elimination of many deadly diseases, increased life expectancy, and a higher standard of living. They also unwisely rejected the objectivity, rationality, and powerful way of thinking that have enabled scientists to investigate thoroughly and solve a wide variety of difficult problems.

SCIENCE: A PROBLEM-SOLVING "ENGINE"

The methods of science, especially its way of thinking, may be thought of as a powerful "engine" for solving many types of problems. The purposes for which this problem-solving engine is used depend on decisions made by governments and ordinary people, not by the engine. If the driver of a car uses his powerful engine to plow into a crowd, we blame the driver, not the engine. In the same way, the engine of scientific thinking can be used for good or evil, and it is up to us to determine what uses are made of it.

Many difficult problems in our world cannot be solved without utilizing science and its ways of thinking through complex situations. We need look no further than the many environmental problems that face us: global warming as carbon dioxide levels increase, destruction of the ozone layer in the atmosphere, increased population levels, denuded forests, and many others. Effective solutions require correct information that only scientific methods of research can provide. We certainly can't get that information by invoking the imaginary magical powers of planets and stars, cards, tea leaves, and crystal balls. What do they know about the environment, or anything else for that matter?

But science is not enough. Complex and difficult political and economic decisions also have to be made, both by governments and professionals, in allocating resources, funding research, enacting taxes to pay for these expenditures, and education to develop new values about the earth's environment.

Most of the activities of science center around the search for causal relationships among different events in our environment. Ancient peoples also sought the causes of various phenomena, but without knowing the real causes of the many mysterious events that occurred, they "explained" them through superstitious belief in the capricious actions of gods, witches, and spirits of all kinds. As a result, ancient peoples fruitlessly sought to placate these supernatural agents with special ceremonies and offerings, which did nothing to improve the community's situation, except, perhaps to make the population feel better.

Today's scientists have discovered the real causes for many mysterious phenomena, and have therefore enabled us to manage and even have some degree of control over them.

CAUSE AND EFFECT

One of the primary aims of scientific research, and often everyday reasoning, is to discover the causes of events. What do we mean when we talk about the "cause" for the occurrence of an event? It is very much like an action sequence: First an action occurs; then we notice that another action follows, perhaps immediately, or sometimes much later. Every time we observe the first action, we also observe the second. We therefore, tend to view the first action as the cause of the second, which we call the "effect."

It is not necessarily true that if one event always follows another then the first event is the cause and the second event is its effect. For example, if a certain type of cloud always precedes rain, it does not follow that this type of cloud is the cause of rain. Actually, scientists have found that the cloud and the rain that accompanies it are both produced when air is cooled and water vapor condenses into tiny droplets. The droplets form the cloud. If they become large enough, they fall rapidly to the ground without evaporating.

Kick a wall hard and your foot hurts. Kick it again and your foot will hurt once again. If you persist in kicking the wall fifty times, you will surely conclude that the cause of the hurt is the kicking of the wall. However, a self-centered child might blame the wall as the cause.

A psychologist might find that the kicker needs to get rid of his aggressions. In that case his mental state may be considered the main cause of his getting hurt. Perhaps the kicker gets pleasure from hurting himself. Since the wall would not have been kicked without that motive, the kicker's mental state could be considered the main cause.

Many people demand simple answers to questions about causality. They grab hold of one simple cause as *the* answer. But life is more complicated than that; there are often many contributory causes for events in complex human affairs. For example, what is the cause of increased crime in the United States? Drugs? Violence dramatically portrayed on television and in the movies? The easy availability of guns? Broken families? Poverty? Slums? Deteriorating value systems? Improper upbringing at home? Laziness and a poor work ethic? Inadequate schools? Could it be that all of them contribute to crime?

Those who insist on one simple cause are bound to fail in finding solutions because when they try their one solution they do not address other contributing causes.

Sometimes we confuse causes and effects, finding ourselves unable to tell which is which, as shown in the amusing cartoon in figure 3.3 (p. 52). From the rabbit's point of view it has trained the lab technician, because every time a button is pressed, it gets food. One day the poor

"He's well trained. Every time I ring a bell he feeds me!"

Figure 3.3 The rabbit sees the cause of his being fed differently than does the scientist. *(Drawing by Arnold Lobel)*

rabbit will find out who is boss; then the true cause for his getting food will be painfully clear.

Knowing the Cause

Knowing about causes and effects of most events is of great value. For example, when a physician examines a patient who is ill, the doctor's first task is to make a "diagnosis," which simply means "finding the nature of the illness." In most cases, these findings also indicate the cause of the patient's complaint.

This is done by measuring and probing with a variety of instruments and "tests," each of which is a small "experiment" designed to produce "observations." These observations provide the essential facts upon which correct judgments may be reached about what is causing the illness.

So the physician probes and pokes the patient; thumps the chest while listening with a stethoscope; and looks into eyes, ears, and throat. The doctor may order an electrocardiogram (a heart test) and perhaps take some blood samples to check chemical substances in the body. Behind these tests is a long history of careful investigative research by scientists, and research based on measurements that make the findings more objective and readily replicated by others.

When the physician has gathered a sufficient number of facts based on observations, he may come to a conclusion: a diagnosis, a judgment of the nature of the illness. When the cause is known, an effective course of treatment may be prescribed to cure, alleviate, or prevent the disease.

This method of solving problems by trying to discover causes for what happens is based on science, which has been developed to a high level during the past few centuries. It is a very powerful and productive process that has transformed not only medical science, but every other aspect of modern life. As noted previously, it may be considered an engine for deriving new knowledge and for solving extremely complex problems.

Science has also dispelled ignorance about the nature of our world. What we now know about the earth, the sun, the planets, the stars, plants, animals, people, disease, air, water, rocks, soil, oceans, light, even the origin of the universe, would astound anyone who lived just a few hundred years ago.

Consider how knowledge of cause and effect is applied to make an automobile work. There are many interconnected parts in a car, each of which works in designed coordination with other parts to cause the engine to move the vehicle. The basic cause of the engine's motion is heat produced by the burning of gasoline. This heat causes gases to expand inside the cylinders, giving rise to high pressures that cause the pistons inside the cylinders to move. This, in turn, causes the crankshaft to rotate. Gears connected to the crankshaft then cause various associated systems to move. A generator causes the battery to be charged. The battery causes electric current to flow to the distributor, which in turn causes properly timed sparks that cause gasoline in the cylinders to ignite. A water pump causes cooling water to circulate in the engine. And so on, in a complex, interrelated chain of causes and effects. The end result of many such causes and effects produces the one main effect we seek—controlled motion of the car.

Obviously, the engineers who design cars, or any other products or structures, must be experts who understand the many possible cause-and-effect relationships for machinery. In like manner, a physician must be an expert in cause-and-effect relationships involving human biology. An economist must be expert in such relationships that involve money, goods, and services. A good psychologist knows the cause-and-effect relationships in human behavior. In fact, the essence of any science, many professions, and a substantial part of business activity is the attempt to discover just such vital relationships.

Difficulties in Discovering the Causes of Effects

Cause-and-effect relationships are not always easy to determine. For example, imagine that you are a member of a tribe in some remote area of the world, cut off from all the information available in modern society. One day an eclipse begins to occur. Someone notices the sky darkening in daytime, and not a cloud in sight. Is the sun about to disappear forever, leaving the community in permanent darkness to die freezing cold with no food to eat?

A hurried meeting is called. Why is the sun getting dark? Is the sun god punishing the community because it has offended him in some way? One of the elders suggests that the sun god be appeased with special offerings and a ceremony (figure 3.4). This is quickly done. And lo! As the ceremony gets under way, the sun god immediately responds by making the sun lighter again. Soon the sun is restored.

Obviously, the wise elder has discovered the correct cause for the darkening sun, and has saved the community from disaster. So, the next time an eclipse begins, you and everyone else will do the same things that "worked" before. In fact, this plan of action will always work because sunlight inevitably returns after an eclipse no matter what anyone on earth does.

Any doubters in the tribe now believe in the existence of the sun god. How much more "proof" does a person need than the outstandingly successful sun god appeasement procedures used during periods of sun-darkening? In this way the tribe has established a set of "facts" that are considered to be absolutely true, yet are totally false and wasteful. It would be hard to change their view because they have obviously "proved" it with a ceremony that is immediately effective.

Now let's suppose that some smart aleck in the tribe tells you that the ritual is hogwash and that no matter what you did the sun would always come back into view. Even if you were swayed a bit by his arguments, would you want to take a chance the next time an eclipse begins? Would you refrain from using a remedy that has thus far shown itself to be successful? Not likely.

More likely than not the members of the tribe would denounce the skeptic as endangering the entire community by insulting and antagonizing the powerful sun god, and obstructing their successful program to save the day when an eclipse begins. They are likely to punish him severely: perhaps banishment, torture, maybe even death.

As we can see, it is not so easy to determine true causes, even in situations that would appear obvious and simple. The more complex the circumstances, the more difficult it is to determine causes for observed effects.

"My father told me what to do when the sun god gets angry with us and takes the daylight away. We have to do a sun dance to bring daylight back."

Figure 3.4 This plan of action will always "work," thereby "proving" that the reason for the eclipse is punishment inflicted by an angry sun god. *(Drawing by Albert Sarney)*

Yet the search for causes is vital if progress in any field of endeavor is to occur. When successful, we gain the power to influence or control effects. For example, when Louis Pasteur discovered that the disease known as anthrax was caused by germs, his findings immediately suggested that other diseases might have a similar cause. This opened the floodgates to germ research. As a result, during the past century, methods of preventing and curing a host of diseases have doubled human life expectancy.

We wash our hands to remove and prevent the spreading of germs. We chlorinate water to neutralize germs. Nurses use antiseptics to clean the skin of patients before surgery. Operating rooms are kept scrupulously clean with disinfectants. A host of germ-killing medicines have been found that destroy the foreign organisms after they enter the body.

Once the noted mathematician and early physicist Isaac Newton had identified the force of gravity as the basic cause of motion of the moon in orbit around the earth, it was possible to calculate orbits for earth satellites and planets, and then to produce rockets that cause them to escape earth's gravity and go into orbit.

How do we know that Newton's theory of gravitation works? Consider the remarkable exploration of the four outer planets by the space probe Voyager II from 1977 to 1989. After two years it reached Jupiter and took many pictures and measurements. Then our space scientists used Jupiter's force of gravity to propel Voyager II toward Saturn. Astronomers calculated exactly how close to Jupiter Voyager II had to come to be swung around by just the right amount of force to be propelled on a long trip to its neighbor planet.

This astonishing process was repeated at Saturn, then at Uranus, so that Voyager II eventually reached Neptune. So precisely were these maneuvers planned that the satellite, after traveling a distance of four billion miles in twelve years, reached the closest point to Neptune within four minutes of the time predicted at the start of its journey!

That's an extraordinary prediction of future events, one that provides strong supporting evidence that Newton's Law of Gravitation and his Laws of Motion, upon which calculations of orbits are based, are true. When we act on these laws, the results can be accurately predicted and we can examine the results to verify the predictions we've made.

In 1905, despite the general belief by scientists that Newton's Laws of Motion and that of Gravitation were absolutely true, the noted physicist Albert Einstein proposed a profound cause-and-effect relationship, which came to be known as the Theory of Relativity; it altered Newton's view of space, time, and motion. Astronomers still use Newton's Laws to calculate orbits for planets and satellites, but only because the differences in calculations for most planetary orbits produced by the Theory of Relativity are generally too small to observe. However, such corrections have to be made for the planet Mercury, which moves around the sun at the highest planetary speed in the solar system. When we shift our attention away from large astronomical bodies to concentrate on the enormous speeds of small particles in nuclear reactions, Newton's Laws of Motion must take relativity into account.

All knowledge grows in this corrective way. The facts and cause-and-effect relationships proposed at one period of time are rarely discarded completely; instead, they are altered to accommodate new circumstances. As scientists probe new areas of knowledge, unknown to previous investigators, they often discover that new conditions and circumstances bring new observations that lead to new theories and new cause-and-effect relationships. This is true in all life situations, as well as in science. You will note many examples of this important fact of life throughout this book.

NOTES

1. Linda R. Caporael, "Ergotism: The Satan Loosed in Salem?" *Science* (April 2, 1976): 21.
2. Ibid.
3. Ibid.
4. Ibid.
5. Advertisement in the *New York Times* magazine, British Airways (March 4, 1990): 10.

QUESTIONS (*Discussion of these Questions Begins on Page 241.*)

1. In this chapter astrology was mentioned as an example of a modern superstition. The extent to which people believe in it is indicated by widespread publication of horoscopes in daily newspapers, the considerable number of books on astrology that are published and purchased, and frequent references by prominent people to their astrological signs. Do you believe there may be some validity to astrology? Explain your answer. (For a more in-depth discussion of astrology see chapter 7.)

2. How do astrologers explain the way stars and planets manage to influence human affairs so selectively, solely on the basis of one's birthdate?

3. How would you design an experiment to provide an objective test for the truth or falsity of astrological claims?

4. List three common superstitions and analyze the likelihood of each of them being true.

5. The controlled motion of a car is due to the operation of many interrelated causes that together produce effects. List three causes of different motions in a car and the effects they produce. For example, if you turn the steering wheel to the left, this causes the front edges of the front wheels to turn and point toward the left. This position causes a moving car to turn to the left.

6. For three household appliances or tools list some of the causes that produce the desired effects. For example, how does a knife cause a slice of bread to be separated from the main part of the loaf?

7. List the known causes for three different diseases; then list the effects they produce. What are the remedies, cures, or preventive measures that physicians apply to remove the causes for each disease?

8. The drunken driver in figure 3.5 (p. 58), whose car crashed into a tree, claims that the tree hit him first. In his stupor he thinks it is the tree's fault. Can the tree be a "cause" for this crash? Analyze the cause-and-effect relationships in this situation.

"I swear, it was the tree that hit me!"

Figure 3.5 Analyze the cause and effect relationships in this situation. *(Drawing by Albert Sarney)*

4

The Reasoning Process

Could a blind man sitting in a car driven by his wife know that she is headed the wrong way on a road, and be right? If so, how could he accomplish this seemingly impossible feat? Let's take an example: One afternoon Arthur Moss, who is blind, was riding in a car driven by his wife, Elaine. They were going to Ridgetown, located to the north, on Barker Turnpike. When Mrs. Moss reached the turnpike entrance she made a mistake in reading the signs and ended up heading south instead of north. After a few minutes Mr. Moss felt the heat of the sun on his right arm, from which he deduced that they were heading south, not north. He told his wife that she was going the wrong way, but his wife disagreed. How could her blind husband tell her which way to go? But nine miles later she finally realized he was right, turned around, and headed in the opposite direction.

How did Mr. Moss do it? Here are the steps in his reasoning to a correct conclusion from the facts he observed and from those learned from previous experience.

1. He sat in the front on the right side of the car.

2. He knew from past experience that sunlight shining on his body makes it warm. Because his right arm got warm, he reasoned that the sun was shining on the right side of the car.

3. This happened in the afternoon. The sun is therefore shining on him mostly from the west.

4. The car was supposed to be heading north to Ridgetown.

Figure 4.1 (p. 60) shows the two possibilities: (A) heading south, or (B) heading north. Which of these situations fits the facts listed above? First look at situation B (heading north). Mr. Moss's arm would be on

59

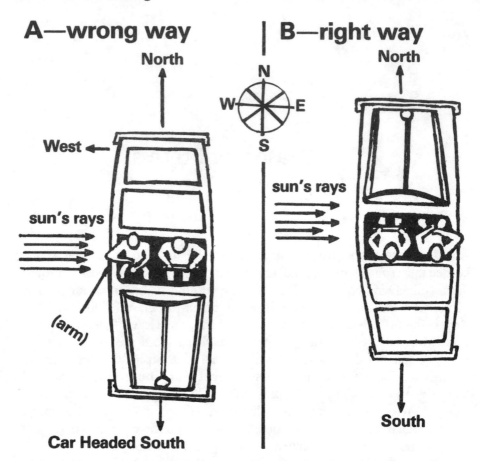

Figure 4.1 The blind man sitting in the passenger's seat uses logical reasoning to conclude that the car is going the wrong way (south). His clue is the observation that his right arm is warmed by the afternoon sun in the west. *(Drawing by Irving Lazarus)*

the east side of the car and sunlight could not reach his right arm because it would be blocked by his body, or the car. Since situation B contradicts (runs contrary to) the fact that he felt the sun on his right arm, it can be ruled out. The car was not heading north as intended.

Situation A matches the facts. With the car heading south Mr. Moss's arm can get sunlight from the west and feel its warmth. Since this is an either-or situation—either the car is heading north, or it is going south—it was possible for Mr. Moss to conclude they were going the wrong way.

Is it possible that Mr. Moss's reasoning might have been wrong? In a real situation, people are rarely certain that all the necessary facts are available. Suppose, for example, that some trickster had placed a heating lamp on the right side of the car, or that Mr. Moss had some special kind of fever that made his right arm feel warmer. These exceptional situations are unlikely. So, if we assume that no unusual facts were present, Mr. Moss's conclusion followed in a logical manner from the facts as stated.

In one sense, all sighted people are "blind" to most of the events that occur in the world. We cannot see atoms, gravity, or electricity; we cannot see events in the past or what is happening far away. But by means of logical reasoning we can discover facts about invisible objects or events, just as Mr. Moss did.

USING CONTRADICTIONS IN REASONING

Mr. Moss was able to conclude correctly that his wife was driving the wrong way because logical reasoning based on his observations led to a *contradiction*. The word *contradict* comes from the Latin *contra,* meaning "against," and *dicere, meaning* "to speak." Therefore, to "contradict" means "to speak against," or "to mean the opposite." A contradiction is a statement or conclusion that is the opposite of another statement or conclusion.

A contradiction sends out a loud signal: STOP. Two contradictory "facts" or conclusions cannot both be right. One or the other is wrong. This is a fundamental principle in reasoning. It provides a powerful tool for finding out when "facts" or conclusions are wrong.

For example, Mrs. Moss didn't believe her blind husband's conclusion about her choice of direction. So, she drove nine miles the wrong way. Then she probably began to notice facts that contradicted her judgment. Perhaps the trip became too long, or the scenery was unfamiliar. Maybe she saw a road sign that indicated she was going south. Such contradictions to her choice eventually convinced her. Only then did she admit that her husband's reasoning was correct and that she was headed in the wrong direction.

The process of proving something untrue by finding contradictions is an important tool in reasoning. For instance, when a lawyer questions a hostile witness on the stand, his main aim is to expose contradictions in the testimony. If the witness cannot explain a contradiction, his story becomes less believable.

A story told about Abraham Lincoln as a young lawyer illustrates the use of contradictions in court trials. Lincoln's client was accused of stealing a horse from a barn. A witness stated that he saw the accused man take the horse from the barn at night. Lincoln asked the witness how he was able to see clearly enough at night to be sure of the identification. The witness said there was a bright moon. Lincoln referred to an almanac and demonstrated that on the night in question there was no moon. This contradiction made the testimony worthless, and Lincoln's client was found not guilty.

An accountant can check the general accuracy of figures in the financial records of a business by seeking contradictions between different sets of figures for sales, inventory, purchases, payroll, and other entries. The figures for all items must be *consistent*. This means they are in agreement and compatible with each other, with no contradictions detected. If any contradictions are found then closer examination of the financial records may be required.

The Treasury Department's Internal Revenue Service (IRS) uses such reasoning to detect income tax cheats. A taxpayer may have an income of $50,000 a year, and report that he has deducted $15,000 for donations to charity. To the IRS examiner, this large amount, almost one-third of the taxpayer's total income, seems much too high. It contradicts—it runs contrary to—experience. How many people give almost a third of their income to charity? A careful investigation of the tax return is likely to be ordered.

Facts that seem obvious are not automatically true. Many "facts" that we think we know are *probably* true, but some are not. A person who keeps an *open mind,* carefully examining contradictions, is more likely to discover errors in "facts" and thereby arrive at correct conclusions. Throughout this book, in many examples of reasoning, we will see that the detection of contradictions is central to logical reasoning.

REASONING FROM GIVEN FACTS

Let's try this problem:

> The children in the Scroggins family are named Tim, Mary, and Sid. Sid is two years older than Mary, who is just beginning first grade. The youngest child is half his brother's age.
>
> From this information, answer the following questions by means of logical reasoning. Evaluate each answer in terms of your estimate of its certainty. Are you sure of your answer? Is it likely or unlikely to be correct?
>
> 1. How many children are in the Scroggins family?

2. How many boys are in this family? How many girls?

3. How old is each child?

4. Can Tim talk?

5. Is Sid in the fifth grade?

6. Can both brothers play a good game of baseball?

After you have tried to answer the questions, check your answers against the reasoning that follows:

1. *How many children?* This information is not given directly, but you know all the children's names: Tim, Mary, and Sid. By counting the names it is clear that there are three children in the family. This answer, arrived at by counting, is about as certain as can be achieved.

2. *How many boys? How many girls?* The names provide clues. Based on memory and experience, we know that Tim and Sid are names of boys, and Mary is a girl's name. So there are two boys and one girl. But are we absolutely sure? Perhaps not. Some parents give their children names that can be used for either boys or girls. Sid (for Sidney) is usually a boy's name, but it also might be the shortened form of a girl's name, perhaps Sidelle. Some girls are also named Sidney or Sydney.

Boys are almost never named Mary, but perhaps there is a female Tim. So we cannot be absolutely sure that there are two boys and one girl in the family. There are *probably* two boys and one girl, but there is a small possibility that the answer might be one boy and two girls— or, if the family likes unusual names, there might even be three girls.

Most judgments in life must be expressed in terms of *probability,* or likelihood. More often than not, some facts are missing, and judgments made without them cannot be considered certain.

But wait. We are also informed that "the youngest child in the family is half *his* brother's age." If "he" has one brother, it follows that there must be two boys in the family, and therefore one girl.

This new fact, which we may have missed at first, provides information allowing us to be more certain that in this family Sid is a boy's name. It now seems practically certain that the Scroggins family has two boys and one girl.

3. *How old is each child?* The problem states that Mary is in first grade. The usual age at which a child begins first grade in the United States is about six years; but if the school year is ending, she might be

closer to seven. Sid, who is two years older, is therefore about eight, and perhaps closer to nine.

The problem states that "the youngest child is half his brother's age." The word "his" tells us that the youngest child is a boy. Sid can't be the youngest child because he is older than Mary. Therefore, Tim must be the youngest. Since the youngest is half his brother's age, Tim must be about half of Sid's age (eight or nine) or about four to four and a half years old.

These answers seem fairly likely.

4. *Can Tim talk?* From experience we know that practically all children can talk at four years of age. However, Tim might be deaf, mute, or so mentally handicapped that he has not yet learned to speak. We can say that Tim most probably talks, but it is possible that he does not.

5. *Is Sid in the fifth grade?* Probably not. If Sid is eight (plus) years old, he is most likely to be in the third grade, not the fifth. However, Sid could be extremely bright and may have been offered advanced placement in school. Or, if Mary is really older than six, Sid might be older than eight. In either case, there is a remote possibility that he is in the fifth grade.

6. *Can both brothers play a good game of baseball?* Experience tells us that most people would think it unlikely that four-year-old Tim could play a good game of baseball. He is too young. As for Sid, at age eight or more, we don't have enough information to give a proper answer. The question is *too general.* To answer it we would need to know a lot more about the Scroggins family. If they live in a specific place where we also know that most boys of eight play baseball, we might answer "probably yes." But if they live in a place where baseball is not often played—perhaps in a crowded city—then the answer might be "probably no."

And what is meant by "a good game"? There is no simple way to compare Sid's game with the way others play without knowing Sid and the others personally. Any judgment about Sid's ability to play baseball must be *subjective*—in other words, based on personal opinion rather than facts. Such opinions are affected by each person's past experiences and ideas of what count as good and bad games of baseball.

There just isn't enough information to make a reasonable judgment. Any answer would therefore be meaningless. In that case we should not feel obligated to find an answer when there is none. Just say, "I don't know."

Note that in answering these questions it was possible to obtain *new* information by reasoning logically from the information contained in the problem to arrive at definite answers for the first two questions.

Isabel: "*The day before yesterday he said there was a 50 percent chance of rain and it didn't rain. Then he did it again yesterday, and again it didn't rain. What's the use of a weather report if they never get it right?*"

Harry: "*Yeah. I wonder why these guys get paid for making predictions that don't come true.*"

Figure 4.2 This couple has a *misconception* about the meaning of "probability," causing them to reach a wrong conclusion. What is the misconception? *(Drawing by Albert Sarney)*

Logical reasoning, by itself, was not sufficient to provide answers to questions 3, 4, and 5 without additional "facts" from the storehouse of information in our minds. But these additional facts are probabilities, so we cannot be sure they apply in these cases. All we can say is that our answers are "likely," or "probable."

Most reasoning situations in life are of just this type. Usually our reasoning processes are fine. The degree of uncertainty in our conclusions is generally determined by the likelihood that the starting assumptions, or facts, are true. In many situations they are not true, or the facts are misinterpreted, thus producing incorrect judgments. Figure 4.2 illustrates such a situation. Isabel has the wrong idea about the meaning of a "50 percent chance of rain." So does her husband, Harry. As a result, they make wrong judgments.

Scientists are keenly aware of the uncertainties when facts are gathered;

that is why they generally state the estimated range of error when reporting measurements for their experiments.

Pollsters who take opinion surveys also estimate the range of uncertainty in their results. For example, in taking a pre-election poll during a campaign for president of the United States in which about fifty million people cast ballots, the pollsters might interview only one or two thousand properly selected people in a "random sample." Obviously, no one can be absolutely certain that a poll of such a small proportion of the voters represents the opinions of the nation. However, the poll is useful to indicate the general trend of opinion.

To indicate the degree of uncertainty, the pollster will announce a figure reflecting public support for a candidate, such as 38 percent, "with a margin of error of plus or minus 4 percent." This means that the pollster estimates the true figure to be somewhere between 38 percent plus 4 percent, or 42 percent, and 38 percent minus 4 percent, or 34 percent. In effect, the pollster feels quite sure that the correct figure is somewhere between 34 percent and 42 percent, and is very unlikely to be outside that range. (See chapter 10 for further discussion of opinion polls.)

WORDS USED IN LOGICAL REASONING

Logic is the science of correct reasoning. In everyday usage, however, the word *logical* simply means "correct reasoning," without any attempt to analyze it in detail. People learn to reason logically by experience. In fact, observations of young children reveal that they seem to have an inborn ability to reason that rapidly develops with experience.

The end results of reasoning may be described with a number of words: *conclusion, deduction, inference, judgment,* or *decision.* Each of these words conveys a slightly different meaning, although they are often employed interchangeably in everyday usage. For example, someone might say, "I concluded that Bill was wrong," or "I (deduced, inferred, judged, decided) that Bill was wrong."

A *conclusion* indicates the end of the reasoning process, while the word *deduction* is used in logic to mean that one has reasoned to a conclusion from given statements of fact or assumptions. The word *inference* implies use of reasoning to reach a conclusion, while the term *judgment* might be used if the facts are complex and weighed carefully, as they might be in a courtroom. *Decision,* like judgment, is often used when the facts are complex. The word *gathered* is also sometimes used to mean "came to a conclusion," as in "I gathered that Sue wants to become a nurse."

Another word frequently used in reasoning is *imply*. It means that the facts (or generalizations) lead logically to an inference or judgment. A detective might *infer* from a set of facts that a suspect is guilty of a crime. The facts *imply* that it is so.

HOW WE GENERALIZE

The only means we have for gaining *direct* knowledge of the world is through our senses: sight, hearing, touch, smell, and taste. This information is stored in our brains as memories, or recorded in books and computers. Later we can recall facts from our memories, look them up in books, call them up on the screen of a computer, and use them in calculations and in devising theories. Let's analyze a simple situation in which new information is obtained by reasoning from knowledge gained by our senses:

Fact 1. House A on my block is box-shaped.

Fact 2. House B on my block is box-shaped.

Fact 3. All the houses on my block are box-shaped.

Fact 4. All the houses in my neighborhood are box-shaped.

Would it be correct reasoning to conclude that all houses are box-shaped? In this case, individual facts were gathered about all the houses on the block and in the neighborhood. Every house was observed to be box-shaped. These observations imply that every house in town is box-shaped. From these facts some people might conclude, "All houses, anywhere, are box-shaped."

Such a statement is called a *generalization*. In other words, we infer that something is true *in general* because we observe many examples of its truth in specific instances. If we count one thousand box-shaped houses in a city to reach a conclusion about *all* houses everywhere, it is possible that around the corner from where we stopped there might be a circular house. In fact, we can never be absolutely sure that there are no houses with other shapes even if we counted a million box-shaped houses without a single exception being noted. The very next town might have a house that is not box-shaped. Somewhere, box-shaped houses might be the exception, not the rule. The validity of such inferences depends heavily on the fairness or representativeness of the instances we observe.

INDUCTIVE REASONING

The kind of reasoning that proceeds from many specific examples to a generalization is called *induction*. Note that when a generalization is formed by induction from many individual observations we can only be sure of it if all instances are observed. If some cases have not been observed, we can only infer its probability of being true. If we have taken a sampling of houses in many towns in many states and have found all houses in the sampling to have been box-shaped, then we could consider the generalization about houses being box-shaped as very likely to be true (figure 4.3).

There are times when we are quite sure of the truth of a generalized fact. Suppose we observe *all* houses in the town of Martinsville and find that they are box-shaped. In that case we may be sure of at least one generalized statement: "All houses in Martinsville are box-shaped."

However, most generalizations are based on a sampling of observa-

INDUCTIVE REASONING

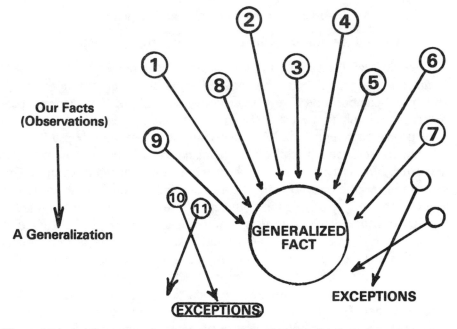

Figure 4.3 Inductive reasoning is the formation of generalizations from a number of observations of similar things or events. All generalized facts are obtained in this way. But we can never be sure these generalizations are absolutely true because it is impossible for us to observe all actual cases, everywhere, in the present, past, and future. *(Drawing by Irving Lazarus)*

tions. In such cases the generalizations based on induction are not known to be *absolutely* true. They have a certain amount of built-in fuzziness and are somewhat tentative, subject to modification, or perhaps likely to be rejected as new observations are accumulated. It should not surprise us if we find occasional exceptions that indicate the presence of a new situation requiring a new generalization or modification of the old one. Such exceptions are important to the investigative process because they often lead to new areas of knowledge.

For example, radioactivity was first discovered in 1896 by Antoine-Henri Becquerel (1852–1908), a French scientist who observed that some small rocks placed on a package of photographic paper caused the paper to be exposed as though light had reached it in some way. This should not have happened, because the black paper in which the photographic material had been packaged was supposed to stop all light from getting through. This fact, a generalization based on many years of experience, had never been violated before. This is another example of a contradiction; in this case, one that led to a major discovery.

An investigation of this exception to an established generalization was made by Marie and Pierre Curie, who discovered a substance, radium, in the rock that was emitting penetrating radiation. In this way, by investigating an exception to a generalized fact, they discovered radioactivity.

Generalizations are the main way we learn the meaning of words. For example, the word *liquid* represents a large group of materials that can be poured. We observe that water, gasoline, oil, alcohol, milk, fruit juice, and many other substances have this similar property; they all behave in a similar way. They require containers like bottles, cans, or cups to hold them. If the container has a hole in the side or bottom, the liquid leaks out. The top surface of a liquid becomes level when it is at rest. The liquid may be poured by tilting its container. Such behavior is not true of solid materials like wood, steel, rock, glass, copper, or hard plastic. At normal temperatures, all solid materials tend to maintain a constant shape. Young children use observations of this kind to infer generalizations about the nature of solids and liquids. Then, by a kind of inborn informal logical deductive process, without realizing it, they begin to apply their generalizations to specific situations—such as efforts to avoid spilling milk from a glass.

If, after many experiences with a certain type of event, we observe that the same things consistently occur, then, by induction, we make a generalization. For example, if we hold a ball in midair and let it go, it falls. If we hold a penny in midair and let it go, it also falls. We have performed similar actions thousands of times in our lives. Each time we dropped an object, it fell. As a result, long ago we—and many other people—concluded, by induction, that "if an object is held in midair and released, it falls." This generalization is accepted as a fact.

Then, one day, some fuzziness in this established fact suddenly appears. We go to a show and watch a magician hold an apple in midair and release it. To our surprise it goes up, not down. This contradicts our generalization. We become suspicious. What is he doing to that apple? Perhaps a thread attached to the apple is manipulated by an assistant who is pulling the apple upward.

Suppose, instead of an apple, someone holds a balloon filled with helium. When it is released, it rises instead of falling. In that case, the generalized "fact" about falling objects needs to be changed in some way, perhaps like this:

1. Objects (except balloons filled with helium) held in midair fall when released.

or,

2. Objects almost always fall when held in midair and released.

Most generalizations that people think are absolutely true wind up having important exceptions. For instance, take one that we might think is absolutely true because it seems to be a definition: "There are twenty-four hours in a day." Scientists have found that the earth's rotation is gradually slowing down. They have good reason to think that sometime in the future a day will last much longer than twenty-four hours. Evidence from fossils indicates that millions of years ago days were shorter than they are now by several hours.

It is important to be aware that such exceptions to generalized facts can occur. Otherwise, errors in reaching conclusions are likely to be made.

DEDUCTIVE REASONING

In contrast to inductive reasoning, which is based on observations, *deductive reasoning* is based on statements called *premises* that may or may not be facts. They could be guessed-at facts (hypotheses, which are based in part on facts), purely speculative statements, or mathematical statements of any kind.

Consider the following example of a simple form of deductive reasoning known as a *syllogism*.

Premise 1: A shrike is a bird.

Premise 2: A bird is an animal with wings and feathers.

Conclusion: Therefore, a shrike is an animal with wings and feathers.

The first two statements, *premises,* provide information from which a logical deduction is to be made. From the premises we *deduce* a third statement, the *conclusion,* which is the end result of the logical process. The conclusion may be brand new information. For example, we may never have heard of a shrike, and may not know that a shrike has wings and feathers. But once we are told that a shrike is a bird and that birds have wings and feathers, we can conclude—even though a shrike has never been seen—that the shrike has wings and feathers.

Formal Logic

More than two thousand years ago philosophers in ancient Greece began analyzing logical reasoning and found many variations in the way it can be utilized in human thought processes. Over the centuries, the basic principles of proper reasoning have been expressed in what is known as "formal logic," a subject that is taught in most colleges. It is not the purpose of this book to detail these principles, but merely to indicate the general direction of such analysis.

The syllogism about the shrike begins with two premises: a *major premise* (A bird is an animal with wings and feathers) and a *minor premise* (A shrike is a bird). We obtain new information from these premises in the form of a conclusion.

In formal logic the different categories of things being discussed (like shrikes, birds, and animals with wings and feathers) are identified with letters, such as A, B, C, etc. Then the reasoning is analyzed in a manner similar to the way letters are used to represent numbers or categories of numbers in algebra. In fact, a kind of algebra has been developed in formal logic to analyze reasoning processes, illustrated as follows:

Minor Premise: (A shrike) is (a bird).
       (A)   is   (B)

Major Premise: (A bird) is (an animal with wings and feathers).
       (B)   is   (C)

Conclusion: Therefore, (a shrike) is (an animal with wings and feathers).
       (A)   is   (C)

In other words, if A is B, and B is C, then A *must be* C. Note that B disappears from the conclusion. Only A and C remain. The fact that A and C are related is the conclusion obtained by deductive reasoning.

This syllogism may be summarized symbolically as follows:

A is B
B is C
Therefore, A . . . is . . . C

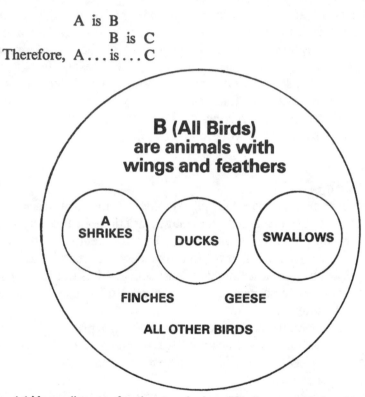

Figure 4.4 Venn diagram for the conclusion, "Shrikes are birds with wings and feathers." *(Drawing by Irving Lazarus)*

The syllogism about shrikes may also be viewed in the form of a "Venn diagram" (figure 4.4). The large circle (B) represents all birds. It contains many smaller circles representing all the different categories of birds, some of which (e.g., ducks, finches, hawks, shrikes) are shown as smaller circles within the big one. We can see that whatever is true of B (all birds) is also true of all shrikes. If all birds have wings and feathers, so do all shrikes.

The statement that "a bird is an animal with wings and feathers" is information about *all* birds, without exception. It is a generalization based on observations and the definition of "birds," obtained by using the inductive method of reasoning.

Syllogisms enable us to apply generalizations to many specific cases. For example, if we know that "objects on earth fall when dropped," then we can apply this generalization, by deductive reasoning, to predict that a rock, a shoe, a ball, or *any* object will fall when dropped. Simple though this seems, because our brains perform the deductive operations so rapidly, it is nevertheless a fundamental part of the reasoning process.

All mathematics is basically deductive, except for a small number of basic premises consisting of definitions and *axioms* that are assumed to be true and which form the foundation of what we understand to be mathematics. Then, by means of deductive reasoning, conclusions are drawn that represent new information. We experienced this process in the disciplines of algebra and geometry in which large bodies of mathematical knowledge are built up from a few accepted axioms and definitions (see figure 4.5, p. 74).

A fascinating example of the power of deductive reasoning in mathematics is provided by the development of non-Euclidean geometry. One of the unproved axioms in the geometry developed by the Greek mathematician Euclid states, in effect, that "parallel lines never meet." This seems obvious because in everyday life we have never experienced them meeting.

Several mathematicians in the 1800s tried to prove the truth of this axiom by assuming that parallel lines *do* meet, logically building up a new geometry with this "wrong" axiom, then hoping to find a contradiction somewhere down the line that would disprove the "wrong" axiom. This would be logical proof that parallel lines do not meet.

To everyone's surprise no contradictions ever developed. Instead, a new "non-Euclidean geometry" was created based on the apparent absurdity that parallel lines meet. Of course, it was assumed that this is a "wrong" kind of geometry in that it does not match the real world, so what good is it?

When Albert Einstein sought to develop his theories about space and time in the General Theory of Relativity, he found that non-Euclidean geometry fit the bill. As a result, today, for everyday purposes, carpenters and navigators use the old-fashioned Euclidean geometry in which parallel lines never meet, while scientists exploring ideas about the beginning of the universe, or the very high speeds of nuclear particles, often turn to non-Euclidean geometry.

Are All Deductions True?

Although deductive reasoning is essential to all thinking it does not ensure the truth of conclusions about the real world. For example, consider the following syllogism:

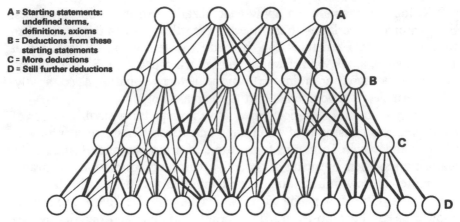

A = Starting statements:
      undefined terms,
      definitions, axioms
B = Deductions from these
      starting statements
C = More deductions
D = Still further deductions

Figure 4.5 In *deductive reasoning* we arrive at conclusions that *must* follow from the premises with which we start. All of mathematics is built up in this way. But we can never be sure our deductions fit the real world, because the assumptions (premises) may not necessarily be "true to life." *(Drawing by Alice Wengrow)*

Premise 1: The Willig family just moved here from Mullinsburg.

Premise 2: People who live in the town of Mullinsburg are loud and pushy.

Conclusion: Therefore, people in the Willig family are loud and pushy.

The logic is correct, but is the conclusion true? Are the Willigs really loud and pushy? This would be true if we really knew that *all* people from Mullinsburg are loud and pushy: but to know that, we would have to know *everybody* in Mullinsburg. So there is a serious problem with Premise 2. The probability that *all* or even most people in Mullinsburg are loud and pushy is extremely low because people vary widely in personal characteristics (figure 4.6).

Then, too, what may be "loud and pushy" to a person brought up in one type of community may be perfectly normal, even a sign of friendliness, to another person who comes from a "loud and pushy" community.

The expression, "loud and pushy" indicates a difference in culture. Each of us grows up in a community and adopts the ways of that community. We have similar ways of speaking loudly or softly, "keeping our distance" from other people or moving closer, asking direct questions or believing it impolite to do so. We carry these modes of behavior with us throughout life.

For that reason, descriptions like "loud and pushy" are subjective terms that depend on each person's background and upbringing. The conclusion about the Willigs being loud and pushy, which seems so obvious to one person, would be considered a *prejudiced* (pre-judged) opinion by others. Such prejudiced reasoning is a major source of conflict throughout the world. This important subject is discussed in chapter 9, dealing with stereotypes and prejudice.

EVERYDAY REASONING

Most reasoning is based on the processes of induction and deduction. We learn generalized facts mainly by inductive reasoning, and then we apply them to new situations by deductive reasoning. But other mental processes are also important. Without *memory,* for example, no facts could be stored in our minds for later use. Another basic ability might be called "creative imagination," or perhaps "intuition." Everybody has experienced moments when, seemingly from nowhere, a solution to a problem leaps to mind in a flash.

Let's see how these different mental abilities work together to solve the following real-life problem:

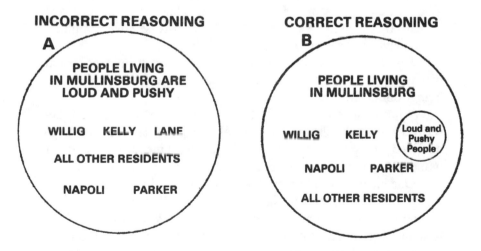

Figure 4.6 The statement in circle A, "People living in Mullinsburg are loud and pushy," is not likely to be true, because it includes *all* people in Mullinsburg. Therefore, the conclusion that the Willigs are loud and pushy, just because they live in Mullinsburg, may or may not correspond with reality. In B, the large circle represents *all* the people in Mullinsburg, but only *some* of them are loud and pushy while others, including the Willigs, are not. *(Drawing by Irving Lazarus)*

The clouds slowly thickened and rain began to fall. Mark, reading a book on the sofa in the living room, reached over to the nearby lamp and turned the switch. Nothing happened.

"The bulb must have burned out," he thought. He got a new bulb from the closet and replaced the old one. Still, nothing happened.

Mark was startled. This had never happened to him before. In the past, a new bulb had always worked. He began to think creatively about what else he could do to fix the lamp.

He had an idea. "Maybe the plug was pulled out." He looked at the wall outlet. The plug was in place. To make sure it wasn't loose he reached down and pushed it in hard. The lamp still did not light.

What now? "I'll bet it's a power outage. A power line must be down." To check this *hypothesis* (a reasonable guess at a possible truth, based on some facts or experiences) Mark tried to turn on several other lamps in the room. None lit up.

"That's the trouble," he thought. "Might as well wait for the electric company to fix it." Mark made sure that the lamp switch was on so he would know when the power had been restored.

After a half hour without electricity Mark began to get nervous. Was the power really off? He phoned his neighbor and was surprised to learn that they had electric power. There was no power outage.

"Maybe the circuit breaker flipped off."

Sure enough, down in the basement the circuit breaker switch was in the "off" position. Mark flipped it on and returned to the living room. The lamp was on.

When Dad returned later that afternoon, Mark proudly described his accomplishment in logical reasoning. He received well-deserved compliments; but then Dad, thinking aloud, said, "I wonder why that circuit breaker flipped off?"

Dad knew more about electricity than Mark did. He understood that a circuit breaker switches off when the flow of electricity is greater than the capacity of wires to carry it. What bothered Dad was that there might still be an intermittent short circuit somewhere in the room. Perhaps an electric line with worn-out insulation allowed bare wires to touch; this could cause a spark and perhaps a fire. If so, it was important to locate the break and fix it.

Mark and Dad began to examine the loose wires in the room. Just then Mom entered. "What are you doing?" she asked. Dad explained.

Mom thought a moment. "Perhaps it was an overload from that portable heater I used to take the chill out of the room while I was using the computer. In fact, I found both off when I came back from answering the phone. I assumed Mark had turned them off while I was out of the room."

That probably explained the mystery. The heater and the computer together may have drawn so much current that they overloaded and overheated the electric wires in the walls. Circuit breakers and fuses are used in electric lines to prevent fires by shutting off such overloaded circuits.

How did inductive and deductive reasoning come into play in this situation? All the elements of reasoning were there, but masked by the rapidity with which people reason about everyday things. Inductive reasoning lay behind the generalizations about electricity, which Mark, Dad, and Mom used to solve the problem. They had gathered facts from personal observation, listening to others, lessons at school, or reading books. These facts had been stored in their memories, ready to be recalled and used as needed. Deductive reasoning was used in each of the tests (small experiments) Mark tried. For example, he knew that electric current does not flow if there is any break or disconnection in the electric line to the lamp. This is a generalization. He tried out a series of premises. A burned-out light bulb breaks the electric circuit and no longer lights up, so he tried changing the bulb. When this did not work he tried another premise and then others, until he found the cause of the lights not working.

These possible explanations for the lamp not lighting were *hypotheses,* reasonable guesses as to why the lamp did not light. Each hypothesis suggests a course of action to get the lamp to light again. So he looked at the plug and found it in the wall receptacle. Then he tried pushing it in harder to see if the prongs of the plug were making good contact with the metal inside the socket. Mark applied the same kind of rapid deductive reasoning to the possibility that there was a power outage, or to the hypothesis that the circuit breaker had been overloaded.

An important part of Mark's reasoning process was creative imagination, in which his mind rapidly produced different ideas that might solve the problem. Mom used creative imagination when she wondered if the electrical problem had been caused by the overload from the heater and the computer being on at the same time.

A mechanic uses similar reasoning processes when attempting to fix a car that won't start. Is it out of gas? Does the ignition system deliver sparks to the spark plugs? Is the distributor wet? Is the carburetor working?

Is the gas line blocked? Is the battery charged? From the generalizations stored in his memory the mechanic makes a hypothesis about what might be wrong. He then tries a number of tests in succession, each designed to supply facts from which he might deduce what prevents the car from starting. Once he knows the cause, he can deduce a procedure to start the car.

Why can't most people fix stalled cars? They haven't learned the necessary generalizations about how cars work, which are the very basis of a mechanic's reasoning processes. Many people can't even think of the premises that might lead to logical deductions to solve the problem of getting the car to run again. Without premises they can't make any reasonable hypotheses to be tested, and therefore cannot even begin to discover what is wrong.

After a mechanic has had a lot of experience, this thinking process becomes almost automatic in most situations. But when a problem arises that does not fit the usual pattern, the mechanic will have to use all his reasoning skills in a creative way to find a solution.

Similarly, a physician uses sight, sound, and touch to observe facts about a patient's body that might indicate the nature of the illness presented. Blood tests, x-rays, cardiograms, and various scans (brain, bone, or body) might be some of the diagnostic procedures ordered. Unusually high or low measurements or other abnormalities are noted. Each physician has in his mind a storehouse of information (generalized facts), which can be called on to supply the premises to which logical reasoning will be applied.

This process of reasoning usually ends with a *diagnosis,* a judgment that identifies the nature of the illness. Then the physician can apply this storehouse of information to prescribe treatment to alleviate or cure the illness.

INTUITION

It sometimes happens that a solution to a difficult problem seems to come in a flash, when least expected. Such sudden insight is often called *intuition.*

An important example of intuition occurred in the late 1800s when Frederich Kekulé (1829–1896), a noted chemist, tried to determine how carbon atoms are arranged in the chemical compound known as benzene. At that time chemists thought that the six carbon atoms of each molecule of benzene were arranged in a straight line, like a chain. This arrangement, however, did not fully explain a number of facts about the compound.

One night Kekulé dreamed of a snake that suddenly curved and put its tail into its mouth, forming a circle. He awoke, instantly realizing that the circle-forming snake represented the six atoms of carbon in benzene, which were linked in the form of a circle instead of a chain. When Kekulé checked out this new idea, he found that it worked beautifully. He had made a major chemical discovery—that some molecules form rings rather than chains.

Such flashes of intuition are likely to occur to someone who thinks about a problem for a long time. It doesn't follow that such intuitive ideas are true. Most are not. But when they do occur to people who are well prepared with excellent information, intuition often leads to new knowledge.

ANALOGIES

One of the most important forms of reasoning is the *analogy,* a kind of logical inference based on the assumption that if two things are similar in one respect, they may be similar in other respects. It is an important form of reasoning when properly used, but is also easily misused, thus resulting in many errors in thinking (see chapter 6).

At a subconscious level, analogies play a fundamental role in the way humans learn what words mean. For example, a one-year-old child sees a large four-legged animal galloping about in a field. It has a long head, pointed ears, big eyes, a mane, a tail, and it neighs. Someone says "horse." Days later the child sees another four-legged animal of similar size and body-shape, although more stocky. This one has a shorter, blunt-shaped head, plods along instead of galloping, constantly chews its cud, moos, and possesses a pendulous udder. Someone says "cow." Thereafter, each time either of these animals is observed, the child mentally compares similarities and differences—a kind of pre-analogy thinking—and says "horse" or "cow" according to similarities it finds with what it learned before.

One day the child sees a donkey, which looks somewhat like a horse. The child points to it and says "horse." But Dad points to it and says "donkey." After a few events of this kind the child has observed the differences between horses and donkeys, and then knows which is which.

A biologist goes through a similar kind of reasoning by analogy when classifying living things into such categories as kingdom, phylum, class, order, family, genus, or species. From the overall similarities horses, donkeys, and zebras demonstrate in appearance, internal organs, body chemistry, and genetic structure, the biologist classifies them as members of the family "equidae," but separates them as being of different species. It is the degree of similarity that determines this classification.

Such classifications by analogy enable us to derive important knowledge of the world. As we have seen, biologists do this when classifying living things, while geologists do it when classifying rocks as igneous, sedimentary, or metamorphic; astronomers do likewise when classifying stars by their similarity of color and spectrum; and everybody does it when attempting to classify people as men, women, children, plumbers, or astronomers. We make such classifications by similarity and analogy for practically every word we learn.

On a more creative level, Newton reasoned by analogy when he observed an apple fall from a tree and wondered if the moon was being pulled toward the earth by the same sort of gravity force he imagined pulled the apple to earth. Both were actions at a distance with no strings attached. This analogy led to the theory that gravity was the cause of both actions.

Analogies often are helpful in judging which political or social policies are likely to solve problems. For example, in 1984 the state of New York passed the first law requiring the use of seat belts in cars. Almost immediately the use of seat belts increased and fewer people died in car crashes. Similar seat belt laws were then introduced and passed in other states. Legislators reasoned by analogy that if a seat belt law was accepted and saved lives in New York State, it was likely to have the same results in their states. There are differences between states, and in some there might be more resistance to the seat belt law than in others, so the analogy is not perfect. Each legislative body must judge for itself.

One purpose for using an analogy is to guide thinking in directions that might be useful. Analogies often suggest possible solutions to problems. If used with proper care, analogies are important aids to reasoning.

All instruments work by using analogies. The passage of time is measured by the rotating hands of a clock or watch around a numbered dial. The rotating motion is not time itself, but is taken to represent time. The angle of rotation of the hands is used as an *analog* for time. One type of thermometer measures temperature from the distance that a liquid such as mercury or red alcohol moves along a narrow tube. The distance the liquid moves is an analog for change in temperature. Another kind of thermometer uses the movement of a rotating pointer around a dial as an analog to indicate temperature. In a cardiogram, the doctor studies the up-and-down marks made by a pen moving across a moving paper. The marks provide an analog of how a patient's heart is beating. Similarly, a calculator uses electric current to produce analogs for numbers. No current represents zero; current represents the number one. Complex calculations can be made by designing electronic switches to turn the current rapidly on and off in patterns that are analogs for mathematical processes like addition, subtraction, multiplication, division, and even for words to be printed out on paper.

Like everything else in our world, analogies, useful though they are, can be misused or abused. Making proper analogies requires the careful selection of similar qualities of different things. A superficial look at a dolphin swimming in the ocean may lead someone to think by analogy that it is a fish. But more careful examination of the dolphin's body structure has led scientists to classify it as a mammal, far more similar to cows and horses than to any fish. The misuse of analogies is discussed in greater detail in chapter 6, "Common Errors in Reasoning," and in chapter 7, "Astrology: A Case Study in Defective Reasoning."

The ability of humans to reason logically at a high level would be impossible without using language to formulate problems, develop premises, and draw conclusions. But the complexities of language make it easy for errors in reasoning to occur. The next chapter explores the important connections between language and reasoning.

QUESTIONS (*Discussion of these Questions Begins on Page 244.*)

1. Consider the situation shown in figure 4.7 on page 82. Use logical reasoning and creative imagination to determine how to save the girl in the burning house.

2. Extend the following sequences by determining the pattern for each. What is the rule for obtaining the next several numbers or letters for each of these sequences? (Note how you mentally "try out" a succession of hypotheses as you seek the pattern for each sequence. Note, too, any flashes of intuition that you experience.)

    (a) 2, 4, 6, 8, 10 . . .

    (b) 1, 2, 4, 7, 11 . . .

    (c) a, b, d, e, g, h, j, k . . .

    (d) 1, z, 2, y, 3, x, 4 . . .

    (e) 1, 2, 3, 1, 1, 2, 2, 3, 3 . . .

    (f) 5, 3, 1, 6, 4, 2, 7 . . .

    (g) 3, c, 4, d, 5, e . . .

    (h) 11, 13, 10, 14, 9, 15 . . .

    (i) c, n, d, r, c, n, d, r, c . . .

    (j) 7, 5, 11, 9, 15, 13 . . .

    (k) b, a, r, e, f, i, n, o, t, u, p, e . . .

Figure 4.7 Clear thinking can save this girl. What would you suggest be done? *(Drawing by Arnold Lobel)*

    (l)   1, 1, 2, 3, 5, 8, 13, 21 . . .

   (m)   9, 6, 4, 3, 10, 7, 5, 4, 11 . . .

   (n)   1, 2, 3, 6, 12, 24, 48 . . .

   (o)   a, b, d, g, k . . .

   3.   There are three large bags—A, B, and C—in figure 4.8. One holds apples, another holds oranges, and the third holds both apples and oranges. All the labels are incorrect: bag A is incorrectly labeled "Apples and Oranges," bag B is incorrectly labeled "Apples," and bag C is incorrectly labeled "Oranges." Switch the labels around to make them indicate the correct contents of the bags, but you are only allowed to reach into one bag and pull out one fruit. You cannot inspect any of the other bags.

     You reach into bag A and pull out an orange. Use logical reasoning to figure out the correct labels for all three bags.

   4.   Mr. Cook, Mr. Taylor, and Mr. Baker met at a party. Mr. Cook observed: "Did you notice that one of us is a cook, another is a tailor, and the third

Figure 4.8 All the labels are wrong. An orange is drawn from bag A. Label all the bags correctly.

is a baker, but none of us has the same name as his occupation?"

"Correct," said the baker. What occupation did each man have?

5. Ms. Brady asked three students in her advanced high school science class to volunteer for an experiment in logical reasoning. Al, Beth, and Carl came up to the front of the room.

Ms. Brady dipped a finger into some black powder and said, "I will touch each of you on the forehead with either this blackened finger or another finger. You may or may not receive a black mark, but at least one of you will have a black mark that he or she will not be able to see. Let me know as soon as you have figured out whether or not you have a black mark on your head. You may not ask any other student to tell you."

Ms. Brady made a black mark on Al's forehead, but not on Beth's or Carl's. Almost immediately Al said, "I have a black mark." How did he know?

6. When you have figured out the answer to Question 5, answer this one: For the next experiment, Ms. Brady gave the same instructions as before and put black marks on the foreheads of Al and Carl, but not on Beth. After a short time Carl announced that he had a black mark. How did he know?

7. When you have completed Question 6, try this: Finally, Ms. Brady put black marks on all three students' foreheads. Beth thought, then declared that she had a black mark on her head. How did she figure it out?

8. Ephemerides, a philosopher in ancient Crete, made the statement, "All Cretans are liars." Can this statement be proven false? Can it be proven true? There is something unusual about it. What is it?

5

Language and Reasoning

Officials at Yosemite National Park once announced that a black bear called Sugarplum was to be shot on sight by rangers. Newspapers printed the report. Letters poured in protesting the death sentence. Some people even went so far as to offer to take the bear as a backyard pet.

Those who protested knew nothing at all about the bear's bad disposition and the danger it posed to patrons of the park, the very concerns that led to its death sentence. The name Sugarplum, selected as a sarcastic joke, caused people to think of the bear as a sweet, lovable, and cuddly teddy bear. If the park officials had called the bear Vicious Sam, there would have been no protests.

To prevent a recurrence of such public misunderstanding, park officials decided to stop naming bears and refer to them only by number. Would anyone protest if bear #293 was to be shot on sight?

WHAT'S IN A NAME?

This incident is an example of the powerful effect names have on the ability of people to make proper judgments. As any businessperson will attest, a good name for a product can greatly boost sales; a poor name can doom it in the marketplace. Consider the experience of a U.S. car manufacturer when its model, the Nova, went on sale in South America. Sales were terrible. The reason? In Spanish, "no va" means "it doesn't go." Would you buy a car whose name meant "no go"?

Market researchers are aware that the name of a product can produce a favorable impression that boosts sales. Names for cars like "Thunderbird," "LeSabre," "Cutlass," "Mustang," and "Triumph" are designed to attract those people to whom power, speed, and adventure are important. Names like "Escort," "Grand Marquis," and "Seville" are designed for less adventuresome people. A car named "Slug" would not find many buyers.[1]

The names parents give their children also make a difference in their lives. A child with what many would consider a strange name may have an extra handicap. Most youngsters surmount it, but for many, an odd name gives mean kids one more way to make fun of them.

Similar problems occur with names for diseases and disabilities. Consider the word *leprosy,* the name of a dreaded disease that was treated in the past by isolating victims from society in separate leper colonies. Today, treatment of the disease has improved so that the effects are much less severe, and exposure to someone who has leprosy is not dangerous. But the old stigma remains.

Medical officials in Brazil therefore started a campaign to substitute the name *hanseniasis* for the common name *leprosy.* They believed that changing the name would help them educate people, encourage preventive measures, and remove some of the stigma from people afflicted with the disease. For the same reasons, "mongolism" has become "Down's Syndrome" and "crippled" has become "physically challenged."

Some occupations have experienced important name changes. Clerks want to be called "office assistants," janitors prefer "maintenance engineer," and garbage collectors are presented to us as "sanitation workers." If these efforts at revised descriptive names seem funny, we might want to ask ourselves why. Is it because we don't think much of people who are clerks, janitors, or garbage collectors, even though they perform important jobs for society? If so, maybe it becomes clearer why people who do these jobs might want to have the titles changed.

Are such changes justified? Everybody wants respect from others for the work they do. *Pejorative* (disparaging or degrading) names for jobs cause people to feel despised. The change of name would seem to be justified if it helps workers adjust to jobs that would otherwise be demeaning.

Long ago what is now called the U.S. "Department of Defense" was called the "War Department." "War" gives the impression of aggression while "defense" suggests peaceful intent. Who can be against defense? But most people try to avoid "war."

"Bombing raids" have been called "protective reactions," and "invasions" have been described with the much milder word "incursions." If opponents are killed, reports have sometimes said that they have been "eliminated," "cleaned out," "wiped out," or "blown away." These terms give the impression of getting rid of insects, rats, or dirt, rather than people with feelings who suffer before dying.

Nuclear missiles generally are given names that attempt to evoke favorable images. The MX missile, capable of destroying ten target cities at once, has been named the "Peacemaker." The name has not been widely accepted because most people can't imagine it as a peaceful device. The name for the "Midgetman" missile, however, has been accepted even though a bomb that can destroy a large city is hardly a "midget."

Whether or not we agree with a particular name depends on the opinions we hold. If most people strongly object to a name, they will refuse to use it. If a name coincides with most people's opinions, the name is likely to be accepted.

THE IMPORTANCE OF LANGUAGE IN REASONING

The influence that names exert on our thinking is just one example of the powerful effect words in general have on our reasoning processes. The main difference between the ability of humans to reason and that of intelligent animals like chimps, dolphins, or elephants lies in our human ability to speak and combine words to form sentences. A major part of the volume of the human brain is devoted to this skill.

A child learns an average of eight new words a day. By age twenty most people have a vocabulary of about 20,000 words, and those who do a lot of reading have learned an even greater number. The main purpose of education in our complex society is the building of vocabulary and combining increasingly abstract words into different combinations of ideas called *concepts*.

Words and sentences are the meat of reasoning; without them we would not be human. Clear, understandable language makes it possible to communicate the results of our creative thinking to others. They, in turn, build on what they know to increase their knowledge and then communicate it to others. This process produces a kind of "chain reaction" that causes the fund of human knowledge to grow. For that reason, one of the main ways to improve reasoning skills is to improve language skills.

Different Meanings of Words

Consider this sentence: "Time flies they go too fast." It seems to make no sense. Can some punctuation be added that will make the sentence meaningful? Give it a minute's thought before you read on.

Let's punctuate it this way: "Time flies? They go too fast!" Suddenly it makes sense. The obstacle to meaning in this case is in the two words,

Figure 5.1 Two different meanings of "line": "Beverly is on the other end of the telephone line," and "Jessica keeps the dog in line with a leash." *(Drawing by Albert Sarney)*

"time flies," which usually go together in the sense of "time" (a noun) "flies" (a verb), meaning "time passes quickly." But when a question mark is put after it—"Time flies?"—followed by "They go too fast," this makes it clear that we are using "time" as a verb (implying that we are timing a speed with a stopwatch). What are we timing? Insects called "flies" (a noun).

This sentence illustrates an important feature of language. Most words have more than one meaning, and we can determine the specific meaning only in *context,* that is, in relation to the other words in the entire sentence. For example, consider the different meanings of the word *line* in the following sentences. Note how each particular meaning is made clear by the other words in the sentence. Some other words with several meanings are also indicated by italics (see figure 5.1).

They formed a *line* around the *block.*

They *ran* an electric *line* across the field.

He follows the *party line.*

Read the last *line* of the poem.

Drop me a *line* when you arrive in London.

He is *descended* from an ancient *line* of kings.

I take the GRB railway *line* to get to work.

What kind of *line* are you *dishing* out?

What's your *line?*

Magnetic *fields* are revealed by *lines* of force.

Throw him a *line*.

That boat has *clean lines*.

We have a full *line* of *goods*.

He hit a *line drive*.

He proceeded to *line* the *walk* with flowers.

He wanted to *line* the coat with silk.

A straight *line* was drawn.

Put it on the *line*.

In *line* with your report, I would say that we should go ahead with the project.

We need to *line* up the votes.

Words in Context

When words have so many different meanings it is remarkable that we are capable of communicating as well as we do. Fortunately the *context,* the way a word is used in relation to other words, usually makes the meaning understandable (see figure 5.2). The sentence "He lifted the wallet from the table" is clear enough. So is the sentence "The pickpocket lifted Joe's wallet," even though the word *lifted* has an entirely different meaning. In each case, the presence of the other words makes the sense of the collection of words clear. Even if the word *pickpocket* is omitted—e.g., "He lifted Joe's wallet"—we may still interpret the word *lifted* correctly as meaning "stole." "Joe" provides the clue. Whoever lifted the wallet, it wasn't Joe, and therefore the wallet didn't belong to the person referred to by "he." This reasoning occurs so rapidly in our minds that the meaning is clear even as we read the sentence.

Different words, spelled the same, may have different meanings: see a bear, or bear it; read a book, or book a burglar; pack a box, or box his ears; write with a pen, or put a pig in a pen. In each case, the other words in the phrase make its meaning clear.

Specialized Words

It is a wonder that there isn't more confusion in communicating thoughts because so many words have more than one meaning. In addition to the

Horace: "Late as usual! Do you know how long I've been waiting?"
Dotty: "But darling, I've been rushing *since three o'clock!*"

Figure 5.2 Dotty and her husband have different ideas about what the word *late* means. *(Drawing by Arnold Lobel)*

words in common use, each business, trade, or profession has a special vocabulary. A lawyer or a police officer, for example, must know the exact meanings of "burglary," "robbery," "misdemeanor," "felony," "assault," "battery," "disorderly conduct," and so on. The police officer who lists a crime improperly could cause a miscarriage of justice.

Physicists discuss the properties of certain particles of atoms called "quarks." They describe the properties of quarks with familiar words like *up, down, top, bottom, charm,* and *flavor.* Each of those words has a special meaning in nuclear physics, entirely different from their ordinary use in the language.

Those who use computers need to understand the specific meanings of terms like *bit, byte, menu,* and *modem.* Newspaper reporters must know about *leads* and *subheads, standard heads* and *running feet.* Plumbers need to know the difference between pipe parts like *elbows* and *unions.*

WORDS WITH FUZZY BOUNDARIES

The word *dog* seems clear. But the first time a wolf, coyote, or fox is seen, we may mistake it for a dog. Wolves look a lot more like German shepherd dogs than German shepherds look like poodles.

Consider the statement "A tomato is a fruit." This may seem false if we classify fruits by taste (usually sweet), or as dessert for a meal. We may consider "tomatoes" to be part of the salad or vegetable part of a meal. But botanists define a "fruit" as that part of a plant that develops from a flower and contains seeds. From this point of view not only is a tomato a fruit, but so is a cucumber, a nut, and a green bean.

Is a houseboat a house? Is an Indian tepee a house? How thick and strong does cord have to be before it is called a "rope"? If someone uses a rock to break the shell of a nut, is the rock a hammer? Is a mature bamboo plant a tree? It is tall enough, and the trunk is thick enough to be mistaken for a tree. Yet botanists classify bamboo as a kind of grass because it is hollow and resembles grasses in other basic ways. In effect, it is necessary to understand the different ways that words are defined in different situations and to apply these definitions properly.

Some words represent large groups, or classes of things or actions. It is difficult to define some of the boundaries in exact terms, and so confusion arises.

Abstract Words

If someone points out a tree and says "This tree flowers in spring," we probably know exactly what the person is talking about. "This tree" is real, and is not exactly like any other tree in the universe. But suppose we begin to note similarities between "this tree" and other trees. It might then be grouped with the other trees as, for example, a "maple," because all members of this group have similar leaves, flowers, seeds, bark, and general shape. The idea of a "maple" is now somewhat *abstract,* a generalized idea of all trees of that type.

Of course, there are many other kinds of trees—oak, pine, redwood, mahogany, and others. All belong to a more general and even more abstract group: "trees." All trees belong to a still broader class of growing things

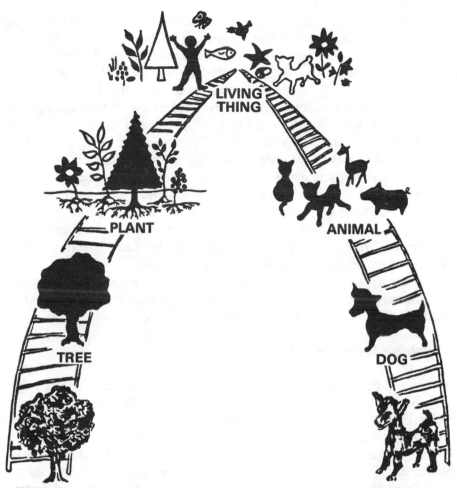

Figure 5.3 The "ladder of abstraction" carries us up and away from real objects toward generalized, abstract words or expressions that give language its great power to communicate ideas. *(Drawing by Alice Wengrow)*

called "plants," a group that also includes grasses, mosses, seaweeds, and others. All plants resemble each other in that they make their food from water and carbon dioxide, with sunlight as the source of energy.

Finally, all plants are living things, a group or category that also includes animals. Perhaps there are even higher levels of abstraction (see figure 5.3).

Communicating the exact meanings of words becomes more difficult when those words refer to ideas rather than to things. People can grasp the concept of a car or a tool more easily than they can ideas like democracy, freedom, treason, truth, God, justice, liberal, conservative, or ecology. Understanding these ideas depends on each person's experience, background, and beliefs.

Such abstract words do not represent actual objects, but qualities or thoughts that cannot be directly observed by our senses. What does "freedom" look like? How does "justice" taste? Or "ecology" feel? Or "truth" smell? The abstract nature of "democracy" is revealed in the varying ideas people of different lands have of its meaning. What does it mean to a "white" person in South Africa, and to a "black" person in the same country? Or in Mexico, the United States, the Soviet Union, Poland, Ethiopia, or Tibet?

The more learning people acquire, the greater the number of abstract words used in their work, everyday conversation, and reasoning. The scholars among us are aware of the great importance of proper meanings in reasoning; they take great pains to define the words they use. International conferences are held to review definitions and to reach agreement about changes made necessary because of new knowledge.

The purpose of a dictionary is to catalog words and to specify their various meanings, thereby reducing confusion in communication and reasoning. Mastery of use of the dictionary is therefore a basic skill in modern life.

Meanings Changed by Sound

When one person speaks to another, hoping to transmit some thought, the speaker must depend on sound waves transmitted through the air. When these sound waves enter the listener's ear they generate electrochemical signals that travel along nerves to the brain. The speaker hopes that what is said evokes the same thoughts in the listener, but this is not always the case. Others may be speaking at the same time, thus confusing the sounds received by the listener. Then again, hard ceilings and walls reflect sounds and cause distortion and confusion.

Then there is the matter of different people giving different meanings to words, depending on where the persons were born: for example, a foreign country, or a rural versus a city area. Different regional accents are often a problem as well.

Confusion in speech is also possible when words that are spelled differently sound the same: *right/write, pail/pale, died/dyed,* and the like. The context will usually provide the correct meaning, but double meanings occur often enough to cause problems. If someone says "The customer's always right," it may be interpreted as "The customers always write." The meaning would be very clear if the sentence were written, not spoken. Another example is illustrated in figure 5.4 in which "attacks on the mayor" is perceived as "a tax on the mayor."

Nancy: *"I don't like attacks on our mayor."*
Charlie: *"A tax on our mayor? . . . H'm . . . Not a bad idea."*

Figure 5.4 The sounds of words may cause semantic confusion. People say one thing and others hear them say something very different. *(Drawing by Albert Sarney)*

For these reasons, what one person says (or writes) may be perceived by another individual as totally different from what was intended. Sometimes this causes friendships to break up, marriages to go on the rocks, and even nations to bristle at each other.

Changed Meanings in Translations

Translations from one language to another pose special problems for the accurate communication of meaning. This is of crucial importance in today's global society. For example, some years ago Nikita Khrushchev, then leader of the Soviet Union, made a speech about U.S.-Soviet relations. In referring to competition between the economic systems of both nations, he included a sentence that was translated into English as "We will bury you." Naturally, people in the United States were outraged at this remark.

Some Russian language experts, however, noted that the phrase "We will bury you" in Russian is an idiomatic expression meaning something similar to "We will beat you" (in the context of the economic competition that was being discussed). To an American, this sense of "beat" means to win, as in a race, not to commit assault. If an American president had said "We will beat you," perhaps that might be incorrectly understood in the Soviet Union as "beat you in a fight," and might cause similar commotion there.

It's hard enough to transfer the thoughts of one person to the mind of another person using speech or writing, but it is even more difficult when different languages are used, thus requiring translations. Much depends on the translator's reading and writing style and which words in a particular language he chooses for his translation.

SEMANTICS: THE STUDY OF MEANINGS

Mac McGill was having his car repaired at Bob's garage in the village of Greenbush. Bob had the hood up and was leaning over the engine making an adjustment. At one point Bob asked Mac to get into the driver's seat, turn on the engine, and step on the gas pedal. A short time later, he asked Mac to "Hold 'er down." So Mac stepped on the gas some more, making the engine run faster.

Bob immediately raised his voice: "Hold 'er down. Hold 'er down!" Mac stepped on the pedal even harder. Now the engine was racing full blast.

Bob, furious, shouted "What's the matter with you? Didn't I tell you to 'hold 'er down'?"

Suddenly Mac realized that Bob wanted him to press *less* heavily on the gas pedal, not more. He also remembered that Bob had originally come from a different part of the country, where the meaning of "Hold 'er down" might be different from what it was in the Greenbush area.

Bob understood "Hold 'er down" to mean "Hold the *power* down by releasing the pedal a bit." But Mac took it to mean "Press the *pedal* down more than before." They agreed on what "down" meant, but differed on *what* was to be kept down.

Semantics is the study of meaning in language. Because Bob and Mac each have a different understanding of the meaning of "Hold 'er down," they experienced what is called *semantic confusion*. This kind of confusion in understanding is common whenever people from different parts of a country, or from different countries, try to communicate. It is an important source of differences among people of diverse backgrounds—especially if they speak different languages, thereby requiring translation.

Even when the same language is used, subtle differences among people—in background, experiences, and attitudes—create different meanings for the same words.

Semantic Confusion

Consider this situation: It is election time. As you walk down the street, you pass a man carrying a sign that reads:

VOTE FOR PARKER
FOR PRESIDENT
PEACE—JOBS—SECURITY

The words *peace, jobs, security* are abstract. Think about some of the different images the abstract words in the sign bring to mind. To one citizen, the word *vote* may produce a good feeling: It is a civic duty and a privilege. Another may think voting is all a sham arranged by political bosses.

What about the word *president*? A person who is generally pleased with the way a current president leads the country is likely to have a favorable impression of the word. That person would be more likely to vote, perhaps for Parker, as the sign suggests. But if his or her attitude toward the office of president is one of distrust, the reaction to an appeal to "Vote for Parker" may be a cynical "Why should I?"

The word *peace* is even more abstract. To one person it may mean an uneasy period of truce while we build up more nuclear weapons. To another the word may mean a hopeful period in which to come to agreement about nuclear weapons while we work to eliminate them. People have all sorts of meanings for "peace."

A person who has always had a good job may ignore the word *jobs* on the sign. But someone who is unemployed or dissatisfied may find it of intense interest, enough to make him consider voting for Parker to help end unemployment.

Confusion in debate and argument is often caused by the fact that each side defines key abstract words in its own way. In such cases it is important to try to clarify the meanings of the terms being used. If wide differences in meaning are deeply ingrained in the minds of debaters, they are likely to find the discussion difficult or perhaps impossible. But the attempt at clarification should be made so that confusion can be reduced.

Self-Contradictory Statements

Many familiar phrases are *self-contradictory*. But even if the words contradict each other, some phrases take on special meanings that make sense. For example, what's an "open secret"? If it's open, it's not a secret. If it's a secret, it can't be open. But as a phrase, "open secret" has come to have a special meaning: a secret that is no longer a secret. Everybody knows about it.

A national leader once referred to his country's "future history." History is about the past. So how can it be in the future? And yet, in a way, this contradiction could make sense, if it referred to what future historians say about the past.

Along these same lines, what's an "athletic scholarship"? Suppose a student whose grades are poor is accepted at a college and given money only because of athletic ability. In what sense could that money be called a "scholarship"? The widespread use of this self-contradictory term has taken on a meaning all its own and is now part of our language.

The word *oxymoron* is used to describe such self-contradictory figures of speech. *Oxy* comes from the Greek, meaning "sharp," and *moros* means "dull or foolish." Therefore, an oxymoron refers to a clear saying that at first view appears foolish, but usually makes sense with some special meaning, as in "thunderous silence" and "sweet sorrow."

People often make self-contradictory statements. For example: "You could not possibly guess what I did this morning." Interpreted literally, this statement is false because every now and then somebody might guess correctly. However, the exaggeration in this case is intended to declare that the speaker did something very surprising this morning.

Figure 5.5 shows a self-contradictory statement: the young lady thinks her boyfriend is "handsome" even though "he doesn't look it." Beauty is in the eye of the beholder. What she is really saying is that her boyfriend is handsome *to her,* if not to other people.

Some self-contradictory statements report "facts" that are impossible. Take, for instance, "Archaeologist Higgins, who has been digging in the ruins of Troy, reports that he has found several old coins bearing the date 1202 B.C." But this is impossible because "B.C." means "before Christ," and 1,202 years before the birth of Christ, no one could have known his future date of birth.

All, None, Always, Never

"Water poured into an open container always falls to the lowest possible level." True or false? Did you say true? But wait a minute! What would happen if water were poured into a container in a spaceship orbiting the earth? The water would not fall at all. So "always" is not absolutely correct.

Perhaps we could change the statement to: "On earth, water poured into a container will always fall to the lowest possible level." True or false? The statement is still not completely true, because water rises slightly above its normal level all along the edges of a container due to its wetting action. We can observe this fact by looking carefully at the places where water is in contact with the glass surface.

"What's the big deal?" you might say. "The effect is so small that there is no need to make a fuss over it." Not so. Your life depends on it. In very narrow tubes the self-rising effect, known as "capillary action," is

"My boy friend doesn't look *it, but he's really handsome!"*

Figure 5.5 This is a self-contradictory statement. *(Drawing by Arnold Lobel)*

substantial. Water soaks into the roots of plants, entering their systems of very narrow tubes, then rising by itself high into the stems or tree trunks and into the leaves where sunlight produces food for the plant and for us.

Development of land plants such as trees, bushes, and grasses would probably not have occurred without the self-rising of water far above its normal level. Indeed, had this not happened, we would have no grains, fruits, or vegetables from land plants; our food supply would have developed from the sea.

As we can see, even in the modified statement, the word *always* introduces a factual error. "Always" means every single time, under any circumstances, without exception. The word should therefore have very limited use in statements that are intended to be accurate. "Never," "all," "none," and "absolutely" resemble "always" in that each implies a certainty that, as we have seen, is rarely if ever achieved in real life.

WRITING MORE CLEARLY

Consider this confusing explanation offered for one cause of rain:

> "When water vapor cools, it becomes rain. It condenses. Winds blow the water vapor over the mountain. Water for the rain came from the ocean. The droplets grow in size and fall as rain. Heating of the

ocean by sunlight caused the water to evaporate. After the water vapor comes from the ocean, it cools and condenses into tiny drops of water."

Although all the sentences are correct statements, they are not in the order of events as they actually occur in nature. As a result, the paragraph is a rambling explanation in which the reader is required to rearrange the sequence of ideas to make sense of the explanation. In addition, there is excessive repetition of words, caused mainly by the sequence of ideas being out-of-order.

In the following rewrite of the above paragraph the ideas are essentially the same, but they follow the sequence of actual events in nature. This produces a much more understandable and readable explanation of rain.

"Sunlight heats water in the ocean, causing it to evaporate into the air. Winds then blow the water vapor over mountains onto the land. As the air rises it is cooled, which causes the water vapor to condense, thus forming tiny droplets of water in clouds. These droplets may grow large enough to fall as rain."

Clear, logical writing requires that thoughts glide along smoothly in an orderly way, without interruptions that break the train of thought.

Some noted writers have a jumpy style that many people like to read. But before deciding to imitate such writing, it is wise to learn how to write smoothly and logically, with every idea in its proper order. Experiment with writing styles later, after mastering the art of communicating ideas to others in a simple and clear manner.

USING WORDS ACCURATELY

We frequently hear or read statements that blur meanings. For example, Jim writes:

"In general, the speed at which an athlete runs an event in a track meet is faster than the time it takes to report the result to the officials."

At first glance, the sentence seems to make sense. But after some analysis, unclear words and expressions can be found. Compare your analysis with this one:

1. When considering the phrase ". . . the speed . . . is faster than the time," there is something amiss. A speed can be faster than another speed, but it isn't possible for a speed to be faster than a time. It's like saying "A speed of 60 miles per hour is faster than a time of two days." Jim probably intended to compare two like quantities: the amount of time it takes to run a race (not the speed at which the race is run), and the amount of time it takes to report the results of the race.

2. With respect to ". . . an athlete running an event in a track meet," is every event in a track meet a running race? Pole vaulting is not. Neither is the broad jump. Jim probably meant "an athlete runs a race in a track meet."

3. "In general" is usually understood to mean "almost every time, perhaps with a few exceptions." But Jim's statement can't be true for long-distance races, which can take hours. The time it takes to report the results of a marathon race is certainly less than the time needed to run the race. So the phrase "in general" would not apply.

Let's rewrite the statement to reflect what Jim probably intended to say:

"In a track meet, athletes run many of the short races in less time than it takes to report the result of the race to the officials."

Certain techniques can help us analyze statements and change words to make them more precise.

1. Ask questions about the unclear details in statements. Examples: Can a speed be faster than a time? Does the statement apply in general to all events at a track meet?

2. Answer the questions. It is helpful to think of specific examples, to determine if the statements are true. For instance, does the statement about running an event in a track meet also apply to pole vaults, broad jumps, and discus throwing?

3. Change the wording so that the answers to the questions are given clearly in your statement.

Note how these techniques can be used to correct the following statement. "The biggest problem everybody in school has now is the problem of getting into college, and how to get into the college he chooses first."

1. Is one particular problem the "biggest" problem for "everybody" in school? Is getting into college a problem for someone who does not plan to go to college?

2. What kind of "school" is involved? Elementary school? High school? Are all fourth graders concerned with the problem of getting into college?

3. Does the sentence mean "chooses first" or "first choice"?

4. Is every student a "he"?

The sentence might be revised as follows: "One of the main problems faced by high school students who plan to go to college is that of getting into any college at all, and, particularly, getting into the one the student prefers."

Confusing Pronouns

Consider this statement: "The French and the English are very different. They are more emotional and dramatic." Does the word *they* refer to the French or the English? The person who wrote the statement undoubtedly knows, but the reader could take it either way. In fact, the reader's interpretation is likely to depend on personal opinions of the French and the English. Someone who considers the French to be more emotional and dramatic than the English will assume that "they" refers to "the French." Most people, however, would just be confused.

To remove any doubt about the meanings of pronouns like "they," "it," "this," "them," "he," and "she," these words need to be tied directly to their *antecedents,* the words that occur earlier in the sentence or paragraph to which the pronouns refer. The two sentences of our example could have been written more clearly as follows: "The French are more emotional and dramatic than the English." Or vice versa, if that is what the writer means.

Out-of-Order Phrases

The following sentence (with the name of the company changed) appeared in a newspaper: "The ABC company was accused of firing a worker who had good reports from his supervisors because he is foreign born." Does the sentence mean that the worker had good reports *because* he was foreign born? Or perhaps he was fired because he was foreign born, despite the good reports.

There is no way to judge what the sentence was meant to convey. The reader must stop to think about which meaning is most likely. A clue could be obtained from the context; it is not likely that a worker would be given good reports *because* he is foreign born. But the flow of thought has to be interrupted to determine the meaning, and many readers find this more difficult and less interesting. It is the writer's (speaker's) responsibility to make the thought clear and comprehensible.

A much better written sentence might read: "The ABC company was accused of firing a worker because he is foreign born, despite good reports from his supervisors." Note that the basic thought, "firing a worker because he is foreign born," was split in two in the original sentence and separated by the less important "who had good reports from his supervisors." The meaning is much clearer when the parts of sentences that belong together are properly joined.

BODY LANGUAGE, AND CUSTOMS

Speech and writing are not the only kinds of language people use to communicate with each other. A nod or a shake of the head often expresses yes or no. A number of other body motions express feelings. Consider these examples:

- At a funeral a friend puts her hand around the widow's shoulder and holds her for a moment, but says nothing. The expression on her face also communicates her sympathy.

- Mom asked Sally to buy some cheese on her way home from school. Sally forgot. When her mother asked for it, Sally suddenly remembered and, instead of answering in words, she put both hands on her head as her face took on an expression of surprise and mortification.

Similarly, the expressions and body positions of the man in figure 5.6 (p. 102) tell a clear story without words. What has just happened?

We may make a number of inferences from the illustration. The golf club on the ground tells us that the man is playing golf. He has obviously just missed an easy putt, dropped his club, and contorted his body in a way that indicates his great displeasure. The man's body conveys a clear message: "How could I have missed that easy putt?" No words are necessary, although he will probably reinforce his feelings with some choice language.

How would body language be used to express each of the following?

Figure 5.6 Body language is an important means of communication, especially when conveying emotions and attitudes. *(Drawing by Albert Sarney)*

A bad smell

Superiority

Shame

Disgust

Doubt about what someone says

Anger

A threat to fight

Fear

Surprise

Feelings are often revealed subconsciously through body language. For example, Pam likes Sid but she doesn't like Jim. When Jim approaches, she pretends not to see him until the last moment. As she talks to Jim she stands farther away than is customary. She shakes his hand limply. But when Sid is around, Pam's body language is different. As he approaches, Pam may stretch out her hand in greeting much earlier than she would with others, and perhaps she would walk toward him. Her face lights up as she talks. She stands closer to Sid than is customary for casual acquaintances.

Nationality and family background alter body language. In some cultures, people tend to stand very close to each other when they talk. In other cultures, speakers and listeners stand farther apart. If people from two different cultures begin talking to one another, both may soon feel uncomfortable. If someone stands further away than is customary while talking, it could give the impression of being cold and aloof, while those who stand too close may seem pushy.

In some cultures people touch each other casually during conversation, hold the listener's arm while making a point, or use a variety of gestures. There are those who speak loudly and who frequently interrupt others. The members of still other societies speak softly, use few gestures, and are generally more reserved. Children tend to pick up the body language, gestures, and speaking style of their parents, friends, and neighbors. They may also imitate body language observed on television.

Communication often begins with a handshake. Some people shake hands very firmly, while others consider limp handshakes acceptable. When two people from different cultures meet and shake hands, both may get an immediate wrong impression from the handshake because their expectations were not met.

Those who have a strong dislike of people from other nationalities or cultures should ask themselves if the cause has something to do with different body language or customs. Obviously, to live in harmony with others it is important to learn about their body language and customs, and take these aspects into account.

Body language can alter the meanings of words. For instance, the word *no,* said without body language, is a simple unemotional response to a question. But if the "no" is uttered loudly while stamping the foot or perhaps pounding a table, that would indicate a highly emotional "absolutely not!" "No" could also be said with a rising inflection, as a question—"No?" A crooked smile and a wave of the hand to accompany the "no" might indicate disbelief. Or, suppose the "no" is given a stretched-out drawl with a dropped jaw. In that case it means "no kidding" or "I already knew that."

Body language is a basic means of communication for many animals. Usually it indicates simple feelings or emotions like anger, fear, joy, or wariness. There's no mistaking the body language of a dog that confronts us with bared teeth and raised hair along its backbone. The snarl sends a message, too, but the body language is usually enough.

Human body language not only expresses feelings and emotion but may also provide information that affects the judgments we make about people and ideas. Complex ideas, however, need words. Without verbal language, we would be unable to communicate our ideas, and our ability to make deductions from facts would be extremely limited. The ability to reason would be crippled. New discoveries could not be conveyed to future generations, and civilization would be impossible.

A number of sources of error in communication were noted in this chapter. Such errors often lead to faulty "facts" that become incorrect premises and produce flawed reasoning. There are many other ways in which people reason incorrectly, as described in the next chapter.

NOTE

1. William Lutz, *Doublespeak* (New York: Harper and Row, 1980).

QUESTIONS (*Discussion of these Questions Begins on Page 247.*)

1. What improvements would you suggest in the following paragraph? Rewrite it to make it shorter as well as easier to read and understand.

Amebas are tiny animals that live on small plants in ponds. You will need a microscope to study them. One week should be allowed to develop them in your culture before experiments are performed. You will often find them in mud scooped from the bottom of a pond. Gather some from a pond and culture them in a jar. A magnification of about 100 times will show them properly.

2. Analyze the following sentences and suggest any improvements that can be made in accuracy or wording.

(a) Babe Ruth was the most unique baseball player of all time.

(b) You can see that the trees are in trouble from a disease of beetles.

3. What is wrong with each of the following statements?

(a) Americans are the most warmhearted people in the world.

(b) Candidate Mary Parker said to the voters in her district, "If you elect me, I will support all the proposals that you want to see go through."

(c) All generalities are false.

(d) When did Eva say she would let us know?

4. One debating team challenged another. Their invitation contained the following paragraph. Find the contradiction.

Each speaker will be allowed fifteen minutes for presentation and three minutes for rebuttal. Two members on each team will debate any timely noncontroversial subject. Judges are to be selected by the principals of the school.

5. What are the contradictions implied by each of the following expressions? What special meanings do they have? (Most are taken from a column by William Safire, who writes about the English language for the *New York Times*.)

Plastic glasses

Alone together

Guest host

Cruel kindness

Thundering silence

6. Words and phrases can sometimes have several meanings. Here are some headlines that actually appeared in newspapers. Can you figure out what they mean?

(a)   Three Tied, 60 Make Cut at Masters

(b)   Madison Piggyback; Base Plus 27

(c)   Indy Diat Is in the Pool for the 500

(d)   Strange Triumphs in Sudden Death

(e)   Young Met Arms Bear Big Burden Again

(f)   Shines Shines

(g)   Chili's Bat Not Cooled by Windy Candlestick

(h)   Stallions Trample Renegades

(i)   Albany Strains at the Tape

(j)   Couples, Strange Stay Tied

6

Common Errors in Reasoning

The worst nuclear accident in the United States occurred in 1979 at the Three Mile Island power plant near Harrisburg, Pennsylvania. Early news accounts of the accident reported some release of radioactive gases, which caused many people to pack up their belongings and flee with their families. For three days operators wrestled with the damaged equipment, trying to prevent the release of huge amounts of radioactive gases and water, not knowing whether the few small explosions of hydrogen gas that had occurred would lead to more extensive damage.

An adjacent containment building held the overflowing radioactive water and saved the day. The nuclear reactions gradually died down until a reasonable level of safety could be assured.

Although no immediate deaths occurred, the cost of cleaning up the radioactive mess—to prevent future deaths from release of radiation—came to a billion dollars over a period of ten years. One question remained: Where could permanent disposal of the debris take place without producing deaths in the future?

The findings of a Presidential Commission on the Accident at Three Mile Island focused on the attitudes of the entire nuclear industry as the main underlying cause of the accident. The report stated in part:

> In the testimony we received, one word occurred over and over again. That word was "mindset." . . . Wherever we looked we found problems with the human beings who operated the plant, with the management that runs the key organization, and with the (federal) agency that is charged with assuring the safety of nuclear power plants. . . .
>
> After many years of operation of nuclear power plants, with no evidence that any member of the public had been hurt, the belief that nuclear power plants are sufficiently safe grew into a conviction. One

must recognize this to understand why many key steps that could have prevented the accident at Three Mile Island were not taken. . . .

Therefore—whether or not operator error "explains" this particular case—given all the above deficiencies we are convinced that an accident like the Three Mile Island was eventually inevitable.[1]

As an illustration, the report notes that the operators were so confident everything was under control during the early stages of the accident that they shut off the emergency water cooling system—the one system that could have prevented the situation from getting worse.

THE DANGERS OF A MINDSET

Although near-accidents of a similar kind had previously occurred in other power plants and warnings had been issued by the investigators to alert the industry, no attention had been paid to them. Everybody was of the mind that the system was foolproof. Therefore, the operators felt that they were protected from accidents by the equipment; a little mistake here or there would do no great harm.

Similar mindsets are clearly the basic causes for other major accidents. For example, in 1986, a disastrous meltdown and fire at an exposed reactor occurred at a nuclear power plant in Chernobyl in the Soviet Union. Radioactive gases and particles were carried by the wind over huge areas of many European countries, directly causing many deaths in the Soviet Union, with many thousands of future cancer deaths expected because of exposure to radioactivity.

An investigation of the cause of this accident showed the same kind of mindset as that of Three Mile Island. The operators seemed to believe that no accident could happen at their facility. While performing a relatively minor test, they deliberately shut off one safety system after another in an effort to push the test to its limits. By the time the operators began to heed the persistent warning readings on their instruments, it was too late to stop a runaway reaction and explosion that ripped off the roof of the plant and set its radioactive carbon burning in open air.

A similar mindset-related tragedy, the deaths of seven astronauts caused by the midflight explosion of America's Challenger space shuttle, is discussed later in this chapter under the heading of "circular reasoning."

It is easy to condemn the operators and workers for carelessness when such big accidents occur. But would any of us have been more alert than they were? When mindsets cloud our thinking because "nothing has ever gone wrong," most people join in the common belief, and probably we would too.

Of course, once a big accident occurs it exposes the mindset; then belated steps are taken to prevent similar accidents in the future. After the Three Mile Island accident, the Nuclear Regulatory Commission (NRC) suddenly awakened to its responsibilities and enacted such strict safety measures for all civilian nuclear power plants that the price of nuclear power rose drastically. All new nuclear facilities were no longer economically competitive and were therefore abandoned, as were many reactors under construction. In effect, the Three Mile Island accident destroyed the nuclear power industry.

However, these lessons fell on the deaf ears of seventeen contractor-operated facilities for making nuclear bombs, owned and paid for by the U.S. government. They were not subject to supervision by the NRC, but by the Department of Energy, which paid no attention to the lessons of Three Mile Island.

For ten years after the Three Mile Island accident in 1979 these facilities were operated so carelessly that most of them had to be shut down in 1989, mainly for reasons of safety. Record-keeping was so poor that no one knows how much radioactive contamination was released over civilian areas during two big fires at the Rocky Flats facility near Denver, Colorado. Thirty pounds of plutonium, a relatively large amount of an extremely dangerous pollutant, are not accounted for and may have been released into the air.

Areas near several of the facilities show very high levels of radioactive contamination. A number of lawsuits are under way over deaths and property damage claimed by people living near these facilities. The official estimate of the cost for cleaning up the seventeen facilities is $200 billion, but such figures often turn out to be much too low.

Mindsets affect our thinking in many more ways than contributing to big accidents. They also apply to most of us in everyday situations, as described in the next section.

MINDSETS AND THE CLOSED MIND

All of us have had a great many personal experiences, rooted in the social, educational, cultural, political, and related environments in which we grew up. These experiences influenced the development of our beliefs and values— ideas about what is right and wrong, good and bad. By adulthood, our minds are "set" in patterns of thinking that affect the way we react to new circumstances and changing situations. These mindsets determine what we think is important, what we read and listen to, and what we choose to ignore. Because we can't pay attention to all the events that occur around us, our minds filter out some observations and facts and let others through to our conscious awareness. As a result we see and hear what we subconsciously want to, and pay little attention to facts or observations that have already been rejected as unimportant.

Mindsets affect everything we do. They tend to become stronger as time goes on, as we continue to select facts that reinforce the ideas we like and with which we feel comfortable. We tend to reject facts and experiences supporting ideas that we find objectionable. It should come as no great surprise that we tend to select friends whose ideas agree with ours. In this way a large number of people can come to hold extremely distorted ideas about specific individuals, other groups, historical events, and so on.

The process of selecting and rejecting facts is unavoidable; actually it is basic to human thinking. But if we are aware of the way mindsets can hinder thinking, we can minimize the problems caused by making judgments that are limited and one-sided.

Some mindsets do perform important functions in our mental structure. For example, we live in a dangerous world, but if we worried about every possible danger, nobody would ever do anything. Our past experience has taught us, then, that if after many repetitions certain potentially dangerous situations do not actually lead to harm, our minds are gradually predisposed against being concerned about them. Then, of course, it may well be at this time that an accident happens and we are shocked out of our complacency.

There have been a number of automobile accidents on interstate highways in which one initial accident causes a chain reaction collision involving dozens of cars. Motorists are frequently warned to allow adequate space between their vehicle and the one in front of them, (about one car-length for every ten-miles-per-hour of speed). But most drivers ignore this basic safety rule, and many tailgate just a few feet behind the car ahead. It is practically impossible for a tailgating driver to react fast enough to prevent crashing into the car ahead. Such drivers pay no attention to this well-known danger because, having done it a thousand times without any accident, they have a mindset that assures them nothing will happen. Young people are particularly prone to such accidents, and insurance rates are therefore very high for these men and women. This point is illustrated in figure 6.1 on p. 110.

What mindsets do you now have? Do you drive much faster than the speed limit? Do you fail to use seat belts? Do you snort a little cocaine

Figure 6.1 This driver, with his arm around the young lady's shoulder, has his mind set on other things. He also wrongly thinks he doesn't have to worry about an accident, because he has never had one before. *(Drawing by Albert Sarney)*

to "try it out," even though you know that some people—but of course, not you—can quickly become addicted? Do you smoke cigarettes despite the warnings on the labels? Watch out! You may have a mindset that will set you up for trouble ahead. All of these mindset attitudes are very similar to those that cause practically all big man-made disasters.

But mindsets go far beyond feelings of invincibility. They apply to practically every realm of ideas and opinion. Familiar relationships and events become so commonplace that we expect them to continue forever. Then we find ourselves completely unprepared to accept changes that are necessary, even when they stare us in the face.

JUMPING TO CONCLUSIONS

One September day, as Sid Newman was leaving school, he remembered that he had left a notebook on his desk. When he returned to retrieve it, he noticed his teacher's purse on the floor. He picked it up and put it on her desk. At that very moment the teacher, Ms. Harris, walked into the room.

"What are you doing with my purse," she demanded.

"Nothing. I just picked it up off the floor."

Ms. Harris looked into her purse. "A five-dollar bill is missing. Let me see what's in your wallet," she said.

Sid turned white as he remembered the five-dollar bill in his wallet that he had been saving to buy a Christmas present for his girlfriend. He refused to show Ms. Harris what was in his wallet.

"Come with me to the principal," said his teacher, glaring at poor Sid, quite sure he was guilty of stealing money from her purse.

There are any number of possible endings to this story; but what interests us here is Ms. Harris's reasoning. She was *jumping to the conclusion* that Sid was guilty of theft.

Why is the word *jumping* used here? The totality of facts do not support Ms. Harris's conclusion. Her error in reasoning arises because she does not have all the facts, and she has closed her mind to what Sid is saying. She did not actually *see* Sid take the money; she does not *know* what really happened or why Sid refuses to show her his wallet. Ms. Harris *did* see Sid holding her purse. She was justified in forming a hypothesis that he was stealing money. But because there were vital missing facts, all she had was *circumstantial evidence*. She could not be sure that her hypothesis was true.

An "open mind" in such situations is vital if we are to do justice to people accused of wrongdoing.

Jumping to conclusions based on "circumstantial" evidence has convicted many an innocent person. Take the case of Willie Jones, who was arrested for sneaking through a subway entrance to avoid paying the fare. His name was entered in the police department computer, which reported that Willie Jones—black, about 30 years old, slim, about 5 feet 10 inches tall, and weighing about 150 pounds—was wanted by police for selling drugs. The description fit the Willie Jones in custody, so he was charged with selling narcotics.

Mr. Jones was a janitor who had no money for lawyers, so he was provided with free legal services. Five lawyers interviewed him at different times. To each he protested that he was the wrong Willie Jones. He pointed out that the police record listed convictions for crimes that he did not commit. None of the five lawyers believed him, because the police description fit him so well, and also because of mindset and probably prejudice. Willie was poor, black, and shabbily dressed. If he had been a white, well-dressed, well-spoken engineer, he would have been out of jail in a jiffy. Nothing poor Willie said altered the lawyers' belief that he was certainly guilty. His counsel didn't even bother to have his identity checked by the police.

Finally, just a day before Willie's trial, one lawyer asked to have his fingerprints compared to those on file for "Willie Jones." It was quickly determined that the wrong Willie Jones was being held.

Figure 6.2 illustrates another everyday error caused by jumping to a conclusion. Kermit sees some "flowers" in a vase. They look like real flowers. So, without making any attempt to check the facts by touching the petals, Kermit jumps to the conclusion that they *are* real. This assumption triggers in his mind his usual allergic reaction to flowers, and he sneezes. The fact that he sneezed then "proves" that the flowers are real. So he yells at Harriet.

Judgments often have to be made even though important facts are missing. But when we cannot be certain that all the facts are available, we should at least be aware that our judgments might be wrong. We

 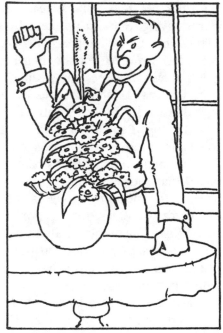

Harriet: "These artificial flowers look very nice on the table."

Kermit: "Aachoo . . . Harriet, you know I'm allergic to flowers. They make me sneeze. Take 'em away."

Figure 6.2 "Jumping to conclusions" is a common error caused by missing or misinterpreted "facts." *(Drawing by Albert Sarney)*

need to keep an *open mind* and to be on the lookout for missing facts that may change our tentative conclusions.

MISCONCEPTIONS

In figure 6.3 on page 114, a member of a school board is shown reporting to the other members what he considers to be serious shortcomings of the students in their district. Apparently a large number of them (50 percent) scored below "average" on a math test. He concludes that the students in town are doing poorly.

This school board member has a misconception about the meaning of "average," as do many other people. The fact is that if 50 percent are "below average" then 50 percent are "above average." An optimist would have said, "Fifty percent of the students in our town are 'above average in math.' " It is similar to the alternative of referring to a half-filled glass of water as "half-empty" or "half-full."

A more meaningful way of looking at the situation would be to refer to the number of students doing math at grade-level or above, as measured by scores on the national test. It is possible for 90 percent of the students in town to be at or above grade level in math, yet at the same time 50 percent are scoring "below average" on a national test.

Misconceptions take on many forms and are often at the root of various wrong ideas, wrong opinions, and incorrect judgments. One class of such misconceptions is discussed in detail in chapter 9 on "Stereotypes, Prejudices, and Discrimination."

By the way, note in the illustration that the school board is composed entirely of white men. Such an illustration tends to reinforce the "stereotype" that they are more capable than women or blacks of making wise decisions about such an important public function as education.

WRONG GENERALIZATIONS

As described in chapter 4, knowledge about the world is obtained by inductive reasoning in which we generalize from many specific observations to form generalizations that provide the factual basis for our reasoning. We then use such generalized facts as premises in deductive reasoning to derive conclusions that provide further information.

However, generalizations are often made improperly, giving us defective facts. Perhaps there are too few observations to justify the generalization,

Chairman of the School Board: *"Our students are not doing well in math. Fifty percent scored lower than average on the national test."*

Figure 6.3 What's wrong with his interpretation of the results of the national math test for the students of his town? *(Drawing by Albert Sarney)*

thus producing numerous exceptions. Or, quite often, biased attitudes or prejudice may cause people improperly to select some observations while subconsciously rejecting others (see chapter 9). Frequently, people get their "facts" from others by hearsay and rumor.

When such incorrect generalizations are used as premises in deductive reasoning, they are very likely to lead to wrong conclusions. The following discussion illustrates this error in reasoning.

"Watch out for that new fellow, Rob Robbins, who came home with your nephew, Bill. Robbins will steal money from your purse while you're not looking."

"Really? How do you know that?"

"Well, he lives in that bad neighborhood down by the railroad tracks. Everyone knows that those people steal whenever they get a chance."

The reasoning in this case may be put in the form of a syllogism as follows:

Major Premise: People who live in the bad neighborhood near the railroad tracks steal.

Minor Premise: Rob Robbins lives in that bad neighborhood.

Conclusion: Therefore, Rob Robbins steals. (So watch out for your purse.)

The major premise is a generalization that is very unlikely to apply to every person, or even to most people living in that neighborhood. People who make such statements as if they were facts may have read newspaper accounts about a higher crime rate in a certain area. Perhaps they were mugged there, or someone they knew had been a victim. It might be correct to say that the neighborhood has a high crime rate, but that does not justify accusing all of the people who live there of being thieves.

Suppose one person in ten from that neighborhood steals. That would produce an extremely high crime rate and make things very difficult for people who live there. The neighborhood might be dangerous to visit. But nine out of ten people living there do not steal, and the Major Premise, therefore, does not apply to them. A generalization has been extended far beyond its proper boundaries. A fact that may be true of some is incorrectly assumed to be true of all.

Many people use the word *generalize* in describing such defective reasoning, as in "Oh, you are generalizing about (whatever the subject may be). . . ." To avoid confusion with the more basic meaning of "generalize" (in the sense of using inductive reasoning to make a general statement from specific observations), we may refer to the erroneous reasoning in this case as *overgeneralizing*. The incorrect generalization may be called an *overgeneralization*. These words convey the meaning that a generalization is faulty because it is being applied beyond its proper limits and is therefore likely to produce wrong conclusions when used in making deductions.

Overgeneralizing about groups of people, specific individuals, and important issues is one of our main sources of misunderstanding. Listen carefully when people talk critically about others. Do the speakers really *know* what all or even most of those other people are like?

Such overgeneralizing leads to, or may be caused by, prejudice, which often leads to injustice, war, and human suffering (see chapter 9).

The United States was founded on the idea of freedom and liberty for all. A true American does not condemn all or most members of particular groups because of the faults or crimes of a few individuals. This attitude has made our country an attractive place to live and work. But we still have a long way to go to eliminate the overgeneralizations and prejudices that continue to make life difficult for some minority groups.

MISTAKING EVIDENCE FOR PROOF

Consider this reasoning:

> Mr. A: "Scrounge is a thief."
>
> Mr. B: "I don't believe it. Prove it."
>
> Mr. A: "He's on trial right now for stealing money from the cash register at Palmer's drug store."

Based on the above account, all we can say is that there is *some evidence* that Scrounge is a thief. What counts as evidence is any fact or observation that is used to support a conclusion, a judgment, or a generalization. No *proof* can be considered reasonable until the evidence for it is overwhelming. Even so, we must remember that in real life the existence of absolute proof leading to complete certainty is for all practical purposes impossible to attain. In everyday reasoning the difference between proof and evidence is usually blurred. People tend to accept a few bits of evidence as proof for their pet beliefs, often ignoring evidence that might disprove their view.

The fact that Scrounge is on trial for theft may be accepted as evidence for a "hypothesis," a reasonable guess that he is a thief. If Scrounge is convicted, this would be considered by most people to be conclusive proof of guilt. But Scrounge could be the victim of mistaken identity. People might even dislike him because of his unfortunate name. The fact that he is on trial is not proof of guilt; there were a significant number of cases where innocent people had been convicted and imprisoned, even executed, for crimes they did not commit.

In court trials great care is taken to make sure juries declare guilt only when the evidence establishes proof "beyond a shadow of a doubt." Yet juries sometimes jump to conclusions and convict people who are innocent. Occasionally, police or prosecutors may be so eager to get a conviction by acting on their own special mindsets that they may overlook or even suppress evidence that tends to cast doubt on the accused person's guilt.

One study of crime in the United States revealed that 343 people are known to have been wrongly convicted of murders. Of these innocent people, 25 were executed. In most of these cases the evidence was circumstantial. It is possible that many other cases of wrong convictions, as yet undiscovered, are likely to have occurred.[2]

People are sometimes *absolutely sure* of generalized facts, based on evidence gathered from a lifetime of observation, yet their "facts" later turn out to be untrue. In the year 1300, for instance, it was considered absolutely certain that the earth was flat and the sun revolved around the earth every day. And what of the prevalent belief just a century ago that women were intellectually inferior to men and were not capable of doing "men's work"? The advances women have made in recent years have shown this belief in the intellectual inferiority of women to be utterly false.

Such beliefs often become "self-fulfilling prophecies." The things people do because of their beliefs often make those beliefs come true. Because women were considered inferior it "made no sense" to educate girls in the same way as boys. Why send them to college, or teach them special skills? As a result, women did not have the same opportunities as men to be trained in skilled professions; therefore, women could not pursue these vocations and were often denied entry to professions because of a persuasive belief in their inferiority. And when those women who were permitted to practice did not do well in these professions, their failure became "proof" that they were inferior. (See chapter 9 for discussion of stereotypes, prejudice, and self-fulfilling prophecies with regard to minorities.)

How Reliable Is Testimony?

From movies and television we are familiar with the police lineup, a procedure that attempts to make identification of suspects for crimes more objective. Surely, the procedure of having an eyewitness select a suspect from a group of similar people in a lineup ought to make identification more reliable. However, in a summary of a number of controlled experiments with lineups, psychologist A. Daniel Yarmey states, "It may be concluded on the basis of experimental evidence that mistaken identity from lineups is often the rule and not the exception."[3] For that reason, identification by one eyewitness is usually an inadequate basis for determining the guilt or innocence of a suspect.

There are many causes for errors in testimony by witnesses to events; much depends on the circumstances. It is much harder to identify strangers than people we know well, and harder to identify people of different racial groups than of our own. When a crime is being committed, eyewitnesses rarely get a good look at the criminal, or may be too excited to note details. Afterward, when the police show them pictures of possible suspects, they may become confused. People often have poor memories for faces, and a photograph is always somewhat different from the actual face.

In a criminal trial, proper identification depends on the care with which the police set up the process by which suspects are identified. Having a witness confront the accused is not necessarily the best procedure. Once a person is accused, an unsure witness may prejudge that he is looking at a guilty person. Being able to pick out a criminal from a lineup often depends on clothing worn by the suspect, the appearance of others in the lineup, or previous remarks. Do police do a good job of selecting fairly similar-looking people for these lineups? Or does the suspect stand out because of one feature (a scar or being bald), perhaps short stature or a wide nose?

Teachers have staged events to demonstrate the unreliability of witnesses. In one such event a student rushed into a classroom and pretended to punch another student. He then dropped some objects to make a loud noise and ran out of the room. The surprised students in the classroom were then asked to describe what they observed. Their reports differed widely. Some even reported that shots had been fired, because of the noise made by the objects that were dropped. Obviously, identification by witnesses, by itself, is not necessarily proof of guilt in a criminal trial.

CIRCULAR REASONING

A common error in reasoning is to rephrase the statement to be proven true and then to use the new, similar statement as "proof" that the original statement is in fact true. This is referred to as *circular reasoning*. For example:

Peter: "Taxation of income is for the common good."

Paul: "Why do you say that?"

Peter: "Because in the long run taxation of income is in the best interest of all citizens."

Peter has offered no real evidence to support his argument. He has simply restated his judgment in different words. "Common good" and "in the best interest of all citizens" are merely different ways of saying the same thing. Consider another example:

Teacher: "Why does the sun give off a lot of light?"

John: "Because it's bright."

Teacher: "Then why is the sun bright?"

John: "Because it shines with a lot of light."

The teacher may expect an answer like "The sun is very hot. Heat causes it to glow and give off a lot of light." John, however, merely substitutes the word *bright* for the phrase "to give off a lot of light." He puts the word *because* in front of the sentence to make it seem as if he has said *why* the sun gives off a lot of light, when he has merely substituted a single word for a group of words. When the teacher pursues the point, John avoids answering the teacher's second question by repeating the words of the first question.

An important example of a more complex form of circular reasoning was noted by Dr. Richard Feynman, a scientist who served as a member of the presidential commission that investigated the explosion of the Challenger space shuttle in 1986 in which seven astronauts died. He was quoted in the newspapers as saying that the fact that the shuttle flew many times without failure was accepted as an argument that it would fly safely again. "Because of this reasoning," he said, "obvious weaknesses were accepted again and again. . . ." In this case circular reasoning reinforced the mindset that there was no danger, despite overwhelming evidence to the contrary.

FALSE ANALOGIES

Here is a newspaper account of a divorce trial:

> Judge Taylor ruled yesterday that while a ship is a she, a she is not a ship.
>
> Such being the case, he granted Mrs. Sue Morley a divorce from Richard Morley, captain of an oil tanker.
>
> Witnesses said Morley's mother told him at a dinner party that he should show his wife more consideration.
>
> "That isn't the point," Morley replied. "There must be a master of the ship and he must be obeyed."
>
> "This is a woman, not a ship," his mother retorted.
>
> The judged agreed.

Let's analyze Mr. Morley's statement: In an analogy it is assumed that if two things are similar in one way, they may also be similar in other ways. For some people the vague hypothesis, "may be," gets converted into "is." Mr. Morley compares his ship with his home because both provide shelter. Arguing by analogy, he declares that if he is the boss on the ship, he ought to be the boss at home.

This is a false, or "stretched" analogy. Morley omits important differences between a ship and a home. A captain or commander of a ship must be obeyed if the ship is to get to port safely in situations where quick decisions have to be made. The lives of the crew and passengers depend on his decisions. The situation in a home is different in most respects. Morley's wife is not a crew member. She should be his loving companion, not his subordinate.

Most people would infer from Mr. Morley's use of this analogy that he is a domineering person who wants to command others. He seeks to transfer the rules of the ship to his home; in effect, treating his home exactly the same as his ship.

Morley could have used other analogies to try to justify bossing his wife. For example, the manager of a factory is supposed to be in command of the employees who work under his supervision. As manager he has the power to tell them what to do in their work. But then, a home is not a factory and a wife is not an employee.

Morley's wife could think of analogies to defend her point of view. In a business partnership, for instance, both partners have an equal say. A wife is a partner in a marriage, and, by analogy, should have an equal say with her spouse.

Stretched analogies are a major source of error in everyday reasoning. In the past, a fisherman hauling in a catch and finding a starfish would chop it up and throw it into the sea. It was assumed this would kill the creature because, by analogy with fish, rats, and other familiar animals, chopping them into several parts does end their lives. This procedure was followed because starfish are predators competing with humans for the food available in mussels on the ocean floor.

Unfortunately, a starfish doesn't necessarily die that way. It can survive loss of limbs if its central mouth remains intact to grow new arms. In this case the analogy with killing fish or rats by random cuts did not apply. The cut had to be through the mouth. The analogy was stretched too far.

Making an analogy based on similarities is fine so long as we understand that at the first stage in the reasoning process the analogy is nothing more than a "hypothesis," a reasonable guess at a possible fact that must be checked and verified before it can be accepted as true. Without these vital steps we can never be sure that any analogy made, or any conclusion drawn, is really on the mark.

USING ANALOGIES IN FORMING JUDGMENTS

Argument by analogy is frequently used in making political judgments. We try to determine correct policies today by examining history to find similar situations that can guide us in knowing what to do. Analogies between the past and the present are less likely to apply if differences have developed over time. In the 1950s, after World War II, many people argued by analogy that Germany and France would continue to be bitter enemies. And history was on their side: in the century before 1945, these two countries had fought three wars over disputed land along their border. There seemed to be little hope for long-term peaceful coexistence.

Today, however, long after the end of the war, the deep enmity between Germany and France seems to have disappeared. Though differences remain, they cooperate frequently. So it appears that the analogy with their warlike past no longer applies.

The sustained peace between Germany and France could be used as an analogy to cause us to be optimistic about the possibility of future peace for the world. If such bitter enemies can become friendly, why not the rest of the world, eventually? It remains to be seen whether such an analogy will apply to the present world situation, though with recent events in Eastern Europe, the Soviet Union, and South Africa, this hope remains very much alive.

Analogies in Proverbs

People may be swayed in an argument by analogies based on proverbs. For instance, if a man is thinking about investing his savings in a business, one of his friends might advise him to "Make hay while the sun shines." This analogy is just a different way of saying "You should buy now before the opportunity is lost." Another friend, who thinks the business should not be bought, could say "Haste makes waste," advising caution. He may think the business is not such a good buy and his friend should be in no hurry to spend hard-earned savings.

Other proverbs could be found to apply to this situation: "Fools rush in where angels fear to tread," "A word to the wise is sufficient," "God helps those who help themselves," "Marry in haste, repent at leisure," "A fool and his money are soon parted." There are enough proverbs, sayings, and quotations to support almost any idea a person might wish to uphold. Such analogies by proverb are not very useful in making judgments, because there are many kinds of problem situations in life requiring very different solutions. If an analogy works in one situation, it does not follow that the same analogy will work in others.

REASONING FROM FALSE "FACTS" OR PREMISES

We might think that if false "facts" are used as premises in reasoning, the conclusion derived from them must therefore be wrong. Although this is usually true, it is not always the case. Observe this reasoning in the form of a syllogism:

1. Animals are rocks.

   All As are Bs

2. Rocks are living things.

   All Bs are Cs

3. Therefore, animals are living things.

   All As are Cs

The conclusion, that animals are living things, is a "true" statement in that it conforms with our experience. It is also a properly deduced logical statement; in other words, the reasoning is "logical," yet it is based on premises that are totally false. In this example it is easy to see that both premises are false. In some cases, however, the falsity of the premises is not so easy to detect. Moreover, if we know that a conclusion is true, we tend to believe that the premises on which it is based are also true.

As we can see from this example, a conclusion that is true does not *prove* that the premises are true. It is usually considered good evidence, but not proof, that premises are correct, and we must watch for exceptions. All we can really say is that the conclusion is *consistent* with the premises, but *the conclusion does not verify the premises.*

Consider this reasoning:

Premise 1: Great thinkers do not come from nations of stupid people.

Premise 2: Gargolia is a nation of stupid people.

Conclusion: Therefore, great thinkers do not come from Gargolia.

Suppose, upon investigating the facts, we find that Gargolia does not appear to have any great thinkers, and we are not aware that it has ever had any. Because the conclusion that follows the premises seems to be true, it may also seem likely that the premises are also true. Some people would infer that "Great thinkers do not come from nations of stupid people" and "Gargolia is a nation of stupid people" are in fact true.

Nevertheless, the premises are likely to be false. The mental achievements of people living in a nation like Gargolia are the result of complex conditions. Perhaps Gargolia has a poor educational system, inadequate natural resources, general poverty, widespread malnutrition and disease, or a combination of these and other factors. The fact that Gargolia has never produced any great thinkers does not prove that it never will. All an investigation can show is that great thinkers have not yet come from Gargolia.

Moreover, no one is justified in calling any large group of people "stupid." The word reveals a prejudice on the part of the person making the statement. The reasoning in this case is oversimplified and based on premises that overgeneralize. A judgment is made about a complex human problem in which many unknown factors are at work. It is almost impossible to prove the truth of overgeneralizations like "Great thinkers do not come from nations of stupid people," or "Gargolia is a nation of stupid people." The word *stupid* is vague, meaning slow-witted or lacking normal intelligence. It is also a *pejorative* word that seeks to belittle people, and is therefore not conducive to objective reasoning.

How does one prove that everyone in a nation is "stupid"? With an IQ test? The scores on such tests are highly dependent on cultural background, degree of literacy, motivation, state of health, and other factors. Give a rural person who has had little schooling a standard IQ test and the test score is likely to be quite low. Some people might mistakenly infer from the low score that the rural person is "stupid." But compare his ability to survive in a remote forest with that of a city person and the latter would seem to be "stupid."

Assume that we could somehow find an objective way to measure "stupidity" and then establish it as a fact that the people in Gargolia are "stupid." Now there is a problem with the words *do not* in the premise "Great thinkers *do not* come from nations of stupid people." What is really meant is that they "*have not* come from nations of stupid people." The words *have not* admit the possibility that great thinkers might yet come from such a nation, while the choice of "do not" implies exclusion of that possibility. Such improper choice of language often introduces confusion in the reasoning process.

A CASE STUDY OF FALSE PREMISES

In 1950, the book *Worlds in Collision* by Immanuel Velikovsky, a psychiatrist, began a controversy in the academic community that raged for twenty-five years until the author's death.[4] He claimed that the planet Venus was originally a comet that somehow broke off from the planet Jupiter, traveled toward the earth, revolved around the earth many times, and then broke away and went off to become a planet unto itself. With this "theory" he tried to explain many events described in the Bible, such as the sun standing still for a day during a battle fought by Joshua, the parting of the Red Sea when Moses escaped from Egypt with the Israelites, and manna (a bread-like food, which Velikovsky claimed came from the "comet") falling from the sky to feed the Israelites.

Many people who knew nothing about astronomy were so impressed by the large number of stories and myths from ancient people, cited by Velikovsky as "evidence," that they believed his astronomical claims about the origins of the planet Venus.[5]

Astronomers unanimously declared that his claims about Venus were false because they violated many long-established principles of science, as well as basic observations in astronomy. Some astronomers considered Velikovsky's claims so outrageous that they made the serious mistake of demanding that the publisher of Velikovsky's book stop publishing and distributing it. Velikovsky then widely publicized this event as a "civil liberties" issue.

The controversy became even more clouded when several of Velikovsky's predictions turned out to be true. He reasoned that Venus would be very hot because it was a new planet only 3,000 years old and would not have had much time to cool off. Later, when the surface of Venus was determined to have a temperature of 900° F., Velikovsky claimed this as "proof" of his theory. It seems, however, that this unexpected high temperature is due to the "greenhouse effect" because the atmosphere of Venus is mainly carbon dioxide, which traps heat.

Velikovsky also predicted that Jupiter would be found to produce radio waves (in the form of noisy "static") because if it threw off the planet Venus, it would have to be an "active" planet. Scientists had not suspected that Jupiter would produce radio waves. Later, astronomers found that Jupiter was actually producing such radio waves.

Although Velikovsky made many other predictions that turned out not to be true, the fact that two of them were supported and widely publicized by him, led many people to believe that his theory, and the premises for his reasoning, were also true. This was a dramatic case of accidentally true conclusions being derived from premises that were totally false.

Velikovsky was an indefatigable campaigner for his ideas, and kept the controversy boiling until his death in 1988. As with many other such controversies based on false premises, it has now subsided and will soon be just a footnote in history.

THE MISUSE OF STATISTICS

Statistics—facts or data in numerical form—are often used to make the reader or listener feel that information is accurate and "scientific." Correct statistics are often purposely misinterpreted in political campaigns and discussions and when people are arguing for their special interests or firmly held points of view. A candidate for office, eager to "prove" that economic conditions are good, may cite a figure of 5 percent unemployment, which is considered reasonably low, and is taken to mean that times are good. His opponent notes another survey that shows 10 percent unemployment when large categories of people, normally left out of the official figures, are included. These categories include the discouraged long-term unemployed who are no longer counted, because they do not apply for unemployment insurance; the homeless, who have no regular addresses; and part-time workers who seek more work but are not counted as unemployed.

"Averages" are also easy to misinterpret. An average of a group of numbers is calculated by adding up all the numbers in a list to find the total, then dividing that figure by the number of items in the list. For example, the average of the ten numbers 1, 2, 2, 3, 3, 4, 5, 7, 7, and 8 is equal to the sum of all the numbers (42) divided by the number of items (10). The average is then 4.2.

Consider the misleading inference that a higher average income for a community means it is "better off." To simplify the calculation assume that there are ten families in Lockville and also ten in Geartown. The incomes of the families in each community are:

ANNUAL INCOMES OF FAMILIES
IN LOCKVILLE AND GEARTOWN

Lockville	Geartown
$10,000	$1,000,000
10,000	5,000
10,000	5,000
10,000	5,000
10,000	5,000
10,000	5,000
10,000	5,000
10,000	5,000

10,000	5,000
10,000	5,000
$100,000	$1,045,000

$$\text{Average} = \frac{\$100,000}{10}$$

$$= \$10,000$$

$$\text{Average} = \frac{\$1,045,000}{10}$$

$$= \$104,500$$

In a speech while campaigning for re-election as mayor of Geartown, Jim Battler declared, "With an average income for Geartown of $104,500, more than ten times as much as for our neighbors across the river in Lockville, my administration has made our citizens ten times better off!"

Mollie Firesome looks at the actual incomes and interprets the statistics differently. "Ninety percent of the families in Geartown earn half as much income ($5,000) as the average income in Lockville ($10,000). Jim Battler favors the rich, who get most of the income in Geartown, while everyone else gets less. Vote for me for mayor."

The reason that averages often mislead is that they are generalized figures that do not give any indication of the actual "distribution" of the numbers. To eliminate this defect with regard to statistics for income, the federal government publishes figures that subdivide the population into "fifths" according to income group (the fifth with the lowest incomes, the fifth with the highest, etc.).

As may be inferred from the above table of incomes, an average tends to increase substantially when just a few large incomes are included. As is often said, "Figures don't lie, but liars can figure." Statistics and numbers are not the problem; people who use them improperly are.

RELATIVE VERSUS ABSOLUTE

A group of hikers reached the top of a hill and gazed down at the magnificent scene below.

"Look at that beautiful lake!" exclaimed Edith.

"That's too small to be a lake," replied Mike. "It's a pond." The rest of the group began to argue the lake/pond issue.

Finally, Ms. Woodward settled the argument. "As far as anyone can tell from up here, it's a pond for those who think it's a pond, and a lake for those who think it's a lake. It's all 'relative.' When we get back, we'll look at a map to see what it's called."

What Ms. Woodward meant by "relative" is that the answer could not be established as an "absolute" yes or no, all or nothing. Someone who lived near the Great Lakes is likely to have a different standard for sizes of lakes and ponds than someone from an area with few large bodies of water. What are called ponds in some areas of the country are considered to be lakes in others. There are no established standards of size.

Much of our reasoning involves situations that are relative, not absolute. The answers to questions usually depend on a number of things. It is precisely for this reason that different people often reach different conclusions from the same information.

EMOTION VERSUS REASONING

Our minds are structured so that we react to events in one of two basic ways: emotionally or by means of reasoning. Both are essential to human survival.

Hormones, special substances produced in the body, play a key role in emotions. For example, when confronted with a dangerous situation that requires one to flee or fight, the adrenal glands release into the bloodstream a hormone known as adrenalin. This substance energizes our muscles to perform more efficiently; we can then run faster or fight more aggressively. This reaction to fear, common to many kinds of animals, is obviously protective and aids in survival.

Hormones are also associated with other emotions such as sexual attraction, parental love, hate, and anger. Unfortunately, emotions often override reasoning power in critical situations and can lead to disaster. For example, driven by fear during a fire in a crowded meeting room or restaurant, people will thoughtlessly jam the exits, so only a few actually escape. In some instances, many people have died primarily because doors could not be opened inward against an onrushing crowd. That is why doors to public places open outward, with a push bar along the entire width of the door. People jammed against the door are then pushed against the bar to open the door automatically.

In some cases people have been crushed underfoot by crowds. At one soccer game a crowd of people tried to get in at an entrance gate that had been temporarily closed. Many were suffocated or crushed by the people behind them who were pushing forward.

In contrast, lives have been saved during a number of ship and airplane crashes as a result of thoughtful action by calm members of the crew and obedience by the passengers.

One of the most powerful of our emotions is love. There is the basic love of most parents for their children, which often leads to personal sacrifice in difficult or dangerous circumstances. That emotion is generally positive because it aids human survival. But there are cases when parental love becomes harmfully overprotective as emotion overrides reasoning power, which indicates that parents should "let go" of children who have become adults.

There is the strong emotion of physical love between the sexes, essential to human procreation. But this emotion sometimes overwhelms reasoning, and those affected do things that others can see will lead to trouble. Frequently, such emotions turn to irrational hatred. Most of us have observed divorce situations in which intense anger festers into long and costly court battles over who gets the family assets or custody of the children. Everyone but the participants can see that mediation or arbitration is essential, but one or both members of the parting couple may be so emotional that they resort to kidnaping children, physical attacks, or even murder.

On a larger scale, human emotions are often deliberately aroused by demagogues and dictators to exert tight control over their people, or even to start wars. They induce the emotion of intense fear by means of imprisonment, torture, and sometimes death. Dictators usually evoke the strong emotion of patriotism in their supporters, aided by control over all sources of information. Obviously, emotion plays a basic role in human behavior, but its excesses must be contained and controlled by use of reasoning.

In many everyday situations we are tugged this way or that by emotional appeals in speeches by public figures, print advertisements, and television or radio commercials. Our ability to reason helps to protect us against the thoughtless actions that emotions often produce. (See chapters 10 and 11 for further discussion of emotion versus reasoning with respect to influencing opinions and in the field of advertising.)

EXTREME JUDGMENTS

A teenager leads a gang into a playground and, in a fight, stabs another youth to death. When he is captured, the gang leader seems to feel no remorse. The boy is condemned to death despite his youth. Most people agree with the verdict and the sentence. Later, however, the governor agrees to commute the death sentence to life imprisonment.

Years later, a study is made of the boy's background. The study finds that he had led a miserable existence from birth, shifting between separated parents, and then through several temporary homes. He often slept in the streets and went without food. He learned to hate comfortable people, whom he blamed for his misery. School meant nothing to this gang leader because he could not see how it could solve his daily problems of survival. He was almost illiterate.

In jail the young man had time to think. He learned to read and write. His attitude toward the world began to change. So did the attitudes of the people who had condemned him. They began to understand that there were important circumstances that led to the seemingly unforgivable crime. Any one of us could have been in similar circumstances.

Such situations are common in life. People are rarely all good or all bad, and their actions are seldom all right or all wrong. The same is true of most attitudes toward important social issues. People often find that the ideas they once held strongly have to be modified on occasion as circumstances change or as new facts come into view.

We must be cautious about making judgments that oversimplify human behavior or problems. Most extreme, either-or, all-or-nothing decisions and solutions to problems tend to be defective because they omit large areas of middle-ground solutions and information that may be vital.

THE ROLE OF ETHICAL VALUES AND ATTITUDES

People hold different views about many concepts: e.g., good and bad, right and wrong, honesty and dishonesty, justice and injustice, democracy and dictatorship, safety and danger. Judgments in such matters often depend upon the *ethical values* of those making the judgments, as well as the meanings given to the words used to convey the problems and the evaluations.

Ethics is the study of what people believe to be morally good and bad behavior. Ethical values, or simply "values," are the beliefs held by persons or groups as to what is good or bad, right or wrong.

Figure 6.4 on page 130 illustrates this point. Mom and Wilbert have different *attitudes* about who is responsible for doing urgent chores. Her attempt to shame Wilbert into helping to shovel snow fails because Wilbert thinks it is the duty of his mom and dad to do *all* the chores around the house. He thinks his "job" is to let mom and dad take care of him.

Ethical values, and the attitudes that derive from them, are learned from many sources: parents, families, teachers, friends, religious leaders, people in the community, newspapers, books, magazines, radio, television, and films. We cannot totally escape our cultural background, and diverse cultural upbringing can cause wide differences in ethical values, which in turn lead to different judgments about events.

People are often classified by their origins. In our country there are

Mother: *"Maybe I can shame Wilbert into doing this job."*
Wilbert: *"Why are you cleaning the walk? Where's Dad?"*

Figure 6.4 Different values often cause people to differ in their attitudes and conclusions, even though they observe the same set of facts. *(Drawing by Arnold Lobel)*

northerners and southerners; city people and country people; rich, poor, and middle-income; Californians and New Yorkers; Indians, Irish, and Italians; blacks, whites, orientals, and hispanics; Catholics, Protestants, Jews, and Muslims; and many more groups. Most of us belong to more than one of these groups. There are obvious differences in ethical values, in what we think and believe, and how we behave. We get along well only when we refrain from making absolute judgments about each other, and when we avoid prejudiced thinking.

The United States is an unusual country because of the diversity of its population. Some conflict among groups is inevitable, but it has been possible for most of us to live together in reasonable harmony because of a basic common belief. We know that in order to live together everyone must seek to understand and be tolerant of the beliefs and values of others.

Today, certain problems threaten the safety of everyone on Earth. Use of nuclear weapons could destroy human life as we know it. Destruction of the earth's environment by various forms of pollution, overpopulation, deforestation, and changes in climate due to the burning of fossil fuels puts everyone in the human family at risk. We have a common interest in solving the problems that threaten our existence. This common goal makes it necessary for all nations to cooperate, even when they disagree strongly about other matters.

THE IMPORTANCE OF AN OPEN MIND

Thus far we have observed the many ways in which people can make mistakes in reasoning. Most of these errors arise from improper use of facts when employed as premises in logical reasoning. The facts themselves may be "fuzzy," with important exceptions ignored. We find ourselves easily slipping into mindsets that frequently produce *closed minds,* excluding entire categories of important facts, even when these facts are obvious to those whose minds are not predisposed against them. We may jump to conclusions prematurely without having enough facts to make a judgment, or indulge in overgeneralization from fuzzy facts, or when facts are missing.

All of these sources of error and the long history of faulty human judgments should lead us to be cautious and to avoid arriving at conclusions too hastily. In large measure, this is the idea behind the concept of an *open mind;* we seek to avoid mindsets and pay close attention to information that contradicts what we believe to be true.

Many people are contemptuous of those with open minds, viewing people who are cautious about accepting unsupported facts as "wishy-washy" or "unable to make up their minds." Of course there are people who are so confused by the complexities of life that they *never* make up their minds. Obstacles scare them so much that they rarely undertake anything new, and they lack any firm opinions on controversial subjects.

A truly open-minded person is not at all indecisive. Decisions are made whenever necessary and are based on the available facts. However, the decision or opinion should not be frozen forever. Without all the facts at our disposal, we must remain open to the presence of new information that could alter our decisions and render previous judgments groundless. With this open-minded attitude we can quickly spot contradictory facts that signal STOP, LOOK, and LISTEN.

In contrast, those with closed minds refuse to consider any contradictory facts, and proceed with their planned course of action, full speed ahead, with their "minds made up" and tightly shut. As an illustration, consider the situation in 1986, prior to the space shuttle Challenger's disastrous launch that killed all seven astronauts aboard. There was a heated telephone debate between two engineers for the company that produced the shuttle booster rockets and top officials of NASA (the federal government's space agency). The engineers insisted that the flight was too risky because of freezing temperatures at the Florida launch site. They explained that some of the seals on the fuel tanks were not designed to withstand such low temperatures and might leak under pressure while in flight, thus endangering the craft and crew.

Despite their pleas to abort the flight, officials at NASA overruled the engineers, who were best qualified to make judgments about the complex technical problems of space flight. The officials gave priority to other, secondary considerations. Several flights had already been postponed and it would not look good to postpone another. Big crowds of people and news reporters were waiting for the launch, and it would be bad public relations to disappoint them. Top government officials were ready to appear on national television and take the credit for another safe flight. So, with their minds absolutely closed to the facts presented by the engineers, NASA officials ordered the Challenger to take off.

Not only did this closed-minded attitude result in the deaths of seven astronauts, but the accident and its repercussions stopped shuttle flights for several years. Suddenly, after the accident, everyone had an open mind about the dangers. Many billions of dollars were spent for thorough redesign of equipment before flights were resumed—because of the closed minds of NASA officials.

There is no virtue in ignoring contradictory facts and "sticking to your guns" when the course taken shows all the signs of being the wrong one. Closed minds are especially noticeable in political campaigns and debates. Many people line up to support one candidate or another and won't listen to any facts presented by an opposing candidate. Whatever the favored candidate says is considered to be the pure truth.

All those with an open mind say is this: "I don't know everything, so I'd better keep my mind, eyes, and ears open to any new facts that may come along." The world would be a much better and safer place if everyone had this attitude. Other sources of error in reasoning are discussed in the chapters that follow.

NOTES

1. Report of the President's Commission on the Accident at Three Mile Island, *New York Times* (October 31, 1979):1:6.

2. H. A. Bedau and M. L. Radelet, "Miscarriages of Justice in Potentially Capital Cases," *Stanford Law Review* 40, No. 1 (November 1987):21–179.

3. A. Daniel Yarmey, *The Psychology of Eyewitness Testimony* (New York: The Free Press, 1979), p. 159.

4. Immanuel Velikovsky, *Worlds in Collision* (Garden City, N.Y.: Doubleday and Co., 1950), pp. 39–86.

5. "Velikovsky: AAAS Forum for a Mild Collision," *Science* 183 (March 15, 1974):1059–62.

QUESTIONS (*Discussion of these Questions Begins on Page 250.*)

Analyze the reasoning in each problem:

1. "I'm in a hurry and Sally is waiting for me. Could I wait for breakfast until after lunch?"

2. "That fellow is stingy."

"How do you know?"

"His name is MacGregor and he is a Scotsman. Everybody knows that Scots are stingy."

3. The phonograph squeaked very loudly when the turntable rotated. So Johnny took it apart, intending to oil it. Unable to find regular lubricating oil, he used some salad oil instead. Thereafter, the phonograph didn't work at all. What was Johnny's error in reasoning?

4. One day Mrs. Bunting happened to see Mike Fialco and Gene Putnam walking down the street together. She turned to her friend Mrs. Reading. "It's a shame, but that nice Fialco boy is friendly with that nasty Putnam fellow. That's the third time I've seen them together. Now he'll be breaking windows, too."

5. "Don't throw out that old refrigerator. It's still working, so keep it as long as it runs. After all, a penny saved is a penny earned."

6. "I'm sure that when Pickering comes in as the new president of the company, he'll fix things up quickly, and we are sure to see a profit next year. After all, a new broom sweeps clean."

7. "I don't trust Roberts. He's one of those fellows who is always smiling and slapping people on the back. When that happens I always say to myself, 'I wonder what he's after.'"

8. "Your Honor, in this trial we have conclusively proven that Tim Tucker is guilty of the holdup at Happy Pizza. He was observed riding in the holdup car a half hour before the crime was committed, only a mile from the scene of the crime. He is known to have visited Happy Pizza on at least four occasions in the past month. And we have also shown that his bank accounts are much larger than his visible income would warrant. The facts are clear and call for conviction."

9. "Unnecessary government control is a wasteful way of minding the business of industries and individuals, who have been proving for over a hundred years that they can manage business affairs better themselves."

"Government control stifles progress, no matter how well-meaning, unselfish, sincere, and intelligent the people are who exercise such control."

10. "Why does a cow give milk?"

"Because otherwise it wouldn't be acting as a cow should."

11. Too much freedom is not good for people.

12. "Are you sure that Pemberton is a member of the ABC party? How do you know?"

"He follows their policies right down the line on every count."

13. "Peck is a skinflint. He never gives any money to charity. And when he does he makes a big show of it so that people will buy insurance from him and he will then make more money than he paid out to charity."

14. "I don't care what anyone says. I'm going after that fellow and punch him in the nose the next time I see him."

15. What reasoning error is hidden in the following election law, similar to one actually enacted in a city?

The mayor shall be elected in alternate years on the first Tuesday after the second Monday in March and will serve a four-year term, providing that he receives an absolute majority of the votes.

7

Astrology:
A Case Study in Defective Reasoning

In her 1990 book titled *What Does Joan Say?* Joan Quigley claims to have been the astrologer who gave advice to Nancy Reagan, wife of former President Ronald Reagan. Quigley states:

> Through Nancy I had a direct line to the president. . . . I was responsible for timing all press conferences, most speeches, the State of the Union addresses, the takeoffs and landings of Air Force One. I picked the time of Ronald Reagan's debate with Carter and the two debates with Walter Mondale, all extended trips abroad as well as the shorter trips . . . briefings for all the summits except Moscow, although I selected the time to begin the Moscow trip."[1]

Quigley also claims that she timed some of President Reagan's press conferences to the second. For example, she says she chose 25 seconds after 11:32 A.M., November 11, 1987, for the president to make an announcement to the press about the appointment of Supreme Court Justice Anthony Kennedy. She states that a man with a stopwatch gave the signal for the president to proceed.[2]

According to the astrologer, when the president was operated on for cancer in 1985, she advised Nancy Reagan to have it delayed for three days. Quigley also declares that she set the date for Mrs. Reagan's mastectomy operation.

The astrologer states that she influenced Nancy Reagan on matters of state and "battled her to the mat" to convince the president to change his view of Soviet Premier Gorbachev. She even went so far as to make a horoscope for Gorbachev, and knew his character because

The placement of his ruler, Mercury, in the 10th house of power and position convinces me that Gorbachev came to power . . . because of his high degree of intelligence. It symbolizes for me that despite his Russian training and origins, he has the instinct of a humanitarian.

Is this a valid basis for determining anyone's character? Are Quigley's astonishing claims true? Did she really have such influence over vital national policies, timing of operations, and the president's major meetings and press conferences?

In her own book, *My Turn,* Nancy Reagan stated that astrologer Quigley was "helpful and comforting . . . a kind of therapist . . . (but) she had influence only on scheduling." This statement confirms the astrologer's effect on at least some aspects of the president's work.[3]

THE WIDESPREAD BELIEF IN ASTROLOGY

If any of Quigley's astonishing claims are true, even with regard to scheduling, they raise very urgent questions about the validity of belief in astrology. Apparently the influential wife of a president took astrology seriously enough to make decisions based on astrological predictions. And from his wife's statements, the president took her advice on at least some of these matters.

Because of astrologer Quigley's claimed influence on Nancy Reagan, one of the questions presidential candidates may be called on to answer in future elections is "Do you believe in astrology?" People who do believe in astrology, and those who don't, would then be able to take this factor into account when casting their ballots.

Apparently, many other people in our country agree with Nancy Reagan in her belief in astrology. Open any newspaper and somewhere on the page devoted to comics and puzzles, it is more likely than not that a daily horoscope will be found with some astrologer's words of wisdom about what those born under the sign of Taurus, Gemini, Capricorn, and the like should look for (or avoid) that particular day. Over 1,000 newspapers publish such columns. Walk into any bookstore and on its shelves can be found a substantial number of impressive-looking books on astrology, many of which sell extremely well.

Obviously, there are many people who believe astrology to be a valid "body of knowledge" that can serve as a guide in their daily lives. In fact, many people believe it to be a "science," just as valid as physics or biology, only in a different realm.

For our purposes astrology provides an excellent case study of how errors in reasoning can produce a "body of knowledge" that is little more than a complex form of superstition. Making such a claim is one thing; showing it to be the case is quite another. How do we know that astrology is more superstition than fact?

The only way to do this is to dig into what astrologers say and do, and objectively examine the "facts" and the reasoning on which their theories are based, much the same way Langmuir did with his proof that the deer fly did not travel at a speed of 700 miles per hour (see chapter 2). Such an analysis of astrology provides an excellent case study of how humans can create imaginative fictional structures and maintain them over thousands of years.

WHAT IS THE THEORY OF ASTROLOGY?

Astrologers assert that the positions of the sun, moon, stars, and planets in the sky "influence" the characters and personalities of the five billion people on Earth today. They claim this was true in the past, and presumably will continue to be true for anyone born in the future. They compose horoscopes for people based on calculations of the positions of these bodies in space at the moment of birth. Since astrologers use standard astronomical data for such calculations, they claim that they are engaged in "scientific" activity.

The first step in making a horoscope is to identify a person's astrological "sign." Table 1 is used for this purpose. It lists the twelve constellations of the zodiac, a band of constellations in the sky through which the sun appears to move each year as the earth revolves around the sun.

Although the constellations are not seen during the daytime, they do become visible during an eclipse. The position of the sun among the stars may also be inferred from the constellations seen just before dawn and after sunset.

Astrologers attach great significance to the constellation in which the sun appears to be at the moment of birth. The name of that constellation— one's astrological "sign"—is the starting point for a *horoscope*. This sign is supposed to be a guide for determining human personality and future events.

To determine a person's "sign," look up the date of birth in table 1. The constellation listed for that date of birth is the astrological sign. For example, note that Virgo is the astrological sign for a person whose birthday is September 4. Pisces is the sign for someone whose birthday is March 11. Check these findings yourself.

Table 1

DATES FOR THE ASTROLOGICAL SIGNS

Constellation in the Zodiac and Astrological Sign	Approximate Dates
Aries (the ram)	March 21 to April 20
Taurus (the bull)	April 21 to May 20
Gemini (the twins)	May 21 to June 21
Cancer (the crab)	June 22 to July 22
Leo (the lion)	July 23 to August 22
Virgo (the virgin)	August 23 to September 22
Libra (the scales)	September 23 to October 22
Scorpio (the scorpion)	October 23 to November 21
Sagittarius (the archer)	November 22 to December 20
Capricorn (the goat)	December 21 to January 19
Aquarius (the water carrier)	January 20 to February 18
Pisces (the fish)	February 19 to March 20

(These dates are approximate, generally within one day, mainly because of leap year.)[4]

Observe that the signs begin with Aries on March 21, the first day of spring. Then each sign follows approximately one month apart. The sign of Cancer begins on June 22, coinciding with the beginning of summer; Libra begins on September 23, the first day of autumn; Capricorn begins on December 21, the first day of winter. Then the twelfth and final sign of the astrological year, Pisces, ends on March 20, to be followed in a new astrological year with Aries on March 21.

These dates, directly linked to the four seasons, served as the key reference points for the charts created by astrologers thousands of years ago, and are used in the same way today.

Unfortunately for today's astrologers, the dates given in the above basic chart for astrological signs are all wrong. They *were* correct when prepared by astrologers long ago, but gradual astronomical changes have occurred during the intervening thousands of years, thus altering the dates when the sun appears in the designated constellations! And even the constellations themselves gradually change shape as very distant stars slowly move in the sky (see figure 7.1, p. 141).

Astrologers have completely ignored these changes and still use the ancient and inaccurate tables. As a result, people today who think their signs are Scorpio, or Aquarius, or Libra, have been misled! They really have other signs.

What were the astronomical changes that caused all the astrological signs to be wrong?

ELEVEN DAYS LOST

When George Washington was a young man his astrological sign was Aquarius (the water carrier) because his birthday was February 11. Later in life he suddenly came under the sign of Pisces (the fish), without changing his personality. How did this remarkable transformation occur?

In the mid-1700s the British government adopted the Gregorian calendar, proposed in 1582 by Pope Gregory XIII to solve a serious calendar problem. The Julian calendar, in effect since the time of Julius Caesar, had been based on a 365-day year. But that number was one-quarter of a day too small. As a result, the calendar gradually fell behind schedule. To correct the substantial error that had accumulated by the mid-1700s, the British government decreed that eleven days be omitted during one year so that the newer, more correct Gregorian calendar could be adopted.

Everybody in the British Empire, including George Washington, suddenly had their birthdays changed by eleven days. His birthday, originally February 11, jumped to February 22, thereby unceremoniously placing Washington under the sign Pisces instead of Aquarius.

This event may seem amusing to most of us but it should be a very serious matter for believers in astrology. The exact moment of birth is the basic factor in determining a horoscope, and here we have the case of birth dates and astrological signs suddenly changing in mid-life for millions of people, and for good reason.

What did astrologers do about this serious challenge to the basic premise of their beliefs? Absolutely nothing! They continued about their usual business, totally ignoring the vanished eleven days. They failed to comprehend the significance of a contradiction to the basic premise of their intellectual structure, which should have said, "STOP. Something's very wrong with your theory. Let's look into it."

CONTRADICTIONS CAUSED BY WRONG ASTROLOGICAL SIGNS

When the system of astrological signs was developed long ago, the dates specified in table 1 for the sun to appear in each of the twelve constellations of the zodiac were correct. Careful astronomical observations over many years seemed to show that the sun returned to the same place year after year in a given constellation of the zodiac.

However, after many centuries of observation, it was found that the sun did not appear to return to *exactly* the same spot in a constellation of the zodiac when the earth completed one revolution around the sun. Instead, the sun moved to a point slightly westward in the sky. This small difference has been accumulating for thousands of years so that the sun is no longer in the constellations listed in table 1 on the specified days of the year. In other words, the information in table 1 is wrong!

Astronomers now know that this has occurred because of a 26,000-year circular "precession" of the earth's axis of rotation, like the wobbling of a spinning top. This precession is produced by the gravitational pull of the moon and sun on the slight bulge at the earth's equator—a bulge caused by the earth's rotation.

This precession is a 26,000-year circular movement among the constellations of the "Celestial North Pole" (the point in the sky directly above the earth's Geographic North Pole). For example, Polaris, now used by navigators as the "North Star," appears to move in a giant circle once every 26,000 years. Several thousand years from now it will have moved too far to be useful for locating north. Other stars will then be nearer to the Celestial North Pole and may then serve as future markers for north. But 26,000 years from now Polaris will be back again as a future North Star.

This wobble of the earth's axis of rotation produces a similar 26,000-year cycle of change in positions in the sky for all stars and constellations, including those of the zodiac, thereby causing all dates in table 1 to be incorrect. As a result, astrologers are confronted with an extremely serious contradiction to astrological theory. On the one hand, they tell people that it is very important for everyone to know the constellation of the zodiac in which the sun happened to be on their birth dates, because that circumstance has a profound effect on human personalities and future events. Consequently, all believers have looked at the equivalent of table 1 and identified their own constellations, which they refer to as their "astrological signs." On the other hand, all those signs are now seen to be wrong, and every believer in astrology has been misled!

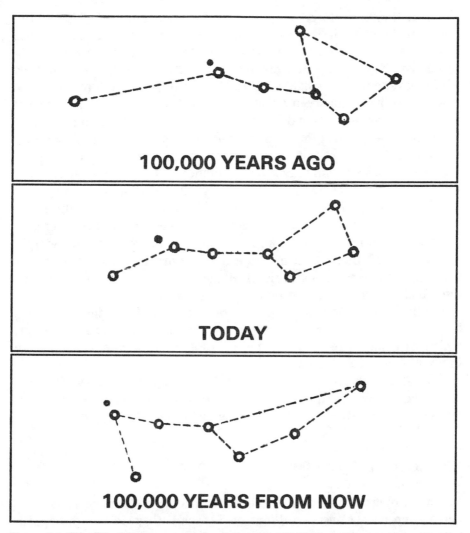

Figure 7.1 The Big Dipper was not a "dipper" 100,000 years ago, and will not be one in another 100,000 years. Ancient astronomers could not detect any motion of the stars, so they pictured them as on a fixed dome that revolved around the earth every day. Now we know that all stars are in motion and are gradually changing their positions in the sky. Astrologers still assume that the stars and constellations do not change. *(Drawing by Irving Lazarus)*

If astrologers were interested in objectivity and truth—in being "scientific"—they would feel compelled to make their theory logically consistent by correcting the old table 1. Instead, they have dodged that urgent task for centuries, preferring to let everyone be wrong about what they believe to be their "signs."

Why don't astrologers make the needed corrections to table 1? Suppose they decide to do that some day. It would require them to announce to all their believers (and customers) that these followers must suddenly switch astrological signs. Imagine the effect that would have on someone who always thought his sign was Aries, but is now told it is really Pisces. And all his life he has been avoiding Pisceans whose horoscopes conflict with his! Astrologers would be busy all day answering telephone calls "explaining" why their profession had misled people for so many centuries.

Rather than make this disastrous correction, astrologers have quietly waved a magic wand and uttered an incantation. They have simply *declared* that astrological signs no longer mean what they were supposed to mean: the signs no longer have any connection with the real world and the actual positions of the sun in constellations of the zodiac. When a believer says his sign is Scorpio, this no longer means that the sun was in Scorpio on the person's date of birth, but actually somewhere else. Astrologers also imply that the actual position of the sun does not matter, but the disembodied word for the astrological sign does.

Here is how one astrology book puts it while describing the twelve "signs" of the zodiac; they are "not to be confused with the constellations, which have the same names as the astrological signs although they are in no other way connected."[5]

What does this tell us about the truth or falsity of astrological theory? It certainly is not logically consistent. It prefers fiction to fact. So it cannot be true, and it surely cannot be considered a "science."

EXAGGERATED CLAIMS OF UNIVERSALITY

When astrologers make predictions about people born under some particular sign (say, Cancer or Virgo or Scorpio), they do not distinguish between Americans, Belgians, or Burmese. They mean *everybody* on earth.

The population of our planet is about five billion, and about one-twelfth of them are born in any given one-month period. As a result, one-twelfth of five billion people, or over 400 million persons, are born under any one of the twelve astrological signs. Any reference to an Aquarian is meant to apply to over 400 million of them *everywhere* on earth! The same is true for the other eleven astrological signs.

On the face of it, one or more specific claims that are to be relevant to at least 400 million people would seem extremely unlikely to be true.

Astrologers also pay no attention to the fact that their "body of knowledge" is still based on the wrong, earth-centered astronomy of 4,000 years ago. They still define the sun and moon as "planets" revolving around the earth, when everyone else defines planets as astronomical bodies, including the earth, that revolve around the sun. Why do astrologers still define the planets in this 4,000-year-old way that includes nonplanets (the sun and moon), merely because they appear to "wander" through the sky along the roadway of the zodiac, just as Mercury, Venus, Mars, Jupiter, and Saturn do?

This is another indication that astrology is not consistent. It ignores reality.

NO UNDERSTANDING OF CAUSE AND EFFECT

How could the positions of the sun, the moon, the planets, and the stars possibly affect the personalities and fates of billions of people on Earth? Is the effect caused by the force of gravity? All objects in the universe attract each other with a force of gravity in proportion to their mass. The force also decreases rapidly with distance (inversely as the square of the distance). Calculations of the force of gravity of Mars or Jupiter on people on Earth show that it is practically zero. A doctor standing near a baby when it is born exerts a greater force of gravitational attraction on the baby than any planet. As for the stars, the *nearest* one (with the exception of our own sun) is twenty-four thousand billion miles away, and its gravitational force is far smaller than for any of the planets in our solar system.

Could the influence be due to electrical or magnetic forces? If that were so, the influence of the electrical lines in one's house would be far greater than from any planet or star. And every time there is an electrical "storm" on the sun, which often disrupts radio and television communication on Earth, we see the strong electrical effects of the *aurora borealis* (northern lights) in the sky. Shouldn't these have a greater effect on babies just being born than the electrical or magnetic effects on any planet? Yet we do not see astrologers taking these "influences" into account.

Could the influence be from x-rays, infrared radiation, ultraviolet rays, "cosmic rays," or other forms of radiation that come to us from the stars in tiny quantities and require very sensitive instruments to detect? Astrologers have never tried to adjust their horoscopes for such influences.

These effects cover the known physical forces that might conceivably exert some kind of "influence" on living things on Earth. But how could *any* such physical force affect the personalities or future events of five billion people? When all is said and done, astrologers are left with just one "explanation" for the effects they claim to predict with their horoscopes, but they are unwilling to talk about it.

Magic is the unmentionable influence. Astrology was devised (created, constructed, invented) in ancient times on the theory that the gods were supposed to pull the sun, the moon, and the planets through the sky, and could exert similar magical influence on people to determine their personalities and fates. Since today's astrologers use the same basic procedures developed in ancient times, based on the magical influences of the gods, whether stated or not, they are basing *their* horoscopes on the magical influences of ancient gods.

Ancient astrologers did not ask "how" the gods managed to influence people's lives. This was a not a pertinent question in ancient times because everyone assumed that the magical ways of the gods were beyond the comprehension of mere humans, and that the gods were capable of producing earthquakes, eruptions of volcanoes, and hurricanes at will. Astrologers today merely accept the results of this ancient superstitious way of thinking, but have dropped all reference to the magical influence of the gods. In effect, the theory of astrology is based on superstition.

THE "STRETCHED ANALOGIES" IN ASTROLOGICAL "HOUSES"

The Greeks believed in a goddess of fortune, Tyche, who rotated a wheel to change "good luck" to bad and perhaps back again to good. Astrologers do the same thing, but they just don't mention the goddess. The entire Earth is their rotating wheel of fortune.

Astrologers declare that the sky is subdivided into sectors, known as "houses," that rotate with the earth. Each house contains different qualities or areas of human affairs, such as health, wealth, temperament, travel, ambition, family, etc. As the earth turns, the houses go with it and different portions of the sky appear to enter these invisible houses and then leave, in regular succession.

As a planet appears to "enter a house," it obviously takes charge of the qualities that that house possesses, and influences human affairs accordingly. After residing in the house for a few hours, the earth has turned enough for the planet to leave the house and enter another one, immediately taking charge of the different qualities in that house. This is the kind of thinking by simplistic analogy that astrologers engage in when they make up a horoscope.

In an analogy, similarities are observed between the characteristics of two or more different things or events. Then, because of these similarities, a hypothesis is made about possible connections among these things or events. As noted in chapter 6, analogies are an important form of reasoning and very useful for making hypotheses about generalized principles or causes for events. But hypotheses may or may not be true; they are not much good unless checked and verified by experimental observation.

This does not bother astrologers. With vivid imagination they make overgeneralizations by the thousands, never checking any of them with reality. We might call this mode of thinking "stretched analogy," expanding analogy-making to its worst extreme, and without ever checking to see if any of the results of this reasoning are true.

Note what astrologers do with those "houses" in the sky. First, they divide the sky into arbitrary sectors (the houses); all are figments of their fertile imaginations. As we shall see, the number of sectors in the sky is something astrologers argue about quite a bit, but most of them agree on twelve.

Then they arbitrarily assign qualities to each house, also by pure imagination. For example, in one system house number 1 is supposed to contain the qualities pertaining to the human self, the person, temperament, and personality; house number 2 contains possessions and feelings, worldly resources, especially money; house number 3 contains short communications, short trips, neighbors, and mental interests. And so on for the other nine houses.[6]

Astrologers then arbitrarily assign human qualities to the planets, each of which is supposed to have major influence over the five billion humans living on Earth. But each planet doesn't get to have its maximum influence over humans until it "enters a house" that contains astrologer-specified areas of human life. The stretched analogy here is that when a powerful influence like a planet enters a house, it naturally takes charge of everything that belongs in that house. So, if the planet Mars, which is supposed to have a violent character (among other qualities), enters house number 1, the region of the sky that is supposed to contain "temperament and personality," the violent planet takes charge of those human qualities and gives all those newborn babies down below a good shot of violence in their characters—another stretched analogy.

As everyone knows, it is not likely that every baby born at that time is going to have a violent temperament, and many will be very sweet and reasonable. However, the astrologer has an out. The planet Venus, in charge of beauty and love, may be in house number 12, which covers the area of "latent talents." Naturally, Venus will give every newborn baby a good shot of reasonableness.

Now the astrologer has to make a judgment as to which influence is stronger, that of Mars or Venus. Is Venus very bright in the sky? By stretched analogy of "bright" to mean "more," the influence of a bright Venus on people may be stronger than that of a dim Mars, and the baby will be more gentle and less violent. Or, if Mars is very bright and Venus is dim, Mars might predominate. The poor kid! What will become of him with all those magic-wielding gods fighting over his fate?

So the astrologer declares, in effect, "On the one hand, Joe Jones, born on (whatever the date and hour), was influenced by Mars in house number 1 to have a violent character. But on the other hand, Venus, in house number 12, counteracts Mars to make Joe sweet and reasonable." Then it might be left to the customer to choose whichever he prefers. If Joe Jones commits murder some day, the astrologer will say, "See, I predicted he would be violent." If he wins the Nobel Peace Prize, the astrologer declares, "See, I predicted he would have a sweet, peaceful temperament."

Astrologers can't lose with such stretched-analogy thinking, especially with ten "planets" (including the sun and the moon), twelve houses (each with several qualities to choose from), all those delicate balancings of hundreds of possible influences, and topped by the many subtle judgments that are possible about "strong" and "weak" influences.

Now, about the question "How many imaginary houses are there in the sky?" According to astronomers R. B. Culver and P. A. Ianna, who have analyzed astrological systems:

> The number of house systems so far proposed is estimated to be as large as fifty (some with as many as 24 or 28 separate houses); however only about twenty apparently have had some use, and just three or four are widely used by astrologers.[7]

So there are fifty different models of the goddess Tyche's wheels of fortune that an astrologer can choose to use in his work. As a result, the horoscope a customer gets from an astrologer who uses a twelve-house system ought to be very different from one who relies on a twenty-house system—unless they both get their horoscope-making computer program from the same company. In any case, the magical influence of goddess Tyche is disguised in horoscopes by using impressive "scientific," astronomical tables and mathematical calculations.

What is the reasoning process by which astrologers decide whether to use a twelve-house system of astrology, or one with twenty, or perhaps twenty-four? They can always find some stretched analogy to justify selecting a number. After all, there are twelve hours on a watch dial, or twenty-four hours in the day. Or people have twenty fingers and toes. Take your pick. Here is the way Culver and Ianna describe how one astrologer figured out that eight houses is best:

> Cyril Fagan has suggested (that) the earliest chart division was not into twelve sectors but rather into eight, arising from an initial splitting of the solar day and night into four periods, subsequently halved. Since these eight "watch" periods provide a measure of the progress around the sky in a clockwise direction, Fagan has argued that the houses should in fact be ordered in the same way, opposite to the common practice.[8]

This eight-house astrologer chooses ancient ideas, the older the better. But he has a problem. How would he assign the human qualities formerly accommodated in twelve houses and jam them into eight? He managed a simple solution by merely lopping off houses numbered 9, 10, 11, and 12 and declaring them null and void!

This kind of thinking reminds us of the Middle Ages when people argued about "How many angels can stand on the head of a pin?"

Different Interpretations of the Signs

What about the practical result of all this hodge-podge thinking? Suppose someone who was born on January 10 wants to get some guidance from an astrology book. First, he looks up the table of astrological signs and discovers that he is a Capricorn. Book A says this about Capricorns:

> The person with a Capricorn Ascendant has need of people with whom he can relate person to person, for without such concretizing meetings and close interpersonal empathy he might feel personally overinvolved in ambitious schemes and large-scale social planning or in mystical and cosmic realizations. Capricorn can refer to experiences and faculties that many people would call "mystical," but the reference is rather to the type of consciousness that is able or desires (*sic*) intensely to operate in terms of a transcendent type of order, of a cosmic and—in the real sense of this much-abused term—occult use of power. He may tend to overwhelm other people with such power, seeking potential subjects in order to fulfill what he considers his destiny. It could be a catabolic kind of destiny.[9]

All clear? Have you figured out the semantic confusion and double-talk in "catabolic kind of destiny," or "transcendent type of order"? About the only bit of practical advice the poor Capricorn can scrounge from the above mystical advice is that he will have "need of people with whom he can relate person to person." Of course, this is good advice for everybody and no one need pay an astrologer to get it.

Astrology book B is more down-to-earth and doesn't hesitate to spell out in simpler language what a Capricorn should expect of himself. Note the very different description of Capricorns as compared with those in Book A.

> Ruled by Saturn and Uranus, natives of this sign are characterized by a cold detachment which grants them a great capacity to view reality from a rational viewpoint. They tend, on the whole to be somewhat unemotional, unforthcoming and always on the defensive, and they are often spurred on by a deep sense of ambition which enables them to realize long-term projects. . . . Unlike the sensitive Cancerians, Capricornians consider the past dead and gone—nothing must be allowed to impede the inexorable journey towards their goals, lonely though those goals may be. . . ."[10]

Each of these statements is supposedly a true generalization that ought to be based on careful observation of many people born between December 21 and January 19. Since astrologers have not done objective investigations to find out if any of these statements are true, their conclusions can be considered nothing more than unproved generalizations derived from little or no data.

When astrologers use such "information" in composing horoscopes for their daily newspaper columns, or by mail, they do not know anything at all about their readers or customers, other than their dates of birth. Nothing is said in horoscopes about the age, national origin, race, cultural background, or conditions of life—or about the two sets of genes inherited from parents born on different days. All these factors, and more, have a lot to do with the personalities children develop. The *only* factor astrologers are concerned about is date and time of birth, from which they might also calculate the positions of the sun, the moon, and planets in the sky at that critical moment. How likely is it that anything they say about people's lives, with so meager an informational base, is meaningful? (See figure 7.2.)

STRETCHED ANALOGIES FOR PLANETS

Every astrology book makes many hundreds of assertions about the kinds of "influences" the sun, the moon, the planets, and the stars have over five billion people on Earth; some make over a thousand. When we look

Expectant mother to her physician: "I don't get along well with Scorpios. Could you see that my baby is born before October 23?"

Figure 7.2 Belief in astrology can be very harmful for those who let its superstitions determine important decisions in their lives. *(Drawing by Albert Sarney)*

through any of these books to find out *how they know* their assertions are true, we find no experiments, no checking, no verification, and no objectivity, all of which are so basic for any statement to be accepted as a fact. All we do find are stretched analogies and overgeneralizations.

The pattern of stretched analogies is particularly clear in the kinds of qualities planets are supposed to impress on people, especially newborn babies. The general approach is to observe the appearance or motion of planets. What are the outstanding qualities that distinguish one planet from the others? Ancient astrologers assumed that these qualities provide clues to the nature of the god responsible for pulling the planet through the sky. So, it seemed natural for ancient cultures to view these characteristics as showing what the gods were like. Then it was a simple step, by stretched analogy, to assume that these are the characteristics the god-planets would impress on people. And today's astrologers have simply borrowed this rigmarole lock, stock, and barrel.

The reasoning here is so obviously defective that we wonder how anyone can believe it, but since so many people *do* believe in these influences, it is important to understand just how they were derived.

Here, for example, is a description of the kinds of "influences" that the red planet Mars is supposed to have on human affairs when it is in certain positions in the sky.

Associations: The aggressive relationship with the outside world, violence, passion, conquest, survival, action, energy, strength, movement, bravery.
Symbolic significance: The vital force of the stage in life in which one must fight to achieve success, the male sex, vitality, heat, action, destruction, destruction and resurrection, rivals, iron tools and weapons, injuries, extroversion.
Physiological relationships: Activity and muscle tone, the external male sex organs, bile, body hair, physical strength, the nose, red corpuscles.[11]

How do astrologers *know* these presumed "facts" about Mars? They borrowed them directly from astrologers of 4,000 years ago. How did the ancients know? They observed that one planet has a distinctly reddish color; red is the color of blood, and blood is shed in war, so they reasoned by stretched analogy (from the similarity in the red color of this planet and of blood) that this bloody planet, called Mars, must be pulled through the sky by the god in charge of war.

Read once again the human characteristics listed above, which astrologers of old (followed by those of today) imagined were governed by Mars. All of these influences match our concept of a tough, vigorous, virile, macho type of soldier.

The analogy is stretched wildly, from the color red to that of blood, to war, to a soldier-god analogous to a superpowerful human. Ancient astrologers might be excused for such defective reasoning because people knew so little about astronomy. But what excuse do today's astrologers have?

We can write the stretched-analogy scenario for Venus ourselves. It is a beautiful, silvery-white planet, brightest in the sky after the sun and the moon. Therefore, the quality of beauty, and anything associated with it, comes under the female Venus-god's dominion of beauty and love. The attributes she governs are: "attraction, harmony, beauty, feelings, physical pleasure, the capacity to love, money, sex, possessions in general."[12]

Our eyebrows are raised a bit by the inclusion of money and possessions in the list. Most of us would not expect that—or would we? Perhaps some ancient (or more recent) astrologer's sexist bias is showing. Note that Venus is a "she."

It is interesting to note that modern astronomers, who have landed satellite probes on the surface of Venus, have found it to be a not-so-beautiful place. The surface is a hellish 900° F. There is no water on the land, because it has all boiled off. The atmosphere is mostly carbon dioxide, with no oxygen. The dense cloud cover that obscures a direct view of the surface contains large quantities of sulfuric acid. Not a beautiful place at all, at least not by human standards. There is plenty of room here for making stretched analogies, but no astrologer has yet taken up this challenge.

The supposed effects of Jupiter on human events follow the same "stretched analogy" pattern as was the case for Mars and Venus. Jupiter, much farther from the sun than Venus or Mars, requires a much longer time to make one orbit around the sun—eleven years, as compared to eight months for Venus and two years for Mars. Therefore, Jupiter appears to us to move much more slowly in the sky than Venus or Mars. So it was viewed by the ancients as a sedate, mature planet. When an analogy is made to the aging process of humans, Jupiter must be the elder statesman of the gods, equivalent to president of Gods, Inc.

Among the characteristics listed for Jupiter's "symbolic significance" are: "maturity, gained through hard-won success, optimism, extroversion, a kind nature, honors, authority, trustworthiness, wisdom, comfort, wealth, decorations, lucky people, luxury, the judge, the master."[13] Each of these stems by stretched analogy from the sedate pace at which Jupiter moves through the sky, as compared with Mercury, Venus, or Mars. By means of such defective reasoning, astrologers produce mountains of groundless "facts" unsupported by experiment or observation. Their "facts" are essentially imaginative fictions in which anything anyone can imagine may be arbitrarily accepted as true.

MAKING A HOROSCOPE RESEMBLES A GAME

The way astrologers make up horoscopes greatly resembles the way people play board games. In addition to the supposed influence of the constellation under which one is born, and of the positions of the planets, astrologers also adjust their horoscopes for three types of factors governed by charts, which they call "polarities," "quadruplicities," and "triplicities."[14]

Let's consider just the "triplicities" to illustrate what astrologers do with them. Figure 7.3 (see p. 152) shows the astrological chart for this kind of influence on people. Note the four words "earth, air, fire, and water" repeated three times around the circle of astrological signs: hence, a *TRI*plicity. Where do these four influences come from? They are the four "elements" that various ancient Greek philosophers believed made up all things on Earth. Since these elements were philosophically important

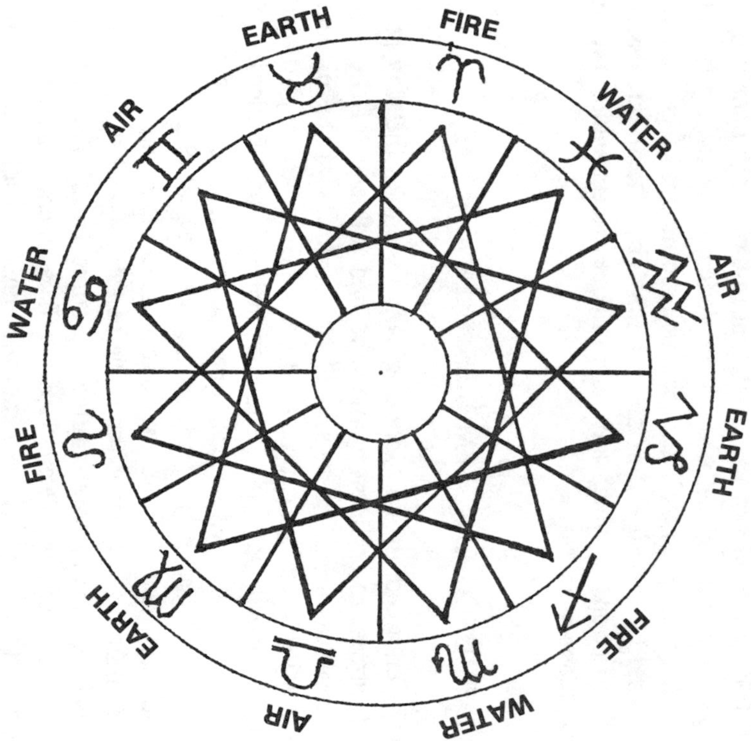

Sign	BIRTH DATES Approximate period
Aries ♈	from 21/3 to 20/4
Taurus ♉	from 21/4 to 20/5
Gemini ♊	from 21/5 to 21/6
Cancer ♋	from 22/6 to 22/7
Leo ♌	from 23/7 to 22/8
Virgo ♍	from 23/8 to 22/9
Libra ♎	from 23/9 to 22/10
Scorpio ♏	from 23/10 to 21/11
Sagittarius ♐	from 22/11 to 20/12
Capricorn ♑	from 21/12 to 19/1
Aquarius ♒	from 20/1 to 18/2
Pisces ♓	from 19/2 to 20/3

Figure 7.3 This chart of "Triplicities" is used by astrologers to determine the "influence" of earth, fire, water, and air on people born under different astrological signs. If "earth" appears over a sign, people born under that sign are supposed to be "earthy." If the word *fire* appears over a sign, they are supposed to be "fiery." Why should any reasonable person believe in such a superstition? (*Drawing by Irving Lazarus*)

to the Greeks, ancient astrologers sought to insert them into the picture as "influences."

How do today's astrologers take these influences into account? Suppose a horoscope is being prepared for a person born on April 9; that individual would have been born under the sign of Aries (the ram). The word *fire* appears above Aries in the triplicity circle. Therefore, by stretched analogy, the person will tend to have a "fiery" personality. As the astrology books put it, the person will tend to have a personality that features "vitality, activity, authority, initiative, energy, enthusiasm, ardor, ambition, excitability."[15]

Now we get the idea: we, too, can be astrologers. Suppose our client was born on September 3, which puts him under the sign of Virgo. In figure 7.3 the word *earth* appears on the triplicity chart above Virgo. Our client will have a "down-to-earth" personality featuring: "resolve, practicality, material interests, laboriousness, concentration, prudence, methodicalness, egoism, obedience."[16] This is an attempt to take into account the influence on people of the four "basic elements." That was a nice try by the ancient Greeks, but today we know that substances are far more complex. There are more than a hundred known chemical elements. Water and most substances found on Earth are chemical compounds: air is a complex mixture of gases, while fire is not an element but rather a visible display of energy released during a chemical change, with liberation of heat and light, and motion of air.

What is an ancient and *incorrect* chemistry doing as the contemporary focal point of forecasts for five billion people? Astrologers haven't changed their erroneous earth-centered astronomy for 500 years, even though the Copernican, sun-centered theory of the solar system has been established for centuries. Their chemistry of the elements has not changed even though its errors have been known for almost 200 years.

The astrological system is further fictionalized with two other charts, each introducing other complicating factors. A "Polarities" chart is supposed to take into account constellations that are opposite each other in the sky. Then a "Quadruplicities" chart is supposed to insert input from the four seasons of the year.

With all these unverified guesses as to unexplained cosmic influences of planets and astrological signs, ancient chemistry, opposite constellations, and the four seasons of the year, astrologers can "predict" virtually anything they please. That's why there are a number of different astrological systems by different practitioners, each with its own rules of the game, producing different horoscopes according to the whim of the astrologer.

ASTROLOGICAL CLAIMS ARE NOT VERIFIED

Does anyone try to verify the many thousands of assertions and predictions about people and their fates that each year pour out of daily astrological columns, individual horoscopes, and books about astrology? Hardly ever. One reason is that astrologers and their believers have little interest in doing so, while those who don't believe in astrology feel they have more important things to do.

There have been a relatively small number of such experiments that met proper standards of objectivity and offered evidence that horoscopes are not valid descriptions of reality. For example, in one experiment several hundred people were each given a number of different horoscopes that described the personality characteristics that supposedly applied to different astrological signs, and were asked to pick the one they thought best described themselves.

If these horoscopes had any validity, the experiment should have revealed at least some tendency for people to select horoscopes pertinent to their own astrological signs. No such effect was found. People were no more able to identify which were supposed to apply to them than if they had made their selections blindfolded, purely at random.[17]

On the other hand, claims by astrologers of successful personality profiles and predictions are generally anecdotal (stories about individual cases), lack scientific controls, and feature selection only of successes while omitting all failures. They do not meet the standards of objectivity for scientific experiments.

In general, the experimental record shows that astrological claims of influences from the sun, the moon, the planets, and the stars on peoples' personalities or behaviors are without merit.

But suppose someone says, "Well, perhaps astrology is not scientific, but maybe there is still something to it." How would we go about conducting an objective investigation of the claims of astrology to see if there is any truth to them?

Let's begin by selecting some "facts" that astrologers claim are true. Suppose our client was born on June 29; this would put him under the sign of Cancer (the crab). Our astrology book tells us that the general characteristics of Cancerians are as follows:

> [They are] strongly attached to their mothers and the families into which they were born. They always feel in some way or other tied to childhood, the past and to their memories. It is only with great difficulty that they manage to cut the umbilical cord and live a life of their own, indeed they may never do so.

[Their] character . . . inclines towards melancholy, introversion and fear of the future, experienced as a dread of the unknown. This is why they prefer the security of the past and cling to tradition and the family. . . .

The real world frightens them and they love to take refuge in dreams, in a fantasy world. . . .

[They] are prone to moodiness and restlessness, constantly swinging from introversion to enthusiasm. They are quick to take offense and are very vulnerable. . . .[18]

The other eleven astrological signs are presented in much the same vein. How can one prove that all 400 million Cancerians on Earth are "prone to moodiness" or "strongly attached to their mothers," or "love to take refuge in their dreams"?

These statements are generally true of everybody to some extent and at some time in life. To prove any of them requires statistical comparisons between Cancerians and people with other astrological signs. Are Cancerians more prone to "moodiness" than Capricornians or Aquarians? How do we find out if Cancerians tend to be more "strongly attached to their mothers" than other people?

First, we would need to find or design psychological tests to evaluate whether or not a person has a particular personality trait. This is not an easy thing to do because people do not give straight answers to questions like "Are you strongly attached to your mother?" Just think about how *you* would answer the question.

Assuming such a test has been designed, we then need to figure out how to study 400 million Cancerians. Social scientists will tell us that it is not necessary to test everybody. We might take a *representative sample* of people, the way political pollsters do before an election. The many people in our sample would then be interviewed, or given questionnaires to fill out, asking personal questions like, "Are you prone to moodiness?" and "Are you strongly attached to your mother?"

If many people balked at answering such personal questions, then we would no longer have a "representative sample." On the other hand, many people would not know how to answer such questions, while some will not give straight answers to a question like "Are you strongly attached to your mother?" There will be serious problems with the accuracy of our results. And when we are through investigating one kind of society, what about the 2,000 others? And we will have checked just a few characteristics claimed by one astrologer for only one of the twelve astrological signs! What a job! It is a hopeless task.

ALL THINGS TO ALL MEN—AND WOMEN

How does it happen that so many people believe in this superstition? One reason is that many daily horoscopes are published in newspapers. People ask themselves, "Would the horoscopes be published every day in my reputable newspaper if there was no merit at all to the advice they give?" Of course, newspapers publish horoscopes because enough readers want them. But since nothing is ever said about astrology being a form of superstitious magic, publication adds to its credibility.

Another reason that statements in horoscopes are taken so seriously is that they are purposely written in such a general way that they could be applied to practically everybody, and therefore are very difficult to prove wrong. Here are excerpts from just one daily horoscope column, typical of any other day's output in any newspaper.

"Capricornians have many opportunities for improving their status. . . ." Doesn't almost everybody, everywhere, have opportunities for improving status, whether they be Capricornian or not? But this statement might do harm if some Geminians think this is not a day for them to look for opportunities because only Capricornians were mentioned.

"Pisceans have a chance to present their views in the evening which is an excellent time for everyone to attend meetings, read books, and do mental work. . . ." This statement also applies to almost everybody.

"Geminians can gain through others if they cooperate, especially with husband or wife or associates in business. . . ." Or with plumbers, landlords, teachers, policemen, and judges in traffic court.

"Tomorrow is a good, constructive time to keep working in practical jobs. . . ." So is today, as was yesterday and July 19, 1892.

"There can be many romantic meetings and interesting opportunities in attracting the attention of the opposite sex. . . ." The writer of the horoscope is careful to use the word *can* rather than *will* because "can" means that romantic meetings may or may not occur. Anything can happen. So the astrologer has a good alibi if no romantic meetings occur.

"Be careful in your social contacts today, as the temptation will be to ignore rules and customs. . . ." Suppose that one horoscope reader waiting in a line pushes ahead of someone else and is punched in the nose for "ignoring rules and customs." He could say that the horoscope was right because the warning was ignored. And if he did not get punched, there would no reason to question the horoscope's prediction.

As these examples show, the astrologer is *always* "right" and can therefore always reasonably claim merit for his or her method of composing horoscopes. There is no way the astrologer can lose with general forecasts.

Is it possible that the astrologers who write these daily horoscopes just write anything that comes into their heads? It would seem that all of us could write our own horoscopes. Would anybody know the difference? Or challenge us by claiming that we are wrong?

NOTES

1. Joan Quigley, *What Does Joan Say?* (New York: Carol Publishing Group, 1990), p. 12.
2. Ibid., p. 171
3. Nancy Reagan, *My Turn* (New York: Random House, 1989), p. 49.
4. Mario Paltrinieri and Elena Rader, with Rosanna Zerilli, *The Book of Practical Astrology* (New York: Macmillan Publishing Company, 1981), p. 25.
5. Ibid.
6. R. B. Culver and P. A. Ianna, *The Gemini Syndrome* (Tucson, Ariz.: Pachart Publishing House, 1979; Buffalo, N.Y.: Prometheus Books, 1984), p. 57.
7. Ibid., p. 58.
8. Ibid.
9. Dane Rudhyar, *The Astrological Houses* (Garden City, N.Y.: Doubleday, 1972), p. 167.
10. Paltrinieri and Rader, *The Book of Practical Astrology*, p. 45.
11. Ibid., p. 60.
12. Ibid., p. 59.
13. Ibid., p. 61.
14. Ibid., p. 31.
15. Ibid.
16. Ibid.
17. Geoffrey Dean, "Does Astrology Need to Be True, Part I: A Look at the Real Thing," *The Skeptical Inquirer* 11 (Winter 1986–7): 179–81.
18. Paltrinieri and Rader, *The Book of Practical Astrology*, p. 37.

QUESTIONS *(Discussion of these Questions Begins on Page 253.)*

1. State four fundamental errors of astrology, borrowed from ancient astrology, whether factual or theoretical, that show modern astrology to be based on false premises.

2. What known forces or effects from stars and planets, scientifically established as fact, might conceivably "influence" events on Earth? Why is it practically impossible for such forces or effects to produce the kinds of "influences" on human personalities and future events claimed by astrologers?

3. Why should astrology be considered a superstitious belief in "magic"?

4. Look at several astrology books in the library. Do they agree on what they claim are the personalities of people born under different astrological signs? In what ways do they differ?

5. For several days obtain daily horoscopes from a newspaper. To what extent does the horoscope for your birthday apply to you? Do the horoscopes for other astrological signs also apply to you? How many of the statements employ qualifications such as "could," "may," and "might" so that the predictions cannot be proved wrong? How are generalizations used so that horoscopes may apply to everybody?

Try to duplicate the style of writing and create your own daily "horoscope."

6. Give three examples of stretched analogies on which predictions of planetary "influences" are based.

7. How is the ancient view of the four elements—earth, air, fire, and water—incorporated into today's astrological system?

8. Describe some of the difficulties of doing an objective investigation of specific claims made by astrologers.

8

Conflicting Opinions

Let's put ourselves in the place of a student in an actual psychology experiment. We enter a room with seven other students and an instructor. The group is repeatedly shown a line and asked which of three other lines is the same length. After a few trials we are astonished when six students ahead of us declare that a line, which seems to us obviously longer, is the same length. The reason for this is unknown to us, but the instructor has asked all the others to lie about which line they think is the same.[1]

What should we do; stick to our own opinion and say what we think, or go along with the others so as not to seem "different"?

CONFORMITY TO OPINION

In a series of such experiments only about one-fourth of all student participants consistently stated what they believed to be true. Of the other three-quarters there were different degrees to which various individuals gave in and accepted some or all of the wrong opinions.

If in such a simple matter people are so influenced by the opinions of others, how much more affected would they be in complicated life situations? Conformity to the opinions of others may affect the results of elections. People tend to vote with the majority. For that reason, a poll showing that one candidate is leading could cause the front runner to gain an even bigger majority. Dictators can stay in office much longer by rewarding conformity and discouraging independent action through threats and punishments.

Figure 8.1 (p. 160) shows a man coming to work in a suit and tie only to discover that most of his co-workers are attired in leisure shorts. He would

159

Figure 8.1 The man in a suit, coming to work and seeing most of his co-workers in shorts, is very likely to conform by coming to work in shorts, too. *(Drawing by Albert Sarney)*

probably feel very uncomfortable being that "different." In all likelihood he would rush to conform by coming to work in shorts the next day.

It is difficult for most people to be different from others and therefore stand out from the crowd. However, there are some people who are quite the opposite: they like being different and go out of their way to flaunt their nonconformity. But they are relatively few in number.

Young people tend to rebel against some established customs of their parents. They may dress in a completely different style. But even then they tend to conform to what other young people their age are wearing. Youngsters are then put under pressure to conform to the way their peers dress.

Of course, conformity in itself is not bad or undesirable. All societies depend on conformity to some extent to ensure that most people perform their responsibilities and adhere to essential social rules or duly ratified laws. For example, most people stop at red traffic lights. Imagine the chaos if everyone decided not to conform to this rule!

Many customs are essential for the survival of people in every society. Those in cold climates wear warm clothing that covers feet, legs, arms, and head, not because it is the fashion of the year, but because they would not survive the cold without it.

Custom notwithstanding, each opinion should stand on its own and be judged on its merits. Majority opinions should be given some weight because if a number of people arrive at the same conclusion then it would seem to be worth careful examination. But relying on the tired phrase "everybody else thinks so" should not be the main reason for forming some particular opinion.

WHAT IS AN OPINION?

One dictionary defines *opinion* as "a belief or judgment based on evidence that is insufficient or uncertain." In other words, it is a case of "missing facts," or perhaps "fuzzy facts," which cannot lead to a verifiable conclusion. There is always some degree of uncertainty in an opinion and many are doubtful at best.

We can judge the extent of doubt from the fact that on many public issues there is often a very wide range of opinions, with some expressing diametrically opposing points of view. Obviously, they can't all be right.

Everybody has opinions—about the weather, about neighbors, about the best way to catch fish, about almost any subject. Opinions are necessary because we often need to make judgments or take action when important facts are missing. Some people hesitate to express opinions because they fear being wrong. Others express hastily formed opinions without bothering to obtain enough facts to support their points of view. Both extremes tend to obstruct the communication of ideas.

To form a reasonable opinion about an important issue, one must gather enough facts. This is not an easy task. How many facts are enough? At the very least, an "objective" opinion means observing carefully (if the problem lends itself to personal observation), making judgments cautiously, reading newspapers and books with different points of view to "get both sides," listening to debates at meetings and on television, and, above all, maintaining an open mind that allows opposing views to be fairly considered.

In any case, there is no escaping the role our value system plays in developing opinions. Many of us exhibit a strong tendency to reject facts that clash with our system of moral values. Some people quickly form opinions on almost any question, and once their opinions have formed, they accept only those facts that tend to prove them "right." An opinion implies that not all the facts are available; therefore, people should be willing to consider new facts even if they contradict old, strongly held opinions.

OPINION POLLS

Opinion polls are taken on a wide variety of subjects. Companies poll people on their reactions to new products and services. Magazines, newspapers, and television stations often use polls to report opinions on elections, political issues, social attitudes, family matters, and life habits. Candidates for public office take polls to judge their chances of winning, as well as to find out which issues to stress and which to soft-pedal.

It would not be very practical for a pollster to question all people in the country (or even all those in a particular state or city) about their opinions. Instead, pollsters and social scientists select a *sample* of people, a group whose members are *representative* of the population they want to poll. Although pollsters sometimes use other types of representative samples, the best type of strategy is to use a *random sample* in which every case (individual, household, etc.) has an equal chance of being chosen. There are various techniques for choosing randomly, but if every case does not have an equal chance, it is not random.

An easy way to imagine a random sample is to think of how the draw of a raffle is conducted. Everyone in the audience is given a card (the raffle ticket) with an identifying name or number. All the raffle cards are thoroughly mixed or shuffled, perhaps in a rotating drum. Finally, a card is pulled out at random to get the winner. If the mixing is very thorough, each person has an equal chance to win (to be chosen at random). Statisticians have found that even in a country with millions of people, a random sample of one thousand or so can usually give a reasonably accurate estimate of the opinions of the whole country.

Should people be called on the phone for interviews or should the poll be conducted person-to-person? Phone calls are much less costly, but there are serious problems to surmount. If people are called during the day, the poll is likely to be distorted by reaching only those people who work at home, are on night shifts, or are housewives. And only those with telephones are reached, thereby excluding all people who do not have telephones—mainly the poor. When a question involves a sharp difference of opinion between the poor and other groups, a poll by telephone tends to be distorted because it does not give adequate weight to opinions of poor people.

Nevertheless, polls by telephone are widely used because the costs are much less than for personal interviews. They may be valid when the answers to questions are not greatly affected by excluding people without telephones. For example, if a car manufacturer is polling people to determine which of a number of names are best for a new type of car, omitting people without telephones would be advantageous because poor people are not likely to buy new cars. But a poll for preference in an election would be a different matter.

Opinion polling can be objective if those taking the poll make good use of *statistics*. Statisticians can calculate how many people need to be surveyed to provide a specified degree of accuracy. For example, suppose a national poll is to be taken of voting preference for candidates for President of the United States and a margin of ± 2 percent error is desired. Statisticians can tell us how many people in a random sample would need to be polled to achieve the required margin of error. If a margin of error of ± 5 percent is desired, fewer people need be polled, and the statistician can calculate the number to be polled in such a case.

How do we know that a poll is reasonably accurate? During elections a final judgment is made by those casting votes at the polling booths. The election ends with a definite fact: one candidate is elected. This is a good check on the validity of the poll. And how do we know that the group doing the polling is really objective and not slanting the poll? We can never be absolutely sure, but, fortunately, there is a self-correcting feature to the business of polling: a professional pollster who makes predictions that turn out to be untrue loses credibility and people tend to be suspicious the next time this polling agency takes a poll of any kind.

This actually happened during the election of 1936 when *Literary Digest* magazine took a poll before the presidential election between Franklin D. Roosevelt and Alf Landon. Ten million sample letters were sent out, asking for opinions on the election, and two million responses came back. The results of the poll indicated that Landon would win. The magazine had conducted similar polls before, and had always been right. Roosevelt won by a landslide—28 million votes to 18 million. The *Literary Digest* became the laughingstock of the country, and went out of business shortly afterward.[2]

Why was the poll so very wrong on this occasion? For one thing, a poll that depends on people mailing back an answer is more likely to be skewed (weighted on one side or the other) than a poll based on interviews. Who answers polls by mail? Perhaps those who work for a living and have to take care of their families after work are less likely to respond than those who have plenty of leisure time. The two million responses out of ten million mailed by the *Literary Digest,* (a 20 percent response rate) was not a representative sample and gave too much weight to people with enough time and inclination to respond by returning a letter. This gave a distorted picture of the opinions of voters in general.

Reputable polling agencies are well aware of the *Literary Digest's* fate and therefore treasure objectivity as their lifeblood. One bad mistake and they could be out of business.

Despite the great care taken by reputable polling companies to make their polls objective, there is always the problem of people not conveying their real opinions in special situations. During the election of 1989, for example, estimates of the preference of votes for governor of Virginia showed Douglas Wilder far ahead of his opponent. Similarly, polls for mayor of New York showed David Dinkins far ahead in the race. Both of these candidates won, but by a much narrower margin than predicted. It would seem that many people in these polls were not revealing their true opinions. Both Wilder and Dinkins are black. Many people may have been ashamed to admit that they are prejudiced against black candidates and thus reported to the poll-taker one preference while actually voting the other way.

A similar error was observed for pre-election polls (taken by a reputable pollster) for the election of the president of Nicaragua in 1990. The polls generally showed incumbent Daniel Ortega and the Sandinista Party strongly in the lead over challenger Violetta Chamorro and the UNO Party. Chamorro won the election by the wide margin of 55 percent to 41 percent. This upset was generally attributed to the highly emotional nature of the election and probable suspicion by many voters that the interviewer, a total stranger, might really be working for the government and there would be retribution if respondents declared support for the opposition candidate.

The Role of Questions in a Poll

The questions in a poll that reports on voting preference are simple: Would you vote for this candidate or that one? But polls about public issues are another matter. The results very much depend on how the questions are worded. A *leading question* can greatly affect the answers given. For example, suppose the question is "Do you favor Jim Marshall's budget proposal for lower income taxes?" This question is likely to get a positive response even if the person answering the question knows nothing about Jim Marshall's proposal. Everybody likes lower income taxes. Jim Marshall's opponent might phrase the question differently: "Do you favor Marshall's budget proposal, which calls for increased sales taxes?" Now the majority vote is likely to come out negative because most people want lower sales taxes. Polls that are slanted in this way utilize a technique called *card-stacking,* which will be discussed in more detail in chapter 10. Only the facts favoring the preferred opinion are presented, while suppressing opposing facts.

The judgments we make about trusting a poll depend in part on who conducts the survey. Polls underwritten by a political candidate or a campaign committee have much less credibility than if those same polls were taken by a polling group having a long record of objectivity.

How Polls Affect Public Opinion

Originally, the purpose of polls was to assess public opinion. However, as their use has increased, so has their influence in affecting public opinion, especially candidates for office and controversial public issues. An interesting example of the role of polls, at an early stage of their development, occurred during the 1948 presidential election when Harry Truman was opposed by Thomas Dewey. Early polls showed Dewey ahead, and he and his followers may have become overconfident. Incumbent President Truman, sensing defeat, was stimulated to undertake a grueling campaign by train to reach people, speaking at many towns along the route. In the days before television, this was an effective campaign technique because the local newspapers publicized each stop as a news event.

Polls taken a week before the election showed Truman catching up fast, but Dewey rested on his laurels and was confident of victory. Truman turned the tables and won the election. This victory taught politicians a lesson: polls must be watched carefully, particularly with regard to the trends they show.

Polls can often help create a *bandwagon effect,* thus giving candidates with money enough to pay for them an important advantage. (See chapter 10 on "How Opinions Are Influenced.") Early polls identify which issues are most likely to attract voters and which are inclined to turn voters away. They also indicate the most effective approaches to take when developing speeches and commercials.

Polls that show a candidate out in front of the pack tend to enhance the bandwagon effect. Voters like to be on the winning side, and undecided voters often shift rapidly to the candidate who seems to be ahead. One effect of this phenomonon has been that elections today often start well before the actual voting day, with candidates desperately trying to pull ahead in the polls. Some excellent candidates have been knocked out of important races, in part because they did not have money for early polls to give them a head start.

The election of 1980, between Ronald Reagan and President Jimmy Carter, illustrates how the speed of communication via television and radio magnified the effect of polls. On the basis of polls of voters as they left the booths (exit polls), the major networks announced that Reagan had won. This occurred before the polls had closed in the western states, three hours after those in the East.

Some people think this may have caused late voters in the West not to go to the polls at all because "the election was over." Although Reagan would have won anyway, it is possible that elections for senators and representatives might have been affected as discouraged Carter voters failed to show up.

As a result of complaints after that election, the networks now refrain from openly predicting the outcome of presidential elections before all polls close. However, people can usually draw their own conclusions about who is winning, from the state by state results broadcast on television.

The "conformity effect" is very strong during elections. People are swayed by what the polls report about voting preferences. Candidates therefore exert much effort to convey a feeling of "momentum" and success to influence undecided voters. The many opinion polls during elections greatly magnify this effect.

One negative effect of polling has been that elections increasingly neglect some basic issues while concentrating on what the polls show would have greatest impact on voters. Often these popular issues are not the most significant ones. Thus, the important educational role of democratic elections is blunted.

The abuse of polls, or the harmful effects of polling—whether intended or not—is an ever more serious problem in our complex society. Citizens must be aware of the influential role that polls play in creating or changing public opinion. Once the power of polling is clearly understood, citizens can try to avoid closing their minds as a result of the impressive message polls can convey.

BETTER OR WORSE?

Many opinion polls call for stating a preference between alternatives, generally expressed as "Which is better . . . ?" followed by the choices. They may take many forms, ranging from judgments about the relative merits of two teams, two products, or two (or more) candidates for office to opinions about such complex issues as capital punishment, abortion, taxes, and deficits.

The range of such opinions is usually wider than just an "either-or" (or "black-or-white") choice, but has large "gray areas" in the middle with varying degrees of confusion caused by many pros and cons. For example, consider an opinion about this question: "Which is better, a small car or a large one?"

The fact that some people buy smaller cars and others buy large cars, while still others buy one of each, suggests that what is "better" for one person (or in one kind of situation), may be considered "worse" by another. Many complex considerations may be involved in opinions on such a question. For instance, the big car may be "better" for tall people who need leg room, for those who can afford one, for those who have a large family, for people who like to show off, or for people who have enough room to park every day. A small car may be "better" for a shorter person, someone with a smaller family, for a person who doesn't have much room for parking, or for the individual who wants to save money (see figure 8.2, p. 168).

People who can afford big cars may nevertheless buy small ones because they believe in conserving energy and resources. They may have strong opinions about curbing pollution and acid rain, which damage the environment. When buying a car the question for some people may be "Better for whom, the individual or society?"

Judgments, and the opinions that flow from them about such "better-or-worse" questions (or choices), get much more complicated when they involve strongly held basic values and ideas about what is "right" or "wrong." Opinions on such matters often lead to rigid, absolutistic positions and then to highly emotional arguments that inhibit discussion of public issues. An open mind and a high degree of tolerance for the opinions of others is essential to avoid breakdowns of democratic procedures.

SEEING THE OTHER PERSON'S POINT OF VIEW

It is important to try to understand differing points of view. Discussion and compromise between those who hold diverse opinions become impossible when people insist that their own view is *the right one,* and any contrary viewpoint is all wrong.

Consider the social controversy over the death penalty. Is it "better for society" if some murderers are sentenced to death? This controversy touches deeply held ethical values. For some people any taking of life—even that of a murderer—is wrong. They believe it is better to put murderers in prison than for society to set a bad moral example by killing them. Others believe that sentencing murderers to death is necessary to deter them and all potiential murderers from killing, or perhaps to avenge the death of the victim.

One example of how people with strong opposing opinions can reach a reasonable compromise occurred in 1986. Conservation groups wanted stronger regulations that would require manufacturers of pesticides and other

Lanky: *"My big car is better. It's got a lot more leg room."*
Shorty: *"My small car is better. At least I can reach the gas pedal."*

Figure 8.2 Opinions based on words like *better* or *worse* are affected by a person's values, attitudes, or conditions of life. *(Drawing by Albert Sarney)*

dangerous chemicals to make their products safer to use. Conservationists sought more rigorous testing for possible harm to people and the environment. The manufacturers claimed that it would take many years and far too much money to test new chemicals in the way that conservationists wanted. To comply with environmentalists' demands would also leave manufacturers with too little time to sell the product during the seventeen-year patent protection period granted for new chemicals. Producers said they could not recoup the money spent on development and testing.

After much discussion, the two groups reached a compromise: The conservationists agreed to support legislation in Congress to extend the patent-protection period, and the manufacturers agreed to accept stricter regulations. If most people could discuss and debate such emotional issues publicly and in a reasonable manner, perhaps solutions could be found more quickly and with less animosity.

Consider the wide differences of opinion about what to do with the large amount of forest land owned by the federal government. Some people believe that this resource should be used for lumber, mining, agriculture, and to promote jobs for nearby residents; others believe that the land must be preserved, that the loss of lush forests threatens fresh water supplies and promotes pollution, erosion, and flooding. The latter group contends that future generations would suffer severely if we allow forests to disappear or deteriorate. Since both views have reasons to commend their respective positions, some way must be found, by means of thoughtful discussion, to solve the dispute in a manner that accommodates the views of each group.

Opinions are likely to clash on almost any occasion in which people come together to share their views. But solutions rather than harsh conflict will be the result if more people try to understand and appreciate the views of those with whom they may disagree. Unfortunately, this does not work unless *both* sides see the need for such understanding. When discussions involve widely differing sets of values, an agreement becomes more difficult to reach. Emotions tend to come to the fore, thus ending calm discussion.

A wide spectrum of religious beliefs and conditions of life produce a vast array of opinions about what is right and what is wrong. For example, in overcrowded China, which has more than a billion people, the government campaigns to limit families to one child. Such a restriction offends the American sense of personal freedom. But, putting ourselves in their shoes, we can see that the Chinese face future disaster if population growth is not curbed; soon there would not be enough arable land to feed the growing numbers of people. What would we do in similar circumstances?

Would the Chinese have any adverse opinions of us? How would we explain to them the sight of so many homeless people sleeping in the streets and train terminals in an affluent nation like ours?

AN OPEN MIND CAN CHANGE OPINIONS

An opinion should be nothing more than a temporary judgment, made before all the relevant facts are known. We should therefore expect many of our opinions to change as time goes by. An *opinionated* person—someone who holds to a fixed view even when new facts point to the need for change—is a person with poor reasoning ability. A "closed mind" with a strong "mindset" can often lead to unreasonable results.

Often, when people demonstrate their vigorous opinions on a subject, the discussion ends with each person sticking to his or her respective opinion. It is not uncommon to hear someone say, "Well, everyone has a right to his own opinion." While it is certainly true to say that we have the right to hold and express our opinions, it is quite another matter to suggest that the opinions we hold are the only ones that are right.

No one should feel justified in having unsound opinions. Our opinions should be checked against reality, debated with others, critically evaluated and changed if necessary. Otherwise, the judgments we make may well be not only unwise but the source of unnecessary problems.

Five hundred years ago people began to be aware that the earth was not the center of the universe. This startling fact opened many minds to new ideas about the physical world and the way people relate to it. The scientific revolution had begun; ideas, beliefs, opinions, and values started to change rapidly.

Opinions have been revised significantly in the past 500 years under the impact of scientific thinking and the industrial revolution. The divine right of kings was once an unquestioned pillar of political thought. In such a climate of opinion the idea that every adult should have the right to participate in choosing a leader would have been considered utterly ridiculous. How could such ignorant peasants know whom to vote for?

But today, with many more educated and literate people in the world, and with vast global sources of information available, choosing leaders is considered a matter of human right.

Opinions do change. In 1933, an opinion poll surveyed the views of U.S. college students regarding 84 traits of ten different national groups of people. The poll was then repeated in 1967. In the 1933 survey, 24 percent thought Germans were extremely nationalistic, while in 1967, 43 percent thought so. This change probably occurred because there had been a world war from 1940 to 1945, one in which Germany had terrorized the world. If the poll had been taken in 1946, just after the war, the percentage believing Germany to be extremely nationalistic would probably have been far greater.[3]

Of those persons surveyed in 1933, 32 percent thought Italians were especially musical; but by 1967, only 9 percent thought so. This significant change probably occurred because the earlier prominence of famous Italian singers, orchestra conductors, and popular Italian songs was overtaken by singers and musicians from other national groups during the intervening years of the survey.

In the earlier survey, 84 percent of those asked thought blacks were superstitious; yet only 13 percent thought so in 1967. The opinion in 1933 had probably been influenced by popular movies that frequently presented blacks as literally quaking with fear at ghosts. In 1967, in the midst of widely publicized civil rights campaigns, most whites had come to see that various "stereotyped" views of blacks were completely without foundation (see chapter 9 on "Stereotypes, Prejudice, and Discrimination").

It is clear that many people do change their opinions when new facts become available. Such changes are facilitated if their minds are open and ready to accept new information. The attitude of an open mind is the key to adjusting to new circumstances and can play an important part in smoothing the path to a better future.

Changes in opinions should take place within a framework of ethical values based on cooperation and consideration of others. Without these basic values, changing opinions can be very destructive and can lead to conflict.

Ethical values, opinions, and attitudes are closely related. *Attitude* refers to the way people reveal their opinions, feelings, and often their ethical values. Consider the seemingly simple situation shown in figure 8.3 (p. 172). In the 1920s men were often arrested for appearing in public in indecent attire if they took off the tops of their bathing suits. The system of values at the time included widespread belief in the sinfulness of "excessive" exposure of the human body. People therefore had a negative *attitude* toward a man who took off the top of his suit. There was a general *opinion* against permitting anyone to appear in public without the top of a bathing suit.

Today the public values regarding exposure of parts of the human body have changed considerably. Nudists, for example, believe that exposure of all parts of the body is a virtue, not a sin. They search for or create beaches where they can follow their beliefs.

Opinions and attitudes have been known to go to extremes. In some countries both sexes are perfectly free to walk about nude on public beaches, while in other more conservative environments, public exposure of the body by women is considered so sinful that they must even cover their faces.

Conflict Resolution

In today's complex world the ability to resolve differences of opinion by "putting yourself in the other fellow's shoes" takes on greater importance than ever before. Human survival may rest upon whether we can understand and appreciate the viewpoints of other people.

We can learn a great deal from the techniques of *conflict resolution* that have been developed to produce acceptable compromises when individuals find themselves in sharp conflict as a result of opposing opinions. In some communities impartial committees of volunteers offer their services to resolve conflicts. They do not pass judgment, but ask questions designed to get each party to see the other's point of view in an objective light.

Figure 8.3 We live in a period of rapidly changing attitudes. In the 1920s men were arrested for removing the tops of their bathing suits. Today, people would laugh if they saw a man wearing a bathing suit with a top. *(Drawing by Arnold Lobel)*

This process frequently leads to mutual understanding and a resolution of the conflict.

Mediation is often utilized by individuals and businesses to resolve disputes that would otherwise result in expensive litigation. The mediator does not render a judgment but seeks to get the two parties to agree on a mutually beneficial compromise.

Arbitration is a similar procedure in which the conflicting parties agree to accept a binding decision by an impartial arbitrator, or committee of arbitrators. This is far less costly and less wearing than long, drawn out legal battles.

In international affairs there is a very hopeful trend toward personal meetings among heads of state on a scale that was not possible before the days of airplane travel. The top leaders of the United States and the Soviet Union are now in constant communication. Discussions now take place at many different levels of government. One of the most astonishing events occurred in 1989 when the top officials of the Soviet armed forces visited their counterparts in the United States and were wined, dined, and shown the formerly secret interiors of the Pentagon. That visit was followed by a delegation of top U.S. armed forces leaders who ventured to the Soviet Union and were taken aboard formerly secret naval vessels.

The heads of state of the seven major democracies now meet regularly to exchange views and to understand each other's domestic and international circumstances. Many potential trade disputes and other economic conflicts are frequently avoided or at least reduced in this way.

The United Nations, which had lost much of its expected influence in the area of conflict resolution, now shows some signs of being rejuvenated as an agent for conciliation. People see the need for ways of resolving international conflicts by discussion and compromise. There is talk of strengthening the World Court as a vehicle for resolving conflicts that arise between nations.

People-to-people exchanges and discussions are accelerating. A number of simultaneous forums have been held via television satellite linkup where groups of Americans and Russians frankly discussed with each other their mutual fears, goals, hopes, dreams, and plans for the future. For the most part, the common ties that bind us as human beings are stronger than the national and political pressures that separate us.

Citizen exchanges of artists, writers, scientists, business people, and managers now occur on a regular basis to share ideas. Increased travel among nations has played a vital role in developing global understanding. In effect, the world is rapidly becoming a "global village." It is not there yet, but it looks as though we are well on the way. With the opening of Eastern Europe to democratic ideas and political freedom, the promise for the future looks bright.

All these positive steps give us hope that civilized people will not repeat the nightmares of the past. No doubt, regional and local conflicts will break out. One need only look to the Soviet provinces, the Middle East, or South Africa to be reminded of how fragile our human community is. But the world has come to realize that we are "one world or none"— an expression that was first heard after the atomic bombs were dropped on Hiroshima and Nagasaki in 1945. A half century later that promise seems to be coming true.

NOTES

1. Solomon Asch, "Studies of Independence and Conformity, A Minority of One Against a Unanimous Majority," *Psychological Monographs* 70 (1956): 1–70.

2. *New York Times* (November 4, 1936): 4:6.

3. Walter G. Stephan and David Rosenfield, "Racial and Ethnic Stereotypes," chapter 3 in the *Eye of the Beholder,* edited by Arthur G. Miller (New York: Praeger Publishers, 1982).

QUESTIONS (*Discussion of these Questions Begins on Page 254.*)

1. Read each of the following statements and decide which are opinions and which are verifiable statements of fact. If the statements are opinions, indicate why you think so.

(a) Foreigners are dirty and loudmouthed, and fill up our jails. Everybody in this town agrees with me.

(b) A dollar is worth one hundred cents.

(c) Always put your money in a bank. Never invest money in stocks, because you could lose it if the price drops or if the company goes bankrupt.

(d) Cities are crowded and dirty. Give me the country any time.

(e) The only car worth the money is a Pronto.

(f) Apples are cheaper than oranges.

(g) That must be Sam Dropleaf in the red sports car. He's the only one in town who has a car like that.

2. How would you evaluate the opinions in the following statements?

(a) In answer to the newspaper reporter's question, "Should a brainy girl hide her knowledge?" Pete S., a student, replied: "If she wants me to date her, she better act dumb. Who wants a brain around? I'm out to have fun, not listen to her spouting her latest ideas on some subject. I get enough of that at school."

(b) The following question and answer appeared in a newspaper advice column:

For nine years I have been married to a man who grinds his teeth in his sleep. I have been putting up with this like a good scout, but sometimes it gets so unbearable that I have to go to sleep on the couch. He claims it is my imagination, but I know it isn't. Is there any cure for this? Maybe a dentist could help? Am I alone in my problem? Can't someone help me? (Signed) Margie.

Dear Margie, I don't know what a dentist could do, short of pulling all your husband's teeth. Your only solution is to sleep apart or get used to the same old grind.

(c) The following was published on the letters-to-the-editor page of a news-paper:

> Why do parents insist on letting small children and babies take up seats on subways and buses? A fare wasn't paid for these toddlers and babies, so why should a fare-paying sucker be deprived of a seat he paid for? Keep those brats on your laps where they belong, you jerks! (Signed) Standee.

(d) The process of education has to be essentially a local and personal re-sponsibility. It cannot be improved by action or funding from the federal government.

3. The following opinion was expressed in a letter to a newspaper: "No one should be paid less than the average wage in his industry." What is wrong with this proposal?

4. What impressions (positive or negative) do you get about people with the following names? Would you be reluctant to have any of these people as your friends?

Sam Brown	Hyman Cohen
Whitney Parsons	Vladimir Sholokovsky
Vito Pappalozzi	Rastus Woodley
Elmer Picklesnuff	Chou Tien
Jose Fernandez	Amiya Gupta
Jon Parker	

5. Is a survey of every tenth house a random sample? If not, how would you select a random sample of houses? Explain your answer.

6. Would a poll conducted over the telephone during the day, on a randomly chosen set of telephone numbers, produce a truly random sampling of opinions?

9

Stereotypes, Prejudice, and Discrimination

An American tourist stopped to glance at a sleeping Mexican peasant who was sitting in a shady spot with his arms around his knees and a big sombrero covering his head.

"Look at that. Asleep in the middle of the day! How can these lazy fellows ever get anywhere?"

The tourist then pulled a camera out of his gadget bag and snapped a photograph of the picturesque peasant.

Nearby, a Mexican shopkeeper glanced out of his window, observed the tourist for a minute, and then turned to his wife.

"These rich Americans. They never work. All they do is take pictures and spend money."

Both men were expressing opinions, but were those opinions based on observation? Only minimally. In the main, both the American and the Mexican had prejudged each other.

Note the contempt with which the American stated his opinion: "Asleep in the middle of the day! How can these lazy fellows ever get anywhere?" Read the sentence aloud and observe the way it makes the American feel superior to those "lazy" Mexicans. Similarly, the Mexican shopkeeper condemns all American tourists for being rich, never working, and always taking pictures and spending money.

Here are some facts that the American tourist did not know about the supposedly lazy peasant. The Mexican had been up since 5 A.M., walking the five miles to market with a heavy load of goods on his back. By noon he had been in the hot sun for many hours. From experience, he had learned that the best thing to do at midday on a hot day is to stay out of the direct rays of the sun and move about as little as possible. Taking a daytime nap was an intelligent and practical solution to his problem. Late that afternoon he would start his two-hour walk home and arrive, weary and footsore, to have a meager supper and a night's rest.

For his part, the Mexican shopkeeper prejudged the tourist while being completely unaware that the American was employed at a small company and earned a modest salary. He had worked hard for many years to save enough money to travel to Mexico.

PREJUDICES AND STEREOTYPES

Both the American tourist and the Mexican shopkeeper expressed *prejudiced opinions* based on *stereotypes* about each other. Think of the word *prejudice* as meaning "prejudgment": an opinion is expressed before the facts are known. It is a case of "missing facts" as well as "jumping to conclusions."

Although prejudiced opinions are usually thought to be unfavorable, that need not be so; they may also be favorable. For example, suppose someone who applies for a job happens to be of the same national origin or cultural group as the person doing the hiring. And suppose, because of that fact, the applicant gets the job. This is an example of prejudice in favor of someone on the basis of national origin. The same could hold in the case of religion, race, sex, or any other characteristic used to discriminate one person or group from another.

A *stereotype* is an opinion, based on limited information, that considers all members of a group to have the same characteristics. This stereotyped opinion is then applied to individual members of the group, whether or not it is really valid for that individual or even for the group as a whole. The American tourist's view of the Mexican peasant as "lazy" was based on a stereotyped opinion of Mexicans in general. So was the Mexican shopkeeper's view of the American tourist.

The word *stereotype* comes from a method of printing. Molten metal is poured into a form to make an exact impression of what is to be printed. This kind of stereotype is a mechanical copy of a prepared form that allows no room for variation. By analogy, when we don't know people individually, but only know that they belong to a certain group, we assume they are copies of people depicted in the stereotyped opinion.

Stereotypes are subject to modification as people acquire more information about individual members of a group. In such cases the stereotype may be considered a *misconception,* a wrong concept. In effect, the stereotype is weakened by proper information, provided prejudice does not obstruct acceptance of information.

Open-minded people are not immune to stereotyping, but they can change their stereotyped opinions when personal experience or new information indicates that they are wrong. People with closed minds, however, have such hardened stereotypes that their prejudices remain regardless of the new information. Such prejudices do the most damage in terms of discriminatory acts.

HOW DO WE ACQUIRE STEREOTYPES?

Our world is far more complex than that of our remote ancestors. They lived in small, isolated communities and had little knowledge of people, events, or objects beyond the distance they could walk. But in today's global environment there is so much more to know, to experience, and to explore. There are hundreds of nations; many groups of people with diverse languages, dialects, and cultures; and a multitude of raw materials, products, and strange new objects that demand our attention and our understanding.

It is impossible to master everything by direct experience. Short-cuts and summaries are necessary, especially when we learn about different groups of people by listening to what parents, teachers, friends, and neighbors say; by reading books, newspapers, and magazines; or listening to the radio or watching movies or television.

Walter Lippmann, a noted journalist, whose book *Public Opinion,* published in 1922, led to the concept of stereotypes, put it this way:

> The real environment is altogether too big, too complex, and too fleeting for direct acquaintance. We are not equipped to deal with so much subtlety, so much variety, so many permutations and combinations. And although we have to act in that environment, we have to reconstruct it on a simpler model before we can manage it.[1]

Lippmann referred to "pictures in our heads," generalized mental images of what people and things are like in the real world, most of which are beyond our direct experience. It is inevitable that the lack of personal knowledge, requiring us to get most of our information second-or third-hand, produces a lot of misinformation, or leaves us with inadequate (missing) information. When judgments are made with such poor information the chances of being wrong increase greatly.

To make sense of life's complexities, we mentally group people, events, and objects into broad or narrow categories about which we then often overgeneralize, or *overcategorize.* Misconceptions are therefore inevitable. Most are quite innocent and do not lead to prejudice. In Gordon W. Allport's *The Nature of Prejudice,* he puts it this way:

Overcategorization is perhaps the commonest trick of the human mind. Given a thimbleful of facts we rush to make generalizations as large as a tub.

Not every overblown generalization is a prejudice. Some are simply *misconceptions* wherein we organize wrong information. One child had the idea that all people living in Minneapolis were "monopolists." And from his father he had learned that monopolists were evil folk. When in later years he discovered the confusion, his dislike of dwellers in Minneapolis vanished.[2]

Misconceptions, intertwined with stereotypes and prejudices that persist over many centuries, intensify many of today's group hatreds and conflicts. For example, a common stereotype about Jews before the 1940s was that they had horns on their heads. Some people who met Jews for the first time would ask them where their horns were. These people had seen statues of Moses (representing Jews) by famous artists like Michaelangelo, Donatello, and others, as well as paintings and reproductions in books, which showed horns on the head of Moses. From this it was inferred—probably stimulated by analogy with the horns on Satan's head—that all Jews had horns.

The stereotype originated during the Middle Ages because of a mistranslation of the Bible from Hebrew into Latin. A passage in Exodus 34:35 describes Moses coming down from the mountain after speaking with God as "sending forth beams of light" from his head. The Hebrew word *karan* usually refers to "light beams," but in other contexts could mean "horns." It was mistranslated as horns. Of course, to prefer horns over beams of light indicates a mindset, perhaps applicable in this case because of the customary view of Satan as having horns on his head.[3]

In general, the stereotype of a minority group is composed of a number of misconceptions of this kind. Since these are usually linked in complex patterns, it does not follow that correction of a misconception automatically destroys a stereotype, although it does tend to weaken it.

After the 1940s, widespread travel by automobile and airplane, as well as increased use of television and radio, helped correct the crudest misconceptions and stereotypes about formerly unfamiliar minorities. Open-minded people capable of correcting misconceptions as they obtain new information, have rapidly shed many stereotypic views. Unfortunately, closed-minded people—and there are many—are resistant to change, and destructive stereotypes often linger in their thoughts for generations.

Children develop racial stereotypes at a very early age. When white preschool children are given black and white dolls and asked which look "nice" and which look "bad," most of them select the white doll as nice and the black one as bad.[4,5]

This stereotype is probably related to the fact that the color black (or dark) is semantically linked with many words and expressions that give the impression of being "bad." In addition to the darkness or blackness of night being associated with danger from evil things lurking in corners, black is also associated with dirt, as well as evil thoughts and deeds, Black Friday (a stock market crash), black clothing at funerals, the black knight of old, blackout, blackguard, black magic, blackmail, black book, blacklist, black comedy, Black Death, blacken (a name), black flag (of pirates), black-hearted, black humor, Black Maria (police van), black market, black money, Black Plague, and black sheep.

In contrast, white is associated with purity and cleanliness: white clothes are worn by nurses. White House, white list, White Knight, white magic and "That's white of you" are all good things. Children pick up this difference very early in life and it reinforces the unfortunate stereotype of black being bad, a concept which then contributes to the stereotype of dark skin color being "bad."

Similar stereotypes develop throughout childhood, so by the time youngsters reach adulthood they have a great number of "pictures in their heads" about what is right or wrong, good or bad, nice or not-nice, big or small, rough or smooth, or any other characteristic of anything within their experience, often beyond direct personal knowledge.

Consider, for example, the role of the concepts of "attractive" and "unattractive" in making pre-judgments about people. In one experiment, male college students were given two essays to rate, one well-written and the other poorly written. Attached to each essay was a photograph of a young woman, previously rated as attractive or unattractive by other students. There was no connection between the photograph and the writer of the essay. When a poorly written essay was accompanied by the photograph of an attractive woman, the ratings were substantially higher than for those with photographs of unattractive women. The ratings for the well-written essays were not significantly different for either type of photograph.[6] In effect, these college students were either prejudiced in favor of the attractive women or prejudiced against the unattractive women.

When we see an individual from a stereotyped group about whom we know very little, many of us assume that the person has the characteristics of the group. When, to our surprise, we meet a number of people from the group and recognize that we have wrong "pictures in our heads," most of us change our views.

Stereotypes are generally accompanied by errors in reasoning that stem from wrong or missing facts, overgeneralization, and jumping to conclusions. For that reason we must be cautious when applying stereotypes, and we must expect to be wrong quite often, perhaps far more often than we are right.

The stereotypes that we form about people are flawed from the start because we apply them to *all* individuals in a group. For all our differences, human beings are basically more alike in their everyday person-to-person dealings with each other than they are different. Of course, cultural differences do exist and people cannot escape their heritage; this may well be the basis of some stereotypes. But many stereotypes are based on so little factual information, or on distorted information, that they are poor guides to what people in different groups are like.

In general, we consider our own "in-group" as good while "out-groups" are bad. Moreover, we tend to like or dislike people in other groups to the degree that we see them as resembling us or as being different from us. The greater the difference in appearance, dress, institutions, views, values, or attitudes, the more likely it is that we will create a stereotyped view of that out-group as "bad."

When stereotypes and the prejudices they produce are invested with strong emotions the combination often becomes deadly. Every society has a minority of people who tend to express their feelings with violent acts, especially against individuals of a stereotyped group. In some situations they form organizations or gangs that attack and perhaps murder stereotyped individuals or groups.

Such attacks generate reactive stereotypes in the attacked group and the violent among them may retaliate with similar acts. In this way violence may escalate, producing fear in the community that, in turn, intensifies stereotypes on both sides. Soon the entire community may be hostage to the alienation produced by the violence. Contacts among the two groups diminish, making it more difficult to overcome the stereotyped opinions that are at the root of the problem.

Stereotypes are generally a contributory cause of nationalistic rivalries and wars. It's hard to kill people we like. Nations usually don't go to war unless the enemy is the subject of strongly adverse stereotypes. Winning the war requires soldiers to hate each other, therefore military training before and during a war generally fosters stereotypes to arouse strong emotions against enemy soldiers—and often civilians—who have to be killed without consideration for their status as human beings.

Prevention of such intra-community violence, and of wars on an international scale, requires overcoming stereotypes. How can this be done?

HOW TO CHANGE STEREOTYPES

One way to change stereotypes and prejudices is for people to be put into situations where they can get to know the people who are stereotyped. This usually works when the cultural differences are not too great and when there is no strong emotional content to the prejudice. However, when there is emotional content, elimination of the prejudice often requires putting people from different groups into situations where they must work together cooperatively for an important common goal. Some private groups, such as Outward Bound, do this by conducting adventurous trips in the wild with people from different groups. In such situations achievement of the goals requires a great deal of cooperative effort. In the process of helping each other, stereotypes and prejudices tend to diminish or disappear altogether.

SOME COMMON STEREOTYPES

Americans harbor many stereotypes about other groups, and not all of these stereotypes are racial in character. For example:

> [U]rban groups tend to see rural groups as unsophisticated, guileless, gullible and ignorant, whereas rural groups view urban groups as sophisticated, urbane, avaricious, dishonest and immoral. . . .
>   [M]anual laborers are seen as strong, stupid, pleasure-loving and improvident, whereas businessmen are thought of as grasping, haughty, cunning and domineering. . . .
>   Upper-class people are viewed as intelligent, ambitious, progressive, and neat, whereas lower-class people are thought of as ignorant, lazy, loud, dirty, and happy-go-lucky.[7]

People living in different regions of the United States often create unfavorable stereotypes about each other. Many people in northern states think people from the south are racist, but many people from the south who visit the north find plenty of racism there, though possibly of a more subtle and insidious nature.

An interesting feature of stereotypes is the similarity of unfavorable features they find in other groups. Gordon W. Allport puts it this way:

> Throughout history and all over the world one of the commonest accusations against out-groups is that they are dishonest, tricky, sneaky. The Egyptian Moslems so accuse the Christian Copts, the Europeans so accuse

the Jews; the Turk points to the Armenian, and the Armenian at the Turk.

The root of this accusation lies in the double standard of ethics that has marked human associations from the beginning of time. One is *expected* to deal more fairly with one's own kind than with out-groups. . . . It is fair and praiseworthy to cheat an outsider. Even among civilized people the double standard is still detectable. Tourists are overcharged; exporters think it is fair to send merchandise of inferior quality overseas.[8]

Walter G. Stephan and David Rosenfield researched various sources to find typical attitudes of whites toward blacks and vice versa. Their findings indicate that each group saw the other as lazy and dirty. The overwhelming view of each for the other was negative, while the view they held of themselves was highly positive. Each thought their own group was intelligent.[9]

Stereotypes and prejudices are often expressed through ethnic jokes, many of which change with the circumstances of each group. All immigrant groups go through difficult periods of adjustment in which they must begin with the lowest-paying jobs, endure poverty, and live in substandard housing. A new language must be learned and customs are generally very difficult to integrate. Frequently, poverty leads to a higher rate of drunkenness, fighting, and crime. Immigrants also have distinctive accents. All of these characteristics become the basis of ethnic jokes.

When Irish immigrants arrived before 1900 they were the butt of jokes about drunkenness and fighting. During a later period, jokes about Italians centered around the Mafia. Jokes about Jews featured money-grubbing. A fad of Polish jokes in the 1970s centered around their imagined stupidity. Jokes about blacks once featured them as slow-witted, with an inordinate love of watermelons. People who tell such jokes about other ethnic groups, or who laugh at such "humor," reveal their own insensitivity in addition to perpetuating these stereotypes and prejudices.

Is there any truth to such stereotypes? Are we wrong to assume that general characteristics exist for specific groups of people? While there may be individuals in each group who fit the general features of the stereotype, mistakes are made when it is assumed that *every* member has all the characteristics. People in all groups differ in personality over such a wide range that there is a great deal of overlapping of qualities among different groups. So, when someone attempts to assign any particular characteristic to *all* members of a group, that judgment is very likely to be wrong.

This is a two-pronged mistake in reasoning. The inductive reasoning is faulty because an overgeneralization is being formed from too-few cases, or because examples for the generalization are selected in a biased manner by subconsciously excluding all those who do not fit the stereotype. A second error is intertwined with the first: a prejudiced person uses deductive reasoning to apply the stereotyped overgeneralization to *every* member of the group. If a person from the stereotyped group is observed not to fit then it may be called an "exception that proves the rule."

Stereotypes about Groups of People

Do *you* have any stereotyped impressions of specific categories of people? Test yourself with the following list. As you read each item on the list stop for a moment and note the initial reaction. Do you get a positive feeling or a negative feeling about the group? Is it pleasant, unpleasant, neutral? Try to be as honest as possible. What is it about the group that you do or do not like? What is the factual basis for your impression? Have you met, worked with, or talked with any people from the group? How much do you really *know* about the group?

garbage collectors	Iowans
Floridians	anarchists
Zulus	Indians
janitors	Jews
Catholics	Protestants
Muslims	humanists
Blacks	welfare mothers
politicians	Russians
Arabs	Vietnamese
atheists	New Yorkers
Ethiopians	Iranians
Puerto Ricans	Frenchmen
Nicaraguans	Englishmen

Have you ever encountered a person from a group about which you had an unfavorable stereotype, only to discover that the person was not at all like what you thought? Stereotypes are present in any prejudice; they are what make prejudice possible, and why prejudice is so difficult to eradicate.

THE CONSEQUENCES OF PREJUDICE

Prejudice is not just mental and passive; it is manifested either in verbal abuse or harmful actions. Gordon W. Allport has identified five levels of intensity for actions that result from prejudice. They can be summarized as follows:[10]

1. *Antilocution* (to "speak against"). The prejudice is expressed verbally, generally among friends. This is the mildest form of unsavory prejudice if it goes no further, but in many cases more intense forms of prejudicial action also occur.

2. *Avoidance.* Members of the prejudiced in-group avoid meeting members of the out-group, against whom the prejudice is directed.

3. *Discrimination.* Members of the in-group discriminate against the out-group in job opportunities; housing; and social, political, and economic rights. Discrimination also includes *segregation* in education, often due to segregation in housing.

4. *Physical Attack.* Individuals or gangs may attack isolated members of disliked groups. There may be vandalism or arson against homes, cars, businesses, or other property. Physical and even sexual abuse may occur.

5. *Extermination.* This may take the form of murder, lynching, or genocide.

Violent acts due to prejudice are punishable under customary legal procedures. However, there have been instances where some prejudiced police and public officials have failed to pursue active investigations of violence against members of out-groups, even in cases of murder. A number of federal and state laws penalizing acts of discrimination were enacted after World War II and especially during and after the civil rights movement of the 1960s. Among the federal actions were the Fair Employment Practices Act (1947), elimination of segregation in the armed forces, an end to all-white primaries in the South, a Supreme Court decision outlawing segregation of schools (1954), the Civil Rights Act (1964), the Voting Rights Act (1965), and the Fair Housing Act (1968), to name a few.

SUBCONSCIOUS STEREOTYPES

Most people are not aware of their racial stereotyping even when those views manifest themselves in active discrimination of some kind. In one experiment, for example, people were asked to view videotapes showing an argument that ends with one person mildly shoving the other. One tape showed an argument between two white people; another depicted the argument between two black people; and a third presented the same argument but this time between a black person and a white person. All the observers were white.

> Observers were asked to code the behavior of and attribute causality to the act of shoving. When a black shoved a white, 75% of the observers (who were white) labeled it as violent; when a black shoved a black, 69% termed it as violent. However, when a white shoved a black only 17% coded the act as violent; when a white shoved a white, only 13% saw the act as violent. Thus when whites were in the role of transgressor, the act was interpreted more leniently—as playing around, dramatizing or being aggressive. The term *violent,* as distinct from and more deprecatory than aggression, was far more readily applied to the same act when the actor was black.[11]

According to some people, statistics indicate that blacks commit more crime than whites; they are therefore more violent. The basic problem with this argument, as with all stereotypes, is that the bad deeds of some blacks are being blamed on *the whole group*. This point is not dependent on the argument that a greater percentage of blacks commit crimes than do whites. As a simple matter of fairness and justice, innocent people should not be condemned because of the crimes of others. Peaceful blacks can no more control their violent minority than can peaceful whites control theirs. Most blacks are just as peaceful as most whites. However, when a peaceful black is confronted by an aggressive white and a fight occurs, white witnesses who are not aware of how the argument arose tend to side with the white person.

The subconscious nature of racial and ethnic stereotypes, when added to their characteristic of applying to *all* members of a group, accounts for the vicious nature of group attacks by members of one race on isolated individuals of another. The members of the gang doing the attacking do not see the person they are attacking as an individual, but as representing everything they think is bad about the group they dislike. They wrongly punish the innocent person for the crimes they attribute to the group.

A vicious circle begins if a white person (or member of any number of other racial/ethnic groups) is attacked by a gang of blacks (or any other racial/ethnic group). A white gang then feels justified in attacking any black they find on the streets of their own neighborhood. Then, of course, a gang of blacks feels justified in attacking an innocent white person who ventures onto their street. This is in part the underpinnings of several traditional battles in contemporary history: Catholics and Protestants in Northern Ireland, Jews and Arabs in the occupied territories, and Armenians and Azerbaijanis in the Soviet Union.

This is not an easy situation to correct because stereotypes are deeply embedded in subconscious mental processes over a long period of time. It will require a lot of education to minimize them.

SELF-FULFILLING PROPHECIES

The writer Thomas Carlyle once said, "Call one a thief and he will steal." This states an important principle in psychology. People react to what is thought about them, often behaving in ways that "confirm" the opinion. Adolescents might react to their mothers' complaints about not keeping their bedrooms clean by deliberately letting them get even messier.

In a well-known experiment by Rosenthal and Jacobson[12] teachers were told at the beginning of the school year that tests given to certain children in their classes showed that these youngsters were likely to do better than past records would indicate. The children had been selected at random without any such indication. At the end of the school year, tests showed that the selected children actually had increased their IQ scores. What happened? The teachers paid special attention to these children, encouraged them to work harder, and made them feel that they could do better. The children responded by working harder to please the teacher by meeting expectations.

The expectancy effect also works to reinforce negative behavior. Suppose a boy is doing poorly at school because he is having problems at home. Perhaps his parents are being divorced, or one of them has died. He may act up in class and, in doing so, acquire the reputation of being a problem child. Other teachers learn about it and then expect him to misbehave in their classes. When the child enters a new class, the teacher who has been forewarned expects trouble and tries to ward it off by saying and doing things to let the boy know he has to be careful in that class. Whereupon the boy meets the expectation by acting up even more.

This expectancy factor—the self-fulfilling prophecy—operates to intensify stereotyped views of other people. If we expect members of a group to act in a certain way toward us, we show it in our behavior toward them. They quickly observe this behavior and react to it by acting similarly toward us. This, of course, "proves" that the stereotype we hold is true, and therefore reinforces it.

Poor self-image and feelings of low self-worth are major reasons for failure among many children at school. This is particularly true of children from minority groups who may also be handicapped by the prejudices of some teachers who subconsciously do not expect them to do as well as others.

How to Counteract Self-Fulfilling Prophecies

An important example of how to counteract stereotypes and prejudice was demonstrated in 1984 by the successful businessman Eugene Lang, who made an unusual offer to aid students of the school he had attended as a child. When he addressed the group of mostly poor black and Hispanic students at an assembly, he offered to pay the costs of their college education if they would graduate from high school and be admitted to a college.

The school was in a very poor neighborhood with mostly children of minority groups who had no expectations of going to college and were therefore not inclined to work hard at school. They were on the road to fulfilling the prophecy that they could not do well in school.

Mr. Lang's offer and his sustained personal interest in this group of children over a period of years stimulated them to such an extent that, of the approximately sixty students who were present when the offer was made, a large majority eventually graduated from high school and went to college. This was astonishing for a school that formerly had almost no students entering institutions of higher learning.

Mr. Lang's action broke the cycle created by the "self-fulfilling prophecy" and thereby led to a successful turnaround for these children.

DISCRIMINATION

Human rights have become a world-wide issue, with oppressed people struggling to liberate themselves, not only from political tyranny but from discrimination based on the prejudice of an "in-group" against an "out-group." For example, in the 1960s, the civil rights campaign of blacks (aided by whites) was directed primarily against discrimination in the South. Blacks in most of the southern states had not been allowed to eat in many restaurants or to stay at most hotels. There were separate toilet facilities for blacks, separate drinking fountains, and segregated schools. Blacks had limited opportunities and were generally excluded from good jobs. Most were poor.

Many states had laws and regulations that prevented most blacks from voting or holding public office. "Poll taxes" were levied before a person could vote, thereby excluding most poor people, but especially blacks. Literacy tests were required when people tried to register to vote, which even black college graduates often failed because prejudiced examiners asked especially difficult questions. These discriminatory acts are now prohibited by federal law. Nevertheless, private acts of discrimination still occur against blacks and against immigrant groups such as Mexicans, Puerto Ricans, and other Hispanics (Spanish-speaking people).

One of the most serious acts of legal discrimination occurred during World War II when many American families of Japanese descent living on the West Coast were forcibly interned in special camps because it was feared that they might spy for Japan. This was in complete violation of their constitutional rights as U.S. citizens. Although we were also at war with Germany and Italy at the time, such internment was not ordered for U.S. citizens who came from those countries. This is a clear indication of a stronger stereotyped prejudice against Americans of Japanese descent. This unequal discrimination favoring those of European descent is probably related to the fact that Germans and Italians look more like most Americans, while differences in the appearance of Japanese are more noticeable. Although there were discriminatory acts against Germans and Italians, they were at a much lower level of intensity. In general we seem to relate closely to people who look like us, and less closely to those who look different.

One reason prejudice and discrimination against blacks is so hard to eradicate is that each new generation cannot escape the difference in appearance the way children of immigrants do. The second- and third-generation descendants of white immigrants speak and look the same as other white Americans; they can get jobs on an essentially equal basis and live where they please. This is not yet possible for blacks whose skin color still effectively excludes them from many jobs and communities. There is also a heritage of slavery and the accompanying stereotype of inferiority that persists.

Stereotypes, prejudice, and the discrimination they produce reached an incredible peak in modern times during World War II in Adolf Hitler's Germany. He pushed the evils of stereotyping to their limit by exploiting the fictitious concept of a superior "Aryan" race to which he supposedly belonged. In his warped view, Jews and Gypsies (among others) were such inferior races that they deserved to be physically exterminated.

Since Jewish Germans could not be readily distinguished from other Germans, Hitler required them to wear yellow armbands. This open identification mark constantly subjected them to discrimination and physical attack. The all-inclusive character of racial stereotypes was absolute under Hitler. It made no difference if a person practiced the Jewish religion or not. All that mattered was that the person had Jewish parents. Even one Jewish parent in a mixed marriage sufficed to condemn a person to death, regardless of any other considerations.

The killings were on a massive scale never before witnessed, with large numbers of men, women, and children herded at one time into huge gas chambers to await death, and all on a regular schedule throughout the day. As in a slaughterhouse, hair was cut from heads and stockpiled for use in industry. Gold was removed from teeth. Shoes and eyeglasses were saved for reuse. Then bodies were burned in large mass crematoria to minimize the waste-disposal problem. The Holocaust would not have been possible without the stereotyped view of all Jews as so evil that they had to be exterminated like pests.

The slaughter was not limited to the Jews. Many millions of civilians in various European nations were also killed, with special fury against anyone who opposed or might oppose the Nazi dictatorship. But the difference for Jews was that *every* Jew was subject to extermination, whether a political opponent or not. This was *genocide,* the extermination of masses of people, not because of anything they did but because they happened to be born to parents of a certain nationality or religion.

There have been many examples in history of extermination programs based on stereotypes and prejudice, but none approached the methodical mass killing technology of the Nazis.

Stereotypes are also intimately linked with extermination policies based on political and economic considerations, not just race or religion. The extermination of people for their political beliefs generally begins with the stereotype that they are "enemies" not worthy of any human rights. For example, a starvation policy in the Ukraine by the Stalin dictatorship in the 1930s was based on viewing the "kulaks," the so-called "rich peasants," as enemies of the people. Their food was taken away, leaving millions in the region to starve to death. Throughout the Stalin era, millions of dissenters, or people suspected of being so, were exiled to Siberian labor camps where many died from hard work and harsh conditions of life.

Similar "enemy" stereotypes are interwoven in the many "disappearances" and murders of political opponents and dissenters by army or police units in a number of nations today, such as South Africa, Guatemala, Haiti, and El Salvador.

Lest we think that our nation is somehow miraculously immune to such inhumanity based on stereotypes of hated enemies, let us ponder the fact that there were an estimated 100 million "Indians" living in the Americas before the white man began to destroy them in the 1500s. Today only a tiny fraction of their number remain. Such a policy of extermination would not have been possible without the evil stereotype of Indians as "savages" unworthy of inalienable human rights. And there is also the shame of centuries of slavery in our nation, with many blacks having been lynched as a consequence of the twisted stereotype of their inferiority.

There is great hope for change in recent widespread international acceptance of universal human rights, but as yet it remains mostly words. Words are not meaningless; they are an important conceptual first step to real change. Words fostering human rights—increasingly followed by deeds—point to a possible future in which the deadly nature of stereotypes and prejudice may be curbed, and perhaps eliminated.

Opinions in general are so important in modern life that a new profession has emerged in which experts in "public relations" play key roles in influencing and changing public opinion in the direction desired by those able to pay high fees. The next chapter considers the techniques used for influencing public opinion, often in ways that mislead people or divert their attention from basic public issues.

NOTES

1. Walter Lippman, *Public Opinion* (New York: The Free Press, 1922, 1949), p. 11.

2. Gordon W. Allport, *The Nature of Prejudice* (Garden City, N.Y.: Doubleday, 1958), p. 9.

3. *Encyclopedia Judaica,* Vol. 12, p. 406.

4. J. C. Brigham, "Views of Black and White Children Concerning the Distribution of Personality Characteristics," *Journal of Personality* 42 (1974):144–58.

5. R. M. Lerner and J. R. Knapp, "The Structure of Racial Attitudes in Children," *Journal of Youth and Adolescence* 5 (1976):283–300.

6. D. Landy and H. Sigall, "Beauty Is Talent: Task Evaluation as a Function of the Performer's Attractiveness," *Journal of Personality and Social Psychology* 29, No. 3 (1974):299–304.

7. Walter G. Stephan and David Rosenfield, "Racial and Ethnic Stereotypes," chapter 3 in *The Eye of the Beholder,* edited by Arthur G. Miller (New York: Praeger Publishers, 1982), p. 99.

8. Allport, *The Nature of Prejudice,* p. 146.

9. Stephan and Rosenfield, "Racial and Ethnic Stereotypes," p. 100.

10. Allport, *The Nature of Prejudice,* pp. 14–15.

11. B. L. Duncan, "Differential Social Perception and Attribution of Intergroup Violence: Testing the Lower Limits of Stereotyping Blacks," *Journal of Personality and Social Psychology* 34 (1976):117.

12. R. Rosenthal and L. Jacobson, *Pygmalion in the Classroom* (New York: Holt, Rinehart, and Winston, 1968).

QUESTIONS (*Discussion of these Questions Begins on p. 257.*)

1. What is a stereotype?

2. How do we acquire stereotypes?

3. How do stereotyped opinions become harmful prejudices?

4. How do stereotypes originate?

5. How do children's books, movies, and television develop and perpetuate stereotypes?

6. List two stereotyped opinions you have had in the past that have changed once you acquired new facts.

7. Read the list of categories of people on page 184. List the groups for whom you have a favorable stereotype. List those for whom you have an unfavorable stereotype. Can you think of other adverse stereotypes that you or others might have? Try to be objective as you explain why you have these stereotypes.

8. Have you personally experienced or observed the good or bad effects of self-fulfilling prophecies? Did you or people you know ever do well because people expected you to; or do poorly for the same reason? Give some examples.

9. How do self-fulfilling prophecies help create stereotypes? Give an example.

10. How might negative stereotyping be eliminated?

11. What is meant by "discrimination"?

12. List three examples of discrimination enforced by institutions, laws, or regulations. List three that are the result of individual or group actions, not sanctioned by law or regulation.

13. What are the five levels of intensity of prejudicial actions, as identified by Gordon W. Allport?

14. List two examples of prejudice in the United States that reached the stage of "extermination" by individuals and/or groups.

10

How Opinions Are Influenced

In 1948, during the re-election campaign of Senator Claude Pepper of Florida, large numbers of leaflets with the following unsigned message were circulated throughout the state just before election day:

> Are you aware that Claude Pepper is known all over Washington as a shameless extrovert? Not only that, but this man is reliably reported to practice nepotism with his sister-in-law and he has a sister who was a thespian in wicked New York City. Worst of all, it is an established fact that Mr. Pepper, before his marriage, habitually practiced celibacy.[1]

In a literal sense, the statements were not false. However, the words *extrovert* (a person who is active and expressive), *nepotism* (favoritism to relatives), *thespian* (an actor or actress) and *celibacy* (being unmarried) were used in contexts that seemed ominous for unschooled people who did not know the meanings of these uncommon words.

A very clever and unscrupulous writer had selected words *deliberately designed* to mislead and to give the impression that Senator Pepper was a very immoral person. The effect was devastating: Senator Pepper was defeated at the polls by George Smathers, who denied that he was involved in this political "dirty tricks" message. However, the damage could not be undone.

This is but one of many examples of opinion-molding tricks that have been played on an unsuspecting public in the past, and are still frequently used. In fact, with today's powerful communications media—mainly television, but also radio, newspapers, and magazines—not only have the benefits of widespread information been magnified, but so have the dangers of misinformation.

This is dramatically revealed in a recent proliferation of "negative cam-

193

paigns" by many candidates for election to public office. According to Curtis Gans, director of the Committee for the Study of the American Electorate,

> Negative, trivial and scurrilous ads are not a new phenomenon nor are present versions necessarily more outrageous than those from other elections. What is different is not the type but the volume.
>
> Where such ads were once limited to the occasional campaign and accompanied by howls of outrage, they are now the staple of all campaigns.[2]

Today, at the height of an annual election campaign there is a flood of about 2,000 political commercials a day, most of which consist of fifteen- to thirty-second "spots" on television. The objective is often not to give information about the important issues in the election, but to find or invent any kind of weakness with which the opponent can be hammered to defeat. In such contests the candidate who has the meanest public relations team and has the most money to spend for a torrent of commercials, often wins the election.

ORGANIZED "PUBLIC RELATIONS"

No source of information about our complex world is completely objective— uninfluenced by personal feelings, values, mindsets, or prejudices. Every writer, speaker, or reporter selects information to include in describing what he or she thinks is important. But what is important or right to one communicator may be unimportant or wrong to some other who is working from different values and knowledge. Moreover, many people deliberately report events in ways that are designed to influence the reader or listener.

The deliberate molding of opinions has become big business. *Public relations* experts are available for hire to generate publicity, advertise products, and to change the way people, products, or public issues are perceived. Many sell their expert services to anyone who has the money to pay.

People who want to become famous hire public relations companies to gain television appearances and "plant" favorable articles in magazines and newspapers. Such "image-making" favors people with enlarged egos; modest people with more talent may not want to push themselves forward in this way.

Candidates for public office generally hire experts to organize publicity for them. "Press conferences" are called, at which time television and newspaper reporters are given "news" to report. Much of this news is justifiable, though some of it is exaggerated or even invented for the purpose of publicity.

Along with the useful information public relations campaigns may supply, there is likely to be *propaganda,* the systematic spreading of ideas and information to advance special interests. To protect our ability to think for ourselves, we need to know about some of the ways public relations campaigns try to change opinions. This chapter describes a number of such opinion-influencing techniques.

CARD-STACKING THE FACTS

The word *card-stacking* comes from the gambler's trick of arranging the order of cards in advance to achieve an advantage in a game. Similarly, card-stacking the facts in a speech, argument, or debate simply means to present only those facts that favor one point of view while hiding or even suppressing facts that favor an opposing perspective. In effect, it means deliberately producing a "missing facts" situation. For example, a salesman for Jumpo cars fails to reveal that these cars have been recalled for more engine corrections than any other cars this year. Instead, he highlights the well-painted body and the low gas mileage, hoping to clinch the sale. If the salesman is asked about a competitor's Speedo, he is likely to mention only its faults. The salesman is stacking the cards, selecting facts solely to convince the customer to buy the Jumpo car. Such card-stacking is illustrated in figure 10.1 (see p. 196).

A glaring example of card-stacking was brought to light in 1986, when the R. J. Reynolds Tobacco Company was charged by the Federal Trade Commission with "unfair or deceptive" advertising because its ads misrepresented the facts reported in a health study of 12,000 men.[3] The ads claimed that the study did not show any link between smoking and heart disease, and stated that the connection was a matter of opinion, not scientific fact.

The tobacco company had card-stacked the facts: it cited only one part of the study (which did not support its conclusion), omitting another part which stated that the danger of a heart attack was cut in half when people quit smoking.

Card-stacking is often practiced in discussions of political and economic issues. Figure 10.2 (see p. 197) shows a chart of business conditions. One opinion-maker wants to discredit the administration in office, so every time business gets worse (at B, D, and F) these facts are reported. But he keeps quiet when business gets better (A, C, and E.) Another opinion-maker who favors the administration in office, does the reverse, citing only the better business conditions when they occur and remaining silent when they get worse.

Figure 10.1 When people have one-sided opinions, or strongly favor one point of view, they try to mold opinions by "card-stacking" the facts: suppressing facts that tend to show their opinions to be wrong. *(Drawing by Arnold Lobel)*

Both are wrong. The graph clearly shows that business conditions remained about the same over more than a year, with some normal ups and downs. Although each person presented some correct facts, by suppressing contrary facts, each was essentially misrepresenting the actual situation.

Subconscious Card-Stacking

Although card-stacking usually refers to the deliberate suppression of unfavorable facts, there is also a more widespread, nondeliberate, or *subconscious* kind of card-stacking. Every person has a system of basic beliefs and values that guides individual judgments of right and wrong. When we discuss or write about matters that involve our values, they have emotional content. We often resist accepting facts that tend to cast doubt on our basic beliefs; we give much greater weight to facts that favor them.

Since this factor also applies to television and newspaper reporters, they cannot avoid subconscious card-stacking. Although most reporters are trained to try to avoid this effect, it plays a role in what they decide to write about, who they interview, and how they write their reports.

As an experiment, have a group of people of different backgrounds watch a televised debate or discussion of a controversial subject and have them discuss it or write a report about it afterward. There will be significant differences in what they choose to say or write about because people generally pay more attention to facts that support their views.

There is a kind of self-fulfilling-prophecy effect, one in which people choose to read or watch only those sources of information with which they agree, while considering all adverse information to be "propaganda." In such cases opinions become hardened and more difficult to change because the individual comes to believe that the facts supporting his view are overwhelming in its favor. As Walter Lippmann put it in his book *Public Opinion:*

> [S]ince my moral system rests on my accepted version of the facts, he who denies either my moral judgments or my version of the facts is to me perverse, alien, dangerous. . . . [T]he last explanation we ever look for is that he sees a different set of facts. . . . It is only when we are in the habit of reorganizing our opinions as a partial experience seen through our own stereotypes that we become truly tolerant of our opponent.[4]

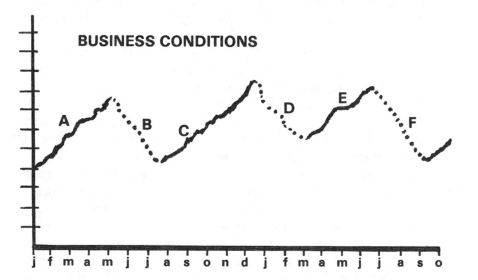

Figure 10.2 To "prove" that business is constantly getting better, note the improvements during periods A, C, and E, but not during B, D, and F. To "prove" that business is declining, note only the periods of decline. In both cases the facts are being "card-stacked." Actually, both views are wrong: business activity remains about the same, with some ups and downs. *(Drawing by Irving Lazarus)*

How to Minimize the Effect of Card-Stacking

The debate method can be used to minimize the effects of card-stacking because different points of view are presented, with each speaker noting facts that the others would normally hide. That is why debates have become a regular feature of elections for political office.

Similarly, procedures in court trials are designed to prevent card-stacking by having opposing lawyers present the strongest case they can make. Each card-stacks the facts, as we would expect from an advocate, but at least the facts on both sides are presented. Each attorney has an opportunity to question the other's witnesses to bring out additional facts that would otherwise be hidden.

Card-stacking also applies to written or printed information. For this reason it is important to read newspapers that present different points of view. Unfortunately, it may happen that on some issues the major sources of information may all be card-stacked one way. In such cases it is very difficult for people to understand the various sides of complex issues.

A primary example of collective card-stacking can be found in the treatment of environmental issues prior to about 1965. Although the environment had been deteriorating for a long time as a result of human activities, little attention was paid to facts that showed this to be happening. Some scientists and a handful of environmental groups tried to make people aware of this vital issue. But prior to 1965, newspaper, radio, and television decision makers practically ignored the problem because they were working within the mindset that believed environmental issues were not important to the public. Not until large numbers of people in cities like Los Angeles and New York began to suffer from polluted air was any attention paid to the environment. Then, suddenly, discussion intensified and formerly hidden facts became known. As a result, today practically everyone is aware that there are serious global environmental problems.

News sources vary widely with regard to their policies on covering issues of the day. Some make a major effort to be objective, to encourage their reporters to present news impartially and to publish opposing viewpoints in letters and columns. However, some owners and publishers have strong points of view and favor news and opinions that support them, or may even completely suppress any news that they consider unfavorable.

There is also a kind of card-stacking-in-reverse in which a newspaper or magazine "gives the readers what they want" to maintain sales. As a purely business proposition, some publishing companies seek a type of readership that offers an untapped market, then they create newspapers or magazines to provide information that those readers seek. This is a very useful freemarket aspect of publishing that is highly effective for providing many special kinds of information.

However, there is a serious defect for such give-them-what-they-want publishing of information on public issues: it is first card-stacked by the reader's preference, then reinforced by the publisher who emphasizes the desired kinds of news and columns. As a result, people may tend to develop hardened opinions because they think they are getting all the vital "facts" on some issues when this is clearly not the case. Thus, they feel no need to modify their opinions.

The large amount of money needed today to publish newspapers and magazines, or to develop technically efficient television and radio stations, tends to favor ownership by the wealthy. This factor may result in card-stacking of news on certain important public issues (such as taxation) where the interests of owners and readers may differ.

Despite these drawbacks, the right of a free press—guaranteeing that any point of view may be disseminated—does give our nation a wide variety of sources of information essential for maintaining a democracy. And many editors, publishers, and journalists do feel an obligation to present news as objectively as they can. Consequently, relatively objective information is available.

The problem for readers and viewers is locating it. When we read an article, or see a television news program, how do we know if it is objective? There are several helpful guidelines. Does a newspaper present columnists with different points of view? Does it have an "Op-Ed" (opinion-editorial) section that presents opposing arguments on issues? Does it publish letters criticizing editorial policies? The presence of such a variety of information is a good sign that the editors and publishers take seriously their responsibility to be objective.

Finally, many people subscribe by mail to newspapers or magazines that have a reputation for objectivity, or provide information that local sources do not offer. Cable television with its wide variety of stations is now available to millions of people who seek additional sources of information. Some radio stations now have programs that feature call-in comments by listeners. Such program formats provide informational outlets for minority points of view—unless an opinionated host cuts off people with whom he or she disagrees.

Card-Stacked Headlines

Every newspaper has "headline writers" whose job it is to write interesting headlines for news items. The job requires a great deal of skill because the headline, although very short, must give a reasonable idea of what the news item is about. It should also be sufficiently interesting to cause a reader to stop and read the item. Another consideration, unknown to most readers, is that the headline must fit neatly into the allotted column width. This is a severe constraint that leads to some peculiar words in headlines. To observe these difficulties yourself, have someone cut out a news item, omitting the headline. Then try to write your own interesting headline for the item.

Here is a fictitious article. What do you think the headline should be?

Debate over the new school construction plan proposed by Mayor Porter got under way yesterday at City Hall.

Frank Calder, President of the Sunrise Community Association, attacked the plan as violating the property rights of about fifty residents whose homes would have to be destroyed to make way for the school building. He declared, "There is plenty of land over at East End. It would cost a lot less money and nobody would lose a home. Children could be bused there the way other children go to school."

Calder concluded, "It's a disgrace for Mayor Porter to support such an unwise plan."

He was followed by Amy Schneider, President of the City-wide Parents Association, who stated, "Mr. Calder knows full well that busing our children is not only inconvenient, but also means a large permanent cost for busing every day. Future school budgets will increase. Where does he think the money for these buses will come from? Mr Calder's proposal is foolish."

Before reading on, take a few minutes to write an interesting headline for that news item.

Here are some possible headlines:

MAYOR'S PROPOSAL ATTACKED AS "DISGRACE"

CALDER PROPOSAL "FOOLISH"

CALDER PROPOSES LONG BUS RIDE FOR KIDS

CALDER PROPOSES LOWER COST PLAN FOR SCHOOL

HOMES TO BE DESTROYED FOR SCHOOL

SCHNEIDER BLASTS CALDER

MAYOR UNDER FIRE FOR SCHOOL PROPOSAL

SCHOOL PROPOSAL DEBATED

All the headlines except the last one are card-stacked in some way giving a one-sided view of the issue under discussion. But the objective headline "SCHOOL PROPOSAL DEBATED" is so dull that most people would not read the item. Perhaps the following, more interesting headlines might help:

BATTLE OVER SCHOOL CONSTRUCTION

CONTROVERSY ERUPTS OVER NEW SCHOOL

NEW SCHOOL PLAN GENERATES DEBATE

Most people skim the newspaper, glance quickly at headlines, instantly decide if they are interested enough to read the item, or turn the page. As a result, most people get their news mainly from headlines. For that reason objective headlines are very important in a newspaper. Card-stacked headlines can give skimmers distorted impressions of what is happening in their world, especially if such card-stacking occurs on a regular basis.

When reading a newspaper or watching television news, note whether or not opposing views are presented. Most media try, but not all. Some feature one-sided presentations of news and commentary. To obtain more open-minded information, try to get information from many sources.

TAKING IT OUT OF CONTEXT

A typical quotation in an ad for a movie might read: "*Great Movie Magazine* calls this magnificent film 'remarkable' with 'talent . . . brilliantly realistic settings . . . top photographers . . . gorgeous pictures.'" It seems clear that *Great Movie Magazine* has given this movie a rave review. But the magazine may really have said:

"This movie is remarkable in showing the way Hollywood can bring together millions of dollars worth of talent, create brilliantly realistic settings, hire top photographers to take gorgeous pictures, and then waste it all on a plot so utterly miserable that we had to walk out in the middle of the show."

Words and phrases in the review have been deliberately "taken out of context." Only those words and phrases have been selected that make the movie seem outstanding, but the crushing conclusion—that the movie is very bad—was deliberately omitted, thereby card-stacking the quotation and turning it into its opposite.

A similar card-stacking process can occur with quotations that are in full sentences. Consider this example of a circular issued by the "Mark Barker for Treasurer Campaign Committee":

VOTE FOR MARK BARKER FOR TREASURER

The *Daily Bugle* says, "We deeply appreciate the important work Mark Barker and his volunteer team have done in beautifying our community. We wish there were more people like him."

DON'T FORGET TO VOTE FOR MARK BARKER

FOR TREASURER ON ELECTION DAY.

What the *Daily Bugle* really said was:

"We deeply appreciate the important work Mark Barker and his volunteer team have done in beautifying our community. We wish there were more people like him.

However, the job of treasurer for our city requires special knowledge and skills, which Mark Barker does not have. We therefore urge our readers to support Ed Mullins, an expert accountant who is eminently qualified for the position."

The lesson with regard to quotations is: "handle with care," especially during election campaigns and other highly emotional opinion situations where the temptation to card-stack and to take statements out of context is very great.

THE WIFE-BEATING QUESTION

Before an audience Mr. Brooks asks mild-mannered Mr. Kostos, "When did you stop beating your wife?" Kostos may love his wife dearly and the thought of beating her may horrify him. But what can he say to avoid the implication that he is a monster who regularly beats his wife? The question puts Mr. Kostos in an untenable position. People are generally quite trusting and find it hard to imagine that the question would be asked without a shred of evidence that Kostos actually does beat his wife. A denial by Kostos could be taken to mean that he did not stop beating his wife. A more complete denial, "I never beat my wife," still leaves the suspicion that he might be lying. If he could beat his wife, he is certainly capable of lying about it. "Where there's smoke there must be fire, right?"

Use of "wife-beating questions" is not common in the pure form illustrated above. However, numerous variations, many of them often quite subtle, play a role in negative election campaigns whose impact has been greatly magnified by television commercials.

NEGATIVE ELECTION CAMPAIGNS

The basic elements of these campaigns are as follows:

1. One candidate uses a variation of the "wife-beating question" to charge (or imply) that his opponent has done something reprehensible, or has allowed it to happen in an area of responsibility that he or she is assumed to control.

2. The opponent may really have little or no control over what happened, or the extent of his/her responsibility for it may be exaggerated.

3. The intended victim's response is directly related to the success or failure of the attack. A weak response to the charge, or excessive delay in responding, is usually very damaging to the person attacked. But if the intended victim can find a fatal flaw in the charge, or deflect it with a clever retort, the attack may rebound to the disadvantage of the attacker.

4. The angry victim often retaliates with a countercharge against the accuser, whereupon a tit-for-tat series of charges may escalate. The negative campaign may then degenerate into charge and countercharge, leaving disillusioned and apathetic voters with a bad taste in their mouths and an attitude of "a plague on both your houses."

Negative campaigns may backfire if used against a well-known, popular candidate. The charge of a misdeed has to be one that people consider serious, and backed up with solid evidence or with a powerful emotional appeal. On the other hand, when one or both candidates are not too well known, flimsy charges may stick. The outcome depends on the agility and cleverness of the attacked candidate in quickly responding to the charges, and, most important, the amount of money available for effective television responses.

Unfortunately, these conditions, together with the long periods of time now required for today's election campaigns and the need for huge sums of money, have converted election process into a grueling endurance contest that discourages many of the best candidates for high public office.

The 1988 presidential contest between Republican George Bush and Democrat Michael Dukakis is instructive in this respect. After the summer nominating conventions the characters of both candidates were relatively vague in voters' minds. Each candidate had to overcome adverse "labels." Because George Bush had been a relatively quiet vice-president and had not taken very strong positions on issues, he had been unfairly tarred by some media commentators as a "wimp." Dukakis had been contemptuously called a "liberal" by conservative pundits.

Bush began his campaign with Dukakis ahead in the polls. His television campaign appeared very early with an extremely effective emotion-arousing, widely shown television commercial that opened with the scene of a revolving prison door that opened to let convicted criminals in and then immediately out again. Then it described how Willie Horton, a black man convicted of murder in Massachusetts, had been let out on a weekend pass granted by his parole board, and soon thereafter proceeded to rape a woman and stab her husband. Since this happened in Massachusetts while Michael Dukakis was governor, the commercial implied that he was "soft on crime" because he had supported an early release program for prisoners in his state. The commercial was very effective because polls had shown that curbing crime was a highly emotional issue of great interest to voters. It also had emotional appeal to those people who are prejudiced against blacks.

The theme of this commercial may be considered a variation of the "wife-beating question" in which a candidate is charged with an act for which he was not directly responsible. Dukakis had not made the decision to let Willie Horton out, but he did have some indirect responsibility because, like many other governors (Republican as well as Democratic) beset by severe prison overcrowding, he had supported early release programs for prisoners.

Practically all political commercials are card-stacked, with candidates presenting only those facts that favor their side. The Willie Horton commercial was card-stacked by giving the impression that Dukakis was directly responsible for crimes committed by prisoners on early-release when, in fact, such crimes have occurred in many states.

It was vital for Dukakis to counteract the effect of this powerful commercial by offering an effective answer. However, he made the fatal error of not seriously responding to the commercial for many weeks while it repeatedly aired on television and quickly turned people against him. The polls suddenly reversed in favor of Bush. By the time Dukakis got around to responding, George Bush had neutralized his public image as a wimp and Dukakis was not only seen as soft on crime, but weak, indecisive, and unable to handle the tough decisions a president must make. After that, Bush never lost his big lead.

In a similar incident in 1990, Bill Nelson, a candidate for the Democratic nomination for governor of Florida, tried to use the early release theme by attacking Republican Governor Bob Martinez for a crime committed by a former early-release prisoner (also a black) who had killed two policemen during a robbery. However, this charge quickly fizzled when it was revealed that the early release of that prisoner had occurred during the administration of a previous governor—a Democrat. Nelson had card-stacked the facts so blatantly that he had left himself wide open for justifiable retaliation by Martinez if he should ever manage to win the Democratic nomination.

Note the use of overgeneralization in both incidents. In each case the charge was based on the major premise that the governor of a state is responsible for crimes committed by prisoners who are released early. When put this way, the premise obviously stretches far beyond reality; the fact is that leaders cannot know what is going on in every state office and should not be held responsible for every decision made by lower-level officials. Modern society is so complex that top leaders usually do not have as much control over events as most people imagine they do.

A number of other opinion-molding techniques are described in the sections that follow.

LOADED WORDS, MUD-SLINGING, AND NAME-CALLING

Mr. Moss, accused in an election campaign of being a political "boss," responded with the following speech about his opponents:

> "It is time to strip these masqueraders of the uniform of the Universal Party under which they parade, and expose them for what they are —self-seeking and deluded demagogues.
>
> We have the fullest faith in the democratic process as represented by the primary elections. We will leave the decision to the voters of Wedgewood City, who will not be misled either by the machinations of this group or by their mud-slinging tactics.
>
> The people of our fair city will decide with their ballots. For only they are the bosses.

First, the fact that Mr. Moss was called a "boss" immediately puts him on the defensive. He responded in kind with emotionally loaded words like *masqueraders, self-seeking, deluded, and demagogues*. These are *name-calling* words and most probably exaggerations. Are all of his opponents really masqueraders, self-seeking, deluded demagogues? There are probably plenty of honest, decent citizens on both sides of this election dispute.

Mr. Moss also uses other words in an emotional way to prejudice the unthinking listener against his opponents. Note the implications of these words or phrases:

"Strip": Violent, emotional removal of a mask that hides something mean.

"Under which they parade": Those sneaks are hiding under a cover.

"Expose them for what they are": Don't let appearances deceive you. They look decent, but underneath they are mean, nasty people.

"Machinations": This word implies a dark plot hatched by someone who pulls the strings behind the scenes while puppets do the dirty work.

"Their mud-slinging tactics": This evokes an image of hoodlums throwing dirt.

A political battle may be healthy for a community when it raises issues, leads to discussion, and requires political leaders to account for their actions. But when the discussion descends to calling names and using emotionally loaded phrases, the real issues are lost. Loaded words are especially effective with people who know little about the matters being discussed, or who are not accustomed to thinking clearly about them.

THE STRAW MAN

Biff took some change from Mom's purse without permission. When Mom discovered this she was furious.

"Now you're going to be punished. No television for a month."

"Aw, why're you picking on me?" said Biff. "You didn't punish Joanie when she left her room all messed up."

In this argument, Biff was setting up a *straw man* by trying to divert attention away from his serious misdeed and toward an entirely different matter involving another person (his sister). The expression *straw man* comes from use on farms of the "scarecrow," the crude figure of a man that flapped in the wind. It was made of a vertical stick and straw stuffed inside old clothes. Its purpose was to distract and scare away birds. By analogy, during a discussion or debate, if someone asks a question or raises an issue that deliberately sidetracks the main discussion and distracts people from considering the merits of an opponent's argument, then the "straw man" technique is being used. (See figure 10.3, p. 207.)

In election campaigns, weak candidates try to divert attention from important issues by raising as many "straw man" issues as possible. Those with large campaign treasuries can often win with such distractions by flooding the airwaves with commercials.

"C'mon, Fred! Knock him down and show how strong you really are."

Figure 10.3 It is easy to knock down a "straw man" set up solely for that purpose. *(Drawing by Arnold Lobel)*

PLAIN FOLKS

The mayor of a city takes off his jacket and digs a few shovels of earth to initiate construction of a new building that had been approved and budgeted while his predecessor was in office. Newspaper reporters, photographers, and television cameras record the event, to appear on-camera that evening and night, and in newspapers the next morning. A movie star discusses her child's school project in an interview. The president of a large corporation sits down to have lunch with some of his workers to show how democratic he is, and all the while television cameras are whirring away. These public relations (PR) activities are designed to send the *plain folks* message that "We're really just like you." But the "image" of the celebrity may or may not bear resemblance to the real person. Like every other group of people, leaders or famous people have much the same range of characteristics or personalities as most other people: pleasant or unpleasant, easy-going or bossy, considerate or inconsiderate, etc.

TRANSFER DEVICE

People are emotional about their flag, their country, mothers, churches, cities, states, communities, helpless children, strong he-men, and beautiful women. They are also emotional about well-known, well-liked people, such as George Washington, Thomas Jefferson, and Abraham Lincoln. In the *transfer device* public relations experts try to connect emotional symbols to whatever ideas, products, or candidates they are publicizing. They seek to "transfer" the favorable emotion from the symbol to the product, person, or idea.

Most commercials utilize this device. For example, an ad for a cigarette may feature a strong, handsome man smoking a cigarette while riding on horseback across an open field with beautiful mountains in the distance. Or the ad may show a beautiful woman in a bathing suit, relaxing on a lovely beach with clear blue water in the background. She has a cigarette in her hand. Such scenes are designed to focus on the good feelings viewers have about the people and scenery and then transfer these feelings to the cigarettes apparently being smoked.

The use of television is so effective in utilizing this technique that it can be spotted in most commercials and political ads. Many recent negative election campaigns feature the transfer device. The television ads of one candidate may concentrate on some unfavorable symbol that can be attached to an opponent, sometimes with a very remote connection. If the television spot proves effective, it is endlessly repeated to build up a reason for people to vote against the opponent.

These ads are harmful because they prevent discussion of important issues, to the detriment of our democracy.

"Plain folks" and "transfer devices" are not necessarily harmful. Many worthy causes that deserve support also use these techniques for influencing public opinion. The point is that people find it difficult to separate truth from falsity when artificial image-building is under way, and they need to be aware of how the process works to protect themselves from being unwisely influenced in their opinions.

GLITTERING GENERALITIES

Here is a statement urging people to vote for a candidate who, in real life, is not much different from the rest of us.

"Bill Baxter is a brilliant leader who constantly battles on your behalf for truth, justice, freedom, and the greater glory of our beautiful city."

Get the idea? There are no real details about what Bill Baxter is or does, only generalities surrounded by glittering words that make him seem wonderful. Advertisers as well as political campaign managers use this technique. By means of *glittering generalities* a speaker or writer can try to wrap his small ideas in emotional words like *freedom, truth, justice, democracy, liberty, brotherhood*. To judge the worth of a reasoning process, try to remove glittering generalities so that the basic ideas can be seen clearly.

THE BANDWAGON EFFECT

A parade marches through town. People are so stirred that they hop on the *bandwagon* and join the parade. That desire to join an exciting event is another emotion that can be used to influence opinions.

During a campaign to promote a product, an idea, or a candidate for election, people who are undecided may look around to see what other people are doing. If a candidate or a product can generate a feeling that many people are joining the parade, this may get enough people on the bandwagon to ensure success (figure 10.4, p. 210).

During recent presidential elections it has become vital for candidates to win early party primaries in several states to start a bandwagon effect. Most people withhold support and contributions until they are sure the candidate has a good chance to win. Campaign "momentum" is highly prized because it creates a bandwagon effect that brings even more supporters into the fold. The long drawn out primary process in fifty states greatly magnifies this effect, thereby putting a premium on the endurance of candidates and the amounts of money they have to spend.

The bandwagon effect is also a factor in getting people to do what they may believe to be wrong—drinking, smoking, and taking drugs, for example. Most people want to be part of the groups around them, and they find it hard to remain different when "everybody's doing it." So they hop on the bandwagon and do it too.

The bandwagon effect is another example of what was described as the "conformity effect" in chapter 8. Recall the experiment in which most people tended to "go along" with others in a wrong opinion about the lengths of lines. They "hopped on a bandwagon" for the same reason.

"Let's join the Green crowd. It's bigger."

Figure 10.4 In the "bandwagon effect" many people tend to join the biggest crowd, favor the majority view, or vote for the candidate leading in the polls. Political candidates try to utilize this effect by getting a big initial lead in the polls. *(Drawing by Arnold Lobel)*

THE TESTIMONIAL

A *testimonial* is a statement of support by a prominent person, designed to influence opinion. People often judge the worthiness of an organization, a cause, a person, or a product on the basis of the people who approve of it. The fact that testimonials are so widely used is an indication of how effective they are.

Some testimonials are useful. Suppose a letter arrives from an unknown organization. The literature is impressive and so is what the organization stands for. But should it be supported with a contribution? Could it be one of those fly-by-night groups just out to collect money, provide cushy jobs for a few people, and spend very little on the cause they espouse? Such letters usually come with lists of sponsors and supporters and testimonials from famous people. If we recognize the names of the sponsors and agree with their statements, then support for the group, and contributions, are more likely.

There certainly have been abuses of testimonials. Prominent people have sometimes had their names listed as sponsors without their permission. In other cases, organizations carried on activities with which some sponsors did not agree. However, this is not very common. By and large, this kind of testimonial is not often abused because the organization risks severe damage if a sponsor should publicly denounce it.

GUILT BY ASSOCIATION

A young man is invited by an acquaintance to go for a ride in what he says is his new car. However, the car has been stolen. A policeman recognizes the license plate, stops the car, arrests both youths, and charges them with car theft. The innocent youth is faced with a situation of *guilt by association*. He is considered guilty because of his accidental association with the youth who was driving the stolen car.

Guilt by association is a widely used opinion-molding technique in election campaigns. In one case, a few days before an election, a photograph appeared in the newspaper showing one candidate smiling and shaking hands with a gangster. That candidate lost the election.

It happens that politicians shake hands with many people whom they do not know. It is quite possible for an unscrupulous candidate or campaign manager deliberately to arrange to photograph such a guilt-by-association handshake, which is then sprung on the electorate at the last moment.

Guilt by association is one of the most dangerous of the many techniques used for manipulating public opinion. One dramatic example, removing Americans of Japanese heritage to camps during World War II, has been described in chapter 9. All were "guilty" of nothing more than being associated with parents or grandparents who came from Japan. But guilt by association was carried to extremes in the 1950s when Senator Joseph McCarthy conducted hearings to investigate Communism. Using his power as chairman of a Senate committee, he forced many people—some of them prominent actors, artists, writers, teachers, and government employees—to answer questions about their political opinions, memberships in organizations, friends and acquaintances. A number of these people, who refused to answer questions about their associations or political opinions, were sent to jail or fired from their jobs. One woman lost her government job because she had the same name as someone McCarthy had listed as a Communist.

Private groups were set up for the purpose of blacklisting thousands of actors and screen-writers who were reported to be Communists or sympathizers ("fellow travelers"). These secret lists were distributed to producers of plays and movies, who quietly acceded to the pressure and stopped employing people whose names appeared on the list. Suddenly, many actors and writers could not get work. This system worked so effectively that it took more than a decade for its effects to wear off. By that time, many careers had been ruined.

It is a fundamental principle of a democratic society that no one should be accused of wrongdoing or punished just because of their national origin, heritage, opinion, or association with others. Each person should be judged on what he or she actually does, not for what others think they might do. Dictatorial regimes destroy dissent and opposition by violating this basic principal. They often persecute relatives and friends of people accused of being dissenters on the theory that relatives and friends are likely to think and act the same way, even if there is no evidence that they do. The deep fear that this wide political net engenders in the population then makes it very difficult for the regime to be changed. Such regimes might maintain themselves for long periods of time.

The recent relatively peaceful overthrow of repressive Communist regimes in Eastern Europe provides strong evidence that democratic governments can replace dictatorial ones without violent revolution. This offers hope for peaceful progress in securing human rights.

SCAPEGOATS

The Bible describes how ancient people sought to rid a community of their sins by symbolically heaping them on the head of a goat, the *scapegoat,* and then sending it out into the wilderness. In effect, the poor goat carried the burden of blame for the sins of the community. By analogy, a majority group that blames the ills or evils of their society on a minority group is making that minority a scapegoat.

Behavior similar to scapegoating exists among some animals. A group of hens generally has a pecking order. The top hen can peck all the others, while the others do not dare to peck her. A second-place hen can peck all the hens except the first, and so on. The poor hen at the bottom of the heap can be pecked by every other hen. If she tries to peck back, the others attack her for daring to get out of line. Sometimes the unfortunate creature is killed by the constant pecking.

Among humans, scapegoating often appears as an attempt to blame the ills of society on minority groups. Like prejudice and stereotyping, scapegoating is an unreasoning response to simple differences in race, religion, sex, national origin, or any number of group characteristics.

In this chapter we considered various ways in which mainly political opinions are deliberately molded. There is another large area of subtle opinion-molding that concerns products we use. In chapter 11 we will consider "reasoning errors in advertising" so that we may protect ourselves from wasting money on products that are often overpriced or, in some cases, worthless.

NOTES

1. Claude Denson Pepper, *Pepper: Eyewitness to A Century* (San Diego: Harcourt Brace Jovanovich, 1987), pp. 203–204.
2. *New York Times* (October 29, 1989). Quoted in the "News of the Week in Review," p. 1
3. Federal Trade Commission, File # 8523143, June 16, 1986.
4. Walter Lippman, *Public Opinion* (New York: The Free Press, 1965), p. 82.

QUESTIONS (*Discussion of these Questions Begins on Page 260.*)

1. Which opinion-molding methods apply to each of the following examples?

   (a) "Our self-seeking mayor's despicable proposal for wasting money on a new subway is just an invitation for still more corruption by the political sharks who infest this town."

   (b) "In the name of our beloved country and for the sake of future generations, I ask you to elect Fred Stiple to the glorious United States Senate so that he can guarantee life, liberty, and the pursuit of happiness for the people of this state."

   (c) "You were seen eating dinner with Joe Hopkins, who spent a three-year term in jail. How long have you been dealing with this known criminal?"

   (d) "This new highway won't improve the traffic situation one bit. Instead, more cars will come into town and choke the city. It will also be bad for business because people will be able to go right through town without stopping. Some of these people would shop in town if they had to drive through the streets."

   (e) "These pious do-gooders have issued a series of slanderous statements that mask their hypocritical attempts at power-grabbing. The honest, hard-working people of this town will throw these rascals out once the truth is known."

2. Read the following report of a baseball game and analyze the ways in which card-stacking and other opinion-molding techniques have been used:

The valiant Pottstown Tigers fought against overwhelming odds before losing the game to the Circleville Eagles.

Everything went wrong for the Tigers. They were out on the field for an extra half-hour of practice while waiting for the Eagle bus to arrive. As a result, they got off to a slow start.

Jim Bates, the Tiger's star hitter, was struck by a pitched ball while batting in the eighth inning and had to leave the game. Jed Belton, their snappy shortstop, tripped while moving over for a fast grounder, and the ball went for a single.

Ultimately, the Eagle's man on first came through for a run. A high drive to left field by Sam Potlow of the Eagles missed being foul by only ten feet. It went over the fence for a home run. A high wind made matters difficult for the Tigers.

BOX SCORE

	Inning 1 2 3 4 5 6 7 8 9	Runs	Hits	Errors
EAGLES	1 0 2 0 0 3 0 4 1	11	16	0
TIGERS	0 0 0 0 1 0 2 1 0	4	5	3

3. Is life today better or worse than it was a century ago? What is your opinion? Ask others for theirs. Analyze how you and others arrived at these opinions.

11

Reasoning Errors in Advertising

The Seaberg family was gathered in the living room watching an exciting program on television. Just as the good guy was about to triumph, the picture shifted to a commercial:

"Prepare for winter now! Aluminum storm windows only $19.95. Buy now before the limited supply is all gone. Call 234-6020. Right now!"

Mr. Seaberg, surprised at the low price, grabbed a pencil and jotted down the number. A few days later, in response to Mr. Seaberg's call, a dapper-looking young fellow came to the house carrying a small model of a storm window. He proceeded to demonstrate it to Mr. Seaberg, who looked at the window skeptically and then remarked, as he shook it a few times, "A pretty poor window. Listen to it rattle."

"Well," said the salesman, "it's a pretty good window for $19.95. There's just one thing you have to watch out for. How far are you from the ocean?"

"About four miles," replied Mr. Seaberg, "Why?"

"Oh," said the salesman, "then you just have to be careful to oil the frame once in a while. Otherwise salt from ocean breezes will corrode and pit the aluminum."

"Oil the aluminum?" gasped Seaberg incredulously. "How often do I have to do that?"

"Only about four times a year," replied the salesman, without any sign of humor.

"Do you mean to say I would have to get outside each of my fifteen windows four times a year and rub the frames down with oil?"

"Well, I can see that you are interested in a quality window. I've got something much better that a person with your quality approach will prefer. It's in the car. Let me get it."

In a few minutes the salesman returned from his car with a shiny aluminum window. It took about an hour, but finally, he convinced Mr. Seaberg to buy fifteen of the more costly windows and arranged for installation the following week.

This is a true story, except that the names have been changed. Advertisers who use this kind of *bait-and-switch* technique have worked out the method in careful detail. They know that people love bargains and become interested if you offer a great deal for little money. So, more people respond to a commercial that promises a big bargain. They also know that a good salesperson, face to face with a prospective customer, is more likely to sell windows than an impersonal commercial would.

The cost of the television commercial was reasonable from the advertiser's point of view because it brought the salesperson and the customer face to face. The salesperson never intended to sell the cheap window. The offer was merely the bait. The salesperson intended to switch the customer's attention quickly to the more expensive window by making the cheap, sale window seem unattractive. He also flattered the customer for his "quality" approach.

Note that bait-and-switch tactics mislead people by card-stacking essential facts. If the commercial that featured the low price had also explained that the frame of this rattling window would require oiling four times a year, nobody in his right mind would have called for a salesperson to come to his house.

Many television commercials, as well as newspaper and magazine advertisements are useful. Notices of sales in reliable stores, and information about new products and special services are an important source of information for the consumer. But advertising can also mislead by means of an assortment of sales tricks. For your protection as a consumer, it's important to be aware of the many ways ads can mislead. At the same time, analyzing these techniques provides interesting practice in reasoning.

THE ROLE OF REPETITION

Repeat, repeat, repeat the message. That's a basic principle of advertising. Eventually repetition has a subconscious effect. People are not even aware that their preferences and opinions have been influenced. Nobody completely escapes the effects of repetition. Even a person who thinks he or she is not affected by an ad campaign tends to pick out the familiar name when confronted with a choice between two brands. We are more comfortable with things we know, and we distrust the unfamiliar.

But which brand is really better? Several consumer organizations perform scientific tests on products to find out. They often report that less well-known and less costly products are superior to some that are widely advertised and purchased.

There are many ways of advertising products: television and radio commercials, newspaper and magazine ads, mailings, contests, giveaways, and so on. All use certain basic principles to try to convince people to buy a product.

ANALYZING ADVERTISEMENTS

Some ads can be harmful. Here is an example:

AT LAST AN ENTIRELY NEW CONCEPT IN MAKEUP

SKIN-O-CREAM was formulated by a leading dermatologist to give you the beauty benefits of cake makeup. Its active medications work where most skin problems start. We call this amazing combination of medications RIDIMINE COMPLEX. It "attractivates" your skin immediately, corrects flaws within 21 days, and if used daily thereafter, your complexion worries are gone forever. Now, no matter what your skin flaw, your complexion looks perfect.

Let's analyze this ad. First, it's possible that the cream will help some, or perhaps even most people. It is also possible that a leading skin doctor invented the cream. But certain exaggerated claims should make us suspicious. Note the statement "corrects flaws within 21 days, and if used daily thereafter, your complexion worries are gone forever." "Forever" is a long time. Note that the cream has to be used every day forever to do what it claims to do and the manufacturer stands to make a lot of money in permanent sales.

The statement "Now, no matter what your skin flaw, your complexion looks perfect" is also suspicious. Suppose a person has the early signs of a skin cancer and, instead of going to a doctor, relies on this cream to hide the blemish caused by the disease. The manufacturer has tried to protect itself somewhat by saying that "your complexion looks perfect," not that it *is* perfect. A person with skin cancer who uses *SKIN-O-CREAM* instead of visiting a doctor may delay treatment long enough to cause death.

If a dermatologist (a physician specializing in skin treatment) did develop the cream, it still doesn't follow that he or she approves of what the ad claims. It is interesting that no physician's name is given. Is the dermatologist ashamed of his creation? Wouldn't the ad be more convincing if it said, "created by Dr. Joe Blow, dermatologist of Watson, Colorado"?

Assuming that the product was developed by a dermatologist, he or she probably didn't write the ad. Well-paid ad writers often know little or nothing about the products they are describing. The writer is usually less concerned with the facts than with card-stacking them to mislead people into buying the product. The presence of serious exaggeration in the advertisement should make us suspect the product. It may be just an ordinary skin cream with a few ingredients added, sold at a higher price because of exaggerated claims.

Many people find it hard to believe that anyone would deliberately mislead by using the printed word. "Doesn't the government stop that sort of thing?" is a familiar question. The federal Food and Drug Administration (FDA), which has this responsibility, does follow up many complaints and does in fact stop false claims, but often its actions are so late that manufacturers can make a lot of money while their claims are being verified.

In 1987, the FDA abandoned an eighty-one-year ban on making specific health claims on packaged foods. Such health claims, generally highly exaggerated, immediately appeared on packaged foods. Among the most glaring was the widely circulated claim by cereal companies that oat bran in their products would reduce heart disease, cancer, and other illnesses. Most of these claims were card-stacked exaggerations of scientific reports. Because of these abuses, in 1989 the Food and Drug Administration (FDA) rescinded its previous policy and once again banned health claims for packaged foods.

READING LABELS

One important consumer skill is knowing how to read product labels. Government regulations require manufacturers of packaged foods and drugs to list ingredients on labels, and to order them according to weight in the package. Unfortunately, the actual percentages of ingredients need not be stated. For example, suppose the ingredients for a soup are listed as: water, mushrooms, soybean oil, wheat flour, cream, salt, corn starch, whey, natural flavoring, and dehydrated garlic. There is more water in this soup than any other ingredient, but that doesn't tell us whether the water content is 25 percent, 50 percent, or 75 percent.

Salt is also on the list. It is a substance that people with high blood pressure or heart problems should avoid. Is there enough in this can of soup to harm such a person? It is far down the list, after cream, but it is listed before cornstarch. Is that a small amount of salt, or too much for someone who must be careful about it? There is no way of knowing based on the labeling.

Consumer organizations have been campaigning for many decades to have the FDA require more complete, quantitative nutritional information on packaged foods, especially for people who would be harmed by excessive amounts of salt, MSG (monosodium glutamate), sulfites, or other ingredients. The FDA is now (1990) taking steps to tighten its regulations in this respect.

However, with an increasing number of alert consumers carefully reading labels, many more manufacturers now include quantitative information on their packaged foods. Read and study labels on packages. It is an important skill to develop and cultivate.

PSEUDOSCIENTIFIC ADS

Modern science has an established reputation for truthfulness and reliability. As a result, people tend to believe statements that are made in the name of science. If a "scientist" makes a favorable statement about a subject in which he is supposed to be competent, then people think it is more likely to be so. Note how this principle is used in the following ad:

> Scientific experiments with the medically acclaimed electromyograph prove APPLICO relieves tired aching muscles twice as fast as when nature take its own course.

The impressive-sounding "electromyograph" makes the "experiment" sound scientific. Actually, this instrument measures electrical voltages in muscles, not aches and pains. It is not "medically acclaimed" at all. It would make just as much sense to refer to a "medically acclaimed thermometer."

What does the ad really say? Not much. The instrument measures something or other about the muscles, which is interpreted to be muscle recovery after exertion. The ad implies that if you let nature take its course, the muscles would recover by themselves, although it does not say how long a time is required. Applico, supposedly, will do it "twice as fast."

If it takes ten minutes for the tired muscles to recover from exertion without Applico, there would be little point in applying the medicine to get the muscles back to normal in five minutes. In that case, by the time you finished putting on the preparation the ten minutes might be up, and you would then feel fine without Applico.

Of course, if it normally takes two days to recover, a one-day reduction in recovery time might be worthwhile. The "experiment," however, is so vague that it is meaningless as described. In all likelihood the ad writers are just card-stacking any kind of flimsy evidence that suits their case. And there may even be some often doubt that any "experiment" was really done; or it may have been done in a card-stacked manner.

Note the misuse of the word *prove*. Proof of a fact in science is difficult to achieve and generally involves research. It usually takes more than a simple measurement with an instrument to prove a point. In this ad it's barely possible that the experiment proved what is claimed, but it is far more likely that it did nothing of the kind.

Note, too, that the ad doesn't refer to a "medically approved experiment," but rather to a "medically acclaimed electromyograph." Physicians may agree that the instrument is useful and important, but that doesn't mean they also believe the "experiment" is of any use. The instrument might have been used improperly, or its use might not apply to the situation.

There are times when important experiments may be cited in selling a worthwhile product. For example, some years ago, after a long period of experimentation, the American Dental Association announced that tests on fluoride as an ingredient in toothpaste showed that it helped to prevent tooth decay. One company was already using this compound in its toothpaste. It immediately brought the association's message to the public by means of an advertising campaign. The ads justifiably quoted the scientific findings as often as they could. Sales of this toothpaste boomed. This ad campaign was socially useful because it really helped reduce tooth decay. But more often, the vague scientific experiments mentioned in ads are meaningless, do not apply, are inadequately performed, or are figments of an ad writer's active imagination.

ENDORSEMENTS

Here is an advertisement in which a famous actor endorses NUTTY Peanut Butter.

How did we get Paul Vibrant to appear in a commercial for NUTTY Peanut Butter? Easy. WE PAID HIM. We approached Mr. Vibrant with a lot of money.

"What?" he shouted. "You ask me to endorse a kid's peanut butter?"

We sent out for more money and finally lured Mr. Vibrant into testing our product. He broke into a big smile.

"It doesn't taste like peanut butter at all. Tastes just like peanuts. It's great."

As we have said, NUTTY is the only peanut butter made just for grownups. That's why you and your kids will go for it in a big way.

This is a clever ad. It assumes people know that when peanut butter is endorsed by a famous actor, this does not mean it is a superior product. Famous people usually get paid for lending their names to products, and may not even use those they endorse. Therefore, we are justified in being skeptical about such endorsements.

The writers of the NUTTY ad took advantage of our skepticism by making the testimonial humorous. They admit what everybody knows. The surprised reader is likely to be amused by the ad and therefore more favorably inclined toward the product. The ad achieves its objective—but that doesn't mean that NUTTY peanut butter is any better than any other brand.

There is no basic error in reasoning here, but the ad does point up the folly of allowing oneself to be influenced to buy a product because some famous actor or athlete has endorsed it.

BETTER/CHEAPER ADS

Here is another type of ad:

BURKE'S is now offering the most stupendous array of the biggest, boldest, and thriftiest bargains imaginable. Huge quantities of all quality furniture styles are arriving daily in boatloads, truckloads, and even trainloads. Because of tremendous incoming quantities, we are forced to sell rapidly. First come, first served for the better selections. Hurry. . . . Hurry. . . . Hurry. . . .

This is an interesting situation. The store managers claim they are hauling in so much furniture by the boatload, truckload, and even trainload, that they have no room to store it. As a result they are "forced" to advertise for people to come and take stupendous bargains away. For this favor the customer is assured a lower price. But why did they stock so much in the first place? We note that there is no description of the actual furniture. Are they unloading boatloads and truckloads of cheap stuff that will be coming apart in a few months? Could be.

The effect of such an ad on unsuspecting readers is to inspire them to rush right to the store in a hurry, hurry, hurry to pick up the "biggest, boldest, thriftiest bargains imaginable" from a "most stupendous array" of goods.

The basis of this type of advertising is exaggeration, as well as an appeal to the emotions.

"FANTABULOUS" ADS

An ad for children's clothes includes the following expressions:

Incredible Pre-Season Savings
Terrific Toddler Buys
Fantastic Values
Fantabulous Bargains

"Fantastic," "terrific," "incredible," and "fantabulous" are highly exaggerated, emotional words, designed to make bargain-hunters rush to the store. How much of a saving would be considered incredible? The word *incredible* means "unbelievable." The savings would be unbelievable only if the store gave away its products at far less than cost. Frequent misuse of such words makes them lose their original meanings. Ad writers constantly try to find new words to replace the misused ones. They even invent new ones, as illustrated by "fantabulous."

SLIPPERY NUMBERS

Another type of ad goes like this:

CLEARANCE SALE. YOU TAKE AN EXTRA 25% DISCOUNT OFF PRESENT PRICE TAGS ON ENTIRE STOCK

Such sales are sometimes legitimate, but some stores raise prices just before the sale so that they can then claim a big discount and still sell the goods at about the same price as before, or only slightly lower. Some customers, responding to ads for sales, have actually found that new labels with higher prices have been carefully pasted over labels with lower prices.

Some stores may simply claim that a 25 percent discount is offered, even if that isn't so. Who will bother to check prices before and after?

Phony figures convey the feeling that a statement is factual. But if the numbers are slippery and can slide up and down, they mean little or nothing. Numbers are often lacking, and that, too, introduces a deceptive element. Consider, for instance a long list of fruit flavors on the label of a can in the supermarket. The list ends with the phrase "plus artificial flavors." Numbers would be useful here. Is 95 percent of the taste due to artificial flavors and 5 percent to tiny amounts of real fruit flavors, or is it some other combination? Without an exact statement of amounts and some objective standard of measure, the consumer cannot judge the information properly. Thus the impressive list of fruits may be completely misleading.

MOUTHWATERING LANGUAGE

An ad writer's most important task is to make an ordinary product seem valuable and appealing. Note the emotional words and phrases in the following:

CABINO SUPERFINISH FINE BEDROOM FURNITURE

So fresh, so exciting that it gives new meaning to "modern." There is a new idea in every crisp line—a satiny-white deluxe Operatone finish, accented with polished brass—the elegance of fluted columns— each piece lifted off the floor on tapered legs. And CABINO'S burn-resistant plastic tops match its wood finish perfectly. Group pieces functionally or use individually. Truly a bedroom to be proud of.

This bedroom set may be very beautiful, but then again it might be just ordinary furniture—or even of poor quality. Note how the following words and phrases contribute to the feeling of fine quality, and beauty: "superfinish," "fresh," "exciting," "new meaning," "crisp line," "satiny-white," "deluxe," "accented," "polished brass," "elegance," "fluted columns," "lifted off the floor," "tapered legs."

If this ad were written accurately and objectively, the description would become flat and uninteresting. Let's try it:

CABINO FINE-FINISH BEDROOM FURNITURE

A modern bedroom set of good quality with white, long-lasting finish, brass hardware, carved columns, and tapered legs. Burn-resistant matching plastic tops prevent cigarette and liquid damage. A good buy in bedroom sets.

This description is certainly more objective, but who would rush out to buy such dull stuff! The emotion-laden words in "mouthwatering" ads are not as objectionable as directly misleading statements. However, consumers must be careful not to be so attracted by the clever use of language that they buy products just on that basis.

The mouthwatering approach is widely used in some types of direct-mail advertising where the customer buys from a catalog or brochure on the basis of a description and a picture that may have been designed to mislead. People are often surprised when they receive the product and find that it is far from what they expected.

THE SCARE TACTIC

Some ads use scare tactics to persuade people to buy. The ads imply that unless people use this product, great harm will result. For example:

OUTBREAK OF COLDS?

Don't wait for the first sneeze or sniffle. Reach for RIDSO right away, keep gargling every few hours until the danger is past.

RIDSO kills germs by the millions. In 12-year tests, those who gargled with RIDSO twice a day had fewer, shorter, and milder colds than those who did not.

The reader might think, "Maybe the ad is right. How can I know?" Logical reasoning provides an answer.

The ad says, "Don't wait for the first sneeze or sniffle. Reach for RIDSO right away. Keep on gargling every few hours until the danger is past." If you don't wait for the first sneeze or sniffle, you have to begin right away. And how will you know when the danger is over? Never. Obviously, keep gargling—and buying Ridso—as long as you live.

Note the attempt to drag in the authority of science: "In 12-year tests, those who gargled with RIDSO twice a day had fewer, shorter, and milder colds than those who did not." No medical source is given for this test. Was it performed by reputable scientists—or even performed at all? Was improvement noted on the basis of objective evidence, or on the assertion of employees of the firm? Would gargling with salt water be just as effective— or perhaps more so?

SUBLIMINAL MESSAGES

Most ads and commercials today are created by teams of creative professionals: writers, photographers, artists, composers, pollsters, economists, and even psychologists and anthropologists. They study the markets, investigate consumer preferences, devise new ways of getting people to buy products, and explore every nook and cranny of the economy, all to develop new ways of influencing people to buy the products they are publicizing.

Much of this work contributes to economic growth, but there are also serious abuses, especially in promoting products that are dangerous or, in some cases, useless. Two of the most deadly products sold are cigarettes (which cause lung cancer and other diseases) and alcoholic beverages (which contribute to about half the deaths caused by drunken drivers).

Direct advertising for cigarettes and hard liquor (distilled spirits) on television has been banned for several decades; nevertheless the cigarette and liquor companies have managed to bypass these bans by using *subliminal* methods (below the level of subconscious perception) to promote their products. People do not realize it when a subliminal message is being communicated.

Cigarette and liquor companies now sponsor a host of major sports events: tennis, soccer, auto racing, horse racing, bowling, sailing, rodeos, ice-skating, and golf. The tournament or event may be named after the cigarette or the company that manufactures it. Numerous banners and signs with the name of the tournament—and the cigarette—are displayed when the games are played, and these signs are seen on television screens in many homes.

The cigarette then gets free television coverage, with the big plus of a stamp of approval by direct association with an important sporting event. Young people, watching the games, become familiar with the name of the cigarette and are then more likely to select that brand if they should ever decide to try smoking. One of the main subliminal messages is: How can it be bad for you if this cigarette is accepted by top athletes?

The brand name of a cigarette or liquor may also appear in giant letters on the back wall of a baseball stadium, observed both by the audience in attendance and those watching via television. Again, the name is made familiar to millions of people, subliminally.

Observe any television commercial and analyze the subliminal message it sends. For example, a commercial for a beer may show the players for a well-known team relaxing after a hard-fought game by drinking beer. That name appears prominently on all the bottles, with labels facing the camera, and the name is spoken many times during a commercial. Everything in the commercial is geared toward sending the subliminal message, especially for impressionable young people: "Virile men relax after a game (or at a party) by drinking beer. That's the model for you to follow."

Beer is not a harmless beverage—drinking a few bottles or cans of beer can make a person drunk. Many accidents are caused by drivers drunk on beer. Is it in the nation's interest to allow commercials on television to encourage young people to begin addiction to alcohol by drinking beer?

Subliminal ads are now being inserted into movies by prominently displaying the names of products being used by the actors. The scene may show the hero drinking Hotsicola, which he pours into a glass. He puts the bottle on the table with the label toward the viewer. The subliminal message is, "Good guys drink Hotsicola." Such subliminal ads are usually paid for by the manufacturers of the products.

Photographs in ads are designed to send subliminal messages. For example, an ad for a cigarette may show a beautiful woman in a bathing suit lounging on a sunny Hawaiian beach, with the sparkling blue sea and graceful sailboats in the background—and, of course, some handsome suitors nearby seeking her attention. A young woman who views the ad relates to the scene thinking, "That's the kind of life I would like." But there's also that insidious cigarette in the photograph, held between the beautiful model's delicate fingers, carrying the subliminal message, "Smoking cigarettes attracts handsome men."

In 1990, Dr. Louis Sullivan, the Secretary of Health and Human Services, launched an attack on several cigarette companies, not only for the subliminal messages they send by sponsoring sports events, but also for their plans to promote several new special brands of cigarettes. The advertising campaign for one was to be directed at young blacks; the other at young working women. Dr. Sullivan's strong criticism of these marketing plans led the company to abandon one cigarette and put the other on hold. Had these plans proceeded, the ads would surely have been designed to send subliminal messages catering to the desires of each targeted group.

New ways to include subliminal messages are constantly sought by the advertising industry. For example, an experiment was tried some years ago in which the picture and name of a product were flashed on the screen during a featured movie. The image was on the screen for too short a time to be observed at a conscious level; it appeared only as a momentary blip. The sponsors hoped that subliminal messages could be inserted in this way into movies and television. Fortunately, nothing came of this experiment, but it is always possible that someone may yet find a way to make such insidious commercials effective. If so, that would raise the serious ethical issue of invasion of privacy.

Subliminal messages are difficult to counteract by means of logical reasoning because they bypass the conscious level of thought and mold opinions about products through subconscious feelings. If people are shown how to detect and analyze subliminal messages in ads and commercials, they would have a better chance to avoid the potentially harmful effects of such campaigns.

OTHER MISLEADING ADS

The following examples of misleading ads have been highlighted in the pages of *Consumer Reports,* which describes and analyzes comparative tests of various products according to quality, price, and defects.[1]

1. One ad stated in large print, "WHY ARE WE GIVING AWAY THIS RUGGED 'NAVIGATOR' STYLE LCD WATCH FOR ONLY $2? THIS IS NOT A MISPRINT." Investigation revealed that this was only an LCD watch. There was no "navigator" watch, only a *picture* that looked like the hands of a watch and the various functions a "navigator" might use. Judging from this deception, one wonders what kind of digital watch would be shipped.[2]

2. An ad for cars stated in enormous letters, "Half Price for 1988," giving the impression that the cars were being sold for half price. In very small print the ad stated that the "Half Price" applied only to the *monthly payments* for a loan on a new car. Most loans would run for three years.[3]

This ad appeared in late summer, so, at most, four payments were to be paid in 1988. A buyer would pay half price *only* on these four payments. Although there would be some savings on what the company *said* was the regular price, this certainly did not approach the offer most people would assume the words *half price* to mean when buying a car. If the car dealer would mislead customers in this way, we might also suspect that their listed prices would be inflated above what other car dealers legitimately charged.

3. A GIANT inflatable Christmas tree was advertised with a large 52″ (52 inches) prominently printed on the ad, implying that this was its height. In tiny print down below, it stated that the 52″ is the "circum.," not the height.[4] With a circumference of 52″ the actual height of the cone-shaped balloon turned out to be 26 inches, not 52. This Christmas tree was not usable as such, but might serve as a toy for a child.

4. A postcard in the mail announces: "CONGRATULATIONS! You Have Been Selected to Receive One of These Four Awards for Participating in Our National Promotion." The four awards were: a car, a $5,000 cashier's check, a fur coat, and a $1,000 U.S. bond. A phone number was listed for more information.[5]

A phone call elicited the information that one had to buy six months worth of vitamins for $299 and would then be eligible to win one of the four prizes in a raffle. These requirements had not been stated in the ad. It turned out that the odds of winning the car were one in 600,000.

5. Someone who had been using a well-known brand of liquid detergent for fabrics found that when she tried to close an old bottle with the cap of a new bottle it no longer fit—it was larger than before.[6]

The detergent was used by measuring out the proper amount in the cap. The larger cap used more detergent and so the same bottle of detergent would no longer last as long as before. It is likely that the cap had been made larger to have consumers use more detergent, thereby increasing sales.

6. An ad for a well-known model of a car showed the apparent price of $6,910 in very large print. The small print said the price was $21,914. The $6,910 was actually a *discount* off what was claimed to be the regular price. The small print also indicated that the car was an "executive driven model"—in other words, a used car.[7]

7. A major telephone company wrote to its customers urging them to continue paying 95 cents a month for a service contract on the length of telephone wire entering the house. The letter warned customers that "if something goes wrong, you'll have to find the source of the problem yourself, and try to fix it yourself. Or pay someone else to do it."[8]

The fact is that the phone company had been required to send this letter by the Federal Communications Commission, in part because excessive charges to customers for this service brought the company an income of $210 million a year while only $30 million was actually spent on such service.

8. A free "Exercise Band" for strengthening arm muscles, stated to be "worth $3.50," was included in a box of cereal. The exerciser turned out to just a large rubber band.[9]

9. A bank advertised a number of "free" services, such as personalized checks, money orders, and traveler's checks, then declared "ALL FOR $3 A MONTH."[10]

10. An ad for an "INDOOR TV DISH ANTENNA FOR ONLY $10" showed a picture of what looked like a big satellite dish antenna. The product turned out to be a small, standard indoor antenna with an attached small, dish-shaped object, which had no electronic function whatsoever and was obviously designed to mislead people into thinking they were getting a real satellite dish antenna.[11]

11. A bank advertised a credit card for "people with poor credit." The small print told the prospective customer that it would have to be "secured" with a savings account that served as collateral for the credit. In other words, the customer would have to keep enough money in the savings account at all times to cover any purchases made with the credit card.[12]

12. A big "25" appeared on a container of flavored low-fat yogurt, giving the impression that there were only 25 calories in the container. Because of the large amount of sugar used in the flavors, eating the yogurt

in this container meant consuming 200 calories. The "25" referred only to the number of calories *per ounce* and there were 8 ounces of yogurt in the container.[13]

13. When opened, a box of "Chocolate-Flavored" candy, labelled as "The Natural Way to Lose Weight," contained a long paper package with large crimps on the ends that made it look much longer. The actual piece of candy inside the paper was about half the length of the box. The larger box led the purchaser to believe that there was a large piece of candy inside.[14]

14. A bag of cat food stated "25% MORE" in large letters. In small print it said "Than 8-LB. Bag." The bag happened to contain 10 pounds. Of course, *any* 10-pound bag would have "25% MORE" cat food than any 8-pound bag.[15]

15. A "Platinum Edition" of a credit card stated eight times that there was "no annual fee." In small print it said, "There is a charge only if you use your card."

Whenever anyone used the card there was a minimum charge of $1.75 a month, or $21 a year. The interest rate, charged from the date of purchase was an excessive 19.8%[16]

16. A customer of a well-known department store received a letter announcing a special one-day sale. When the customer went to the sale and selected some picture frames, he found that he could read an old price of $10 underneath the thin paper of a $14 label pasted on top. A frame marked $17 had the price of $11 underneath.[17]

Apparently, new labels had been put on for the sale with higher prices than before. The discounts brought the price to just about what they had been before the sale.

17. The contract for a "low-priced" rented car declared, ". . . rental rates are based on a calendar day." One would assume that a car rented in the afternoon and returned the next morning would be charged for at most one day. Not so. Once the car was kept past midnight it was in a new "calendar day" and the rental charge was then for *two full days.*[18]

18. A well-known tire company advertised its sale for radial tires with the phrase, "The tire America needs, the price America wants." In small print the ad indicated that this tire would no longer be sold after the inventory was gone. In other words, production of this tire had been discontinued *before* the sale—a fact that contradicted the glowing report that this was the "tire America needs."[19]

NOTES

1. *Consumer Reports* is published by Consumer's Union of the United States, 256 Washington Street, Mount Vernon, New York, 10553. Copies are available in most libraries.

2. *Consumer Reports* (November 1989): 739.

3. Ibid. (April 1989): 279.

4. Ibid. (November 1989): 739.

5. Ibid. (April 1988): Inside back cover.

6. Ibid. (July 1989): 483.

7. Ibid. (October 1989): 671.

8. Ibid.

9. Ibid. (May 1989): 347.

10. Ibid.

11. Ibid. (August 1989): 543.

12. Ibid.

13. Ibid (January 1989): 67.

14. Ibid.

15. Ibid. (September 1989): 603.

16. Ibid. (July 1988): 475.

17. Ibid. (February 1989): 127.

18. Ibid.

19. Ibid. (April 1989): 279.

QUESTIONS (*Discussion of these Questions Begins on Page 261.*)

From the consumer's point of view, how are the following ads defective, misleading, or exaggerated? Compare your answers with those at the back of the book.

1. "Knowledgeable people buy CALIGULO shirts because they have educated taste and a sense of value."

2.   LIVE PRACTICALLY RENT-FREE

Beautiful brick homes. Approximately $800 a month pays all.
2 HUGE playrooms plus extra bath*

from $99,990

(*optional)

3.   TO BE HEALTHY, TAKE UNITO VITAMINS

Take the vitamins that start where meals leave off. A single UNITO multiple vitamin tablet, taken once a day, supplies all the vitamins any adult or child normally needs. Even apparently well-balanced meals often don't contain enough vitamins. Take UNITO.

4.   "How smoothly WHITE KNIGHT'S rye whiskey
ends a day or begins an evening.

After a hard day, join the millions who welcome the calming hour, the twilight tradition of WHITE KNIGHT'S smooth taste. Whether you are where home fires burn or out with friends, you deserve to relax and savor America's most sought-after and satisfying whiskey."

5. "CONSUELO cigarettes give satisfying flavor . . . A friendly taste . . . No "filtered-out" flavor or dry taste. Never too weak . . . always just right."

6. "One menthol cigarette has to TASTE BEST—and that's SAHARA: 7 out of 10 smokers say SAHARA has just enough menthol—just enough."

7. A picture shows a lemon being squeezed toward a candle flame. The oils from the lemon catch fire. The copy reads:

"SEE" THE FLAVOR

Visible proof. Twisting peel of lemon or lime produces volatile mist—Gingero's natural essence—which candle flame ignites. Here is proof that these volatile oils are found in the peel of these natural, fresh fruits.

TASTE THE QUALITY OF GINGERO'S SODA

8. "TESTS OF FOUR LEADING PAIN RELIEVERS PROVED PRONTO STARTS FASTER TO EASE PAIN."

9. "Why pay an extra 19¢ for blades? ZIPPY blades are the finest blades made, yet cost 19¢ less."

10. "THREE TIMES MORE fresh beef protein in one can of PUP'S DOG FOOD than in any dry dog food, and most canned foods."

11. "It took 30 years to create today's EPITOME brand whiskey."

12. Find five advertising tricks in this ad:

Cover your exterior walls with
PURE-STONE
Goodbye to painting—ends all maintenance—cuts fuel bills 30%—
cools homes 25 degrees

NO MONEY DOWN

Any 4 sections only $299.95

13. "Highest quality at our lowest prices"

14. "Doctors approve REMIDEX for head colds"

15. "NOTHING LIKE IT IN THE HISTORY OF SHOW BUSINESS. CRITICS AND THE PUBLIC AGREE, THIS IS THE GREATEST ENTERTAINMENT OF ALL TIME."

12

The Big Picture

The many sources of error in reasoning described in this book may leave some people feeling much too skeptical about the body of knowledge that we possess. They may wonder how much of it is really true. Such an attitude is not realistic, because we would never accomplish anything if every fact and conclusion had to be checked and verified before decisions were made. Fortunately, most of the thinking we do in solving everyday problems is very effective and needs no basic overhaul.

OUR EFFECTIVE EVERYDAY REASONING

Consider how effectively young children reason as they learn the very complex skill of communicating through speech. Many of the cute "errors" they make are actually correct deductions from observations. Children say "I goed home" instead of "I went home." Why do they say this? Reasoning inductively, they develop a correct generalized concept of a verb as a word describing an action. Later, with additional observations and inductive reasoning, they extend this to the generalization that words may indicate the present, past, or future. Further observation leads them to generalize that the past tense of a verb is often formed by adding an "ed" to it, as in want-wanted, help-helped, and jump-jumped. Then, using deductive reasoning correctly, they apply this self-learned principle to the word *go* by adding an "ed," and get "goed." This is an A-plus level of correct reasoning. And no one has to teach our three- and four-year-olds to think this way. It is an inborn skill that almost all of us possess.

The word *goed* is "wrong" only because the English language has many grammatical exceptions. Eventually, by additional observation and inductive reasoning, children learn to replace "goed" with "went." With similar reasoning they learn many hundreds of other grammatical exceptions, master different meanings for many different words, determine the meanings of idioms from their context, and overcome many other complexities of modern language. Such high-quality reasoning and learning is typical of the way almost all people learn to adapt to everyday life. And it is so habitual that we are not aware of the mental processes by which we do it.

We would be mentally paralyzed if every fact and conclusion in our reasoning had to be checked and verified. So, the challenging question "How do you know it's true?" is reserved for those special occasions, such as debates, or for times when contradictions develop. And occasionally, some original thinkers like Copernicus and Galileo ask questions about accepted "facts," and answer them, to make giant leaps in human knowledge.

TODAY'S WORLD OF ABSTRACTIONS

Ten thousand years ago our ancestors lived in small, isolated groups, facing problems that were very concrete and down-to-earth. They struggled directly with the forces of nature: getting enough food, finding adequate shelter, and staying alive in the face of many dangers.

In contrast, today we live in a world in which mastery of abstract concepts is essential in many professions and occupations—very different from those our prehistoric brethren had to manage. Think of the kinds of abstract problems an engineer solves to build a big bridge, or a doctor confronts when diagnosing an illness, or the manager of a business faces in bringing together hundreds of parts and organizing their assembly into a refrigerator. A poet creates abstract metaphors and a lawyer deals with many abstract ideas when planning his presentation in court. A teacher does the same when planning a lesson about the Civil War. And, as citizens in a democracy, we have to form judgments about very abstract policies, such as budgets, taxation, environment, education, peace, and war.

Today it is in this area of abstractions that facts often get very fuzzy, premises are easy to get wrong, and we arrive at incorrect conclusions that are counterproductive.

We obtain this abstract knowledge from a host of communication sources that bring us indirect information about events far away or data observed by other people, perhaps reprocessed by still others. We get much of our abstract information from teachers at school. We read books, newspapers, and magazines that are loaded with abstractions. All sorts of subliminal messages come to us from movies and television. And now the information revolution is exploding with ever more powerful computers and increasingly abstract information.

The consequences of some reasoning errors today tend to be more dangerous and costly. The mistaken judgment at the Three Mile Island nuclear plant cost a billion dollars. An incorrect navigational judgment in steering the Exxon oil tanker *Valdez* through Alaskan waters produced immense environmental damage that cost two billion dollars for a partial clean up. A wrong judgment by the commander of a nuclear submarine could send off a volley of missiles that might start a world war.

Skill in abstract thinking, the base for "critical thinking," is therefore essential for adaptation to today's world. We need such skills to solve the many new problems in our modern world.

THE VITAL ROLE OF THE OPEN MIND

If this book does nothing else, it warns us not to be absolutely certain about our facts and conclusions. The main corrective is to have an open mind that can alert us to indications that we are wrong. We smell mental trouble when exceptions and contradictions appear. We think something should happen and it doesn't; or we "know" that something should not happen, and it does. Or someone disagrees sharply with a strong opinion we have. Then we need to think long and hard about why these differences have occurred. Such contradictions tell us that facts or conclusions may be wrong. Then we have to trouble-shoot to locate the flaws that obstruct reasoning and problem solving.

There is a vital role in society for the constructive gadfly who challenges facts, conclusions, or opinions that the rest of us take for granted. The probers and questioners may be right, or perhaps there is some germ of truth in what they say that may cause us to modify what we think and do.

However, some people carry the role of gadfly to an extreme by challenging every fact or accepted generalization. They delight in tripping us up to show how smart they are. They abuse and trivialize the vital question "How do you know?" until it blocks objective analysis.

We have much to learn from the methods of science, which have been so successful in giving us new knowledge. Science has taught us the importance of objectivity in gathering, checking, and verifying facts, and drawing conclusions. It has given us tools that help us determine the truth or falsity of facts and conclusions. Science also reinforces respect for the truth and contempt for cheating and dishonesty. These methods and attitudes contribute to human knowledge and to our ability to solve the difficult problems we face.

REMEMBER THESE BASIC PRINCIPLES

An open mind is the heart of clear thinking. Open-minded people know these important principles:

• Facts, especially generalized facts, should not be considered true until adequately checked and verified, preferably by many people.

• STOP, LOOK, and LISTEN whenever contradictions are encountered that indicate wrong or fuzzy facts or flawed reasoning.

• Mindsets often put blinders on our thinking and obstruct problem solving.

• Accurate communication by means of the written or spoken word is not easy. We must be alert to the many ways that wrong messages are being sent or received because of improper use of language or semantic confusion.

• Rational thought processes can go astray because of wrong or fuzzy facts or premises, overgeneralization, jumping to conclusions, and illogical or circular reasoning.

• Many people or groups try to influence our opinions and actions by card-stacking facts, making emotional appeals not founded on facts, as well as using subliminal messages and other techniques described in this book.

• History teaches us to be "tolerant" of contrary opinions. There is usually some truth in an opposing viewpoint. Our task is to find points of agreement and use them constructively to solve social and political problems cooperatively.

Five billion people on earth believe in about half a dozen different major religions and hundreds of lesser ones. There are thousands of different cultures and backgrounds, each claiming some degree of superiority. In today's new kind of global community, solving the world's urgent problems of achieving peace and preserving the environment can only be accomplished by a constant effort to understand each other and to compromise when differences arise.

Clear thinking is essential if we are to achieve this vital goal.

Discussion of the Questions

CHAPTER 2

1. "To see the sun at noon, face south."

First, a caution: *Do not look at the sun directly.* Your eyes may be permanently damaged by doing so.

The sun is always seen at noon in the southern part of the sky only in those places in the Northern Hemisphere located north of latitude 23.5° N. Since all parts of the United States are north of that latitude, the above statement is true for the United States, Canada, and parts of Mexcio. It is also true for Europe, most of Asia, and some northern parts of Africa.

However, this statement is never true for people who live in the Southern Hemisphere south of latitude 23.5° S. These people have to look north to see the sun at noon.

At the equator the sun appears mainly overhead, but shifts position north or south with the seasons.

All of these effects occur because of the 23.5° tilt of the earth's axis, combined with the once-a-year revolution of the earth around the sun.

Moreover, several factors, such as use of daylight savings time, time zones and changes in the earth's velocity as it orbits the sun, all combine so that "true noon" (the moment when the sun reaches its highest point in the sky) rarely occurs exactly at 12 noon as shown by clocks. True noon—when the sun is highest in the sky—may occur as much as an hour and half before or after noon shown on clocks.

For that reason we rarely see the sun at clock-time noon directly south, but somewhat east or west of south.

One way to correct the statement would be to make the following revision: "In the United States the sun is always seen south of the observer when it is highest in the sky for the day."

2. If the statement refers to a ruler then, yes, "One foot is 12 inches long." But if the word *foot* refers to a human foot, then the statement is rarely true. So this is a very fuzzy fact, with confusion caused by two meanings of the word *foot*.

3. The mathematical statement "10 + 10 = 100" is correct in the "binary number system" in which the only digits used are 1 and 0. In our customary decimal number system with digits—1, 2, 3, 4, 5, 6, 7, 8, 9 and 0—the number ten is written as "10." This means "one ten in the tens place and 0." The number 11 means: "one ten and 1." The number 12 means "one ten and 2."

Similarly in the binary number system (with only 1 and 0 as digits):

Number in Binary System	Equivalent Number in Decimal System
1	1
10	2
11	3
100	4
101	5
110	6
111	7
1000	8

From this table it may be seen that in the binary system the sum of 10 (meaning 2 in the decimal system) and 10 (2 in the decimal system) does equal 100 (4 in the tens system).

4. The statement "14 + 14 = 33" is mathematically false in our customary number system based on ten. But it happens to be a true statement in a system based only on the digits 1, 2, 3, 4, and 0. In such a system the "base" is said to be five. What we call five is written as "10," not "5." In that number system "10" means: "one 5 plus 0." The number 6 is written as "11," meaning "one 5 and 1." The number 7 is written as a "12," meaning "one 5 and 2."

In the number system based on five, the number written as "14" means "one 5 and 4," equal in value to 9 in our customary decimal system. So "14 + 14" in the system based on five is the same as "9 + 9" in the decimal system, with a true value of 18.

How would we translate the number 18 (in our tens system) to a number in the system based on five? Make a table from 1 to 18 in the decimal system and write the equivalents for the number system based on five, as was done for the binary system in question 3 above. You will find that the number 18 in the decimal system is equivalent to 33 [three 5s (or 15) plus 3] in the number system based on five. So the statement "14 + 14 = 33" is correct in the number system based on five.

5. Bacteria and other one-celled organisms do not "die" in the same sense as do living things like cats and maple trees. If conditions are favorable for life, a bacterium grows; then through "fission" it divides to form two bacteria. Each of these organisms then repeats the process. This could go on for a very long time—theoretically, forever—so long as conditions for bacterial life remain suitable. In fact, this process has continued ever since the first bacterium appeared on earth more than a billion years ago.

When one bacterium divides to form two, it cannot be said to "die" in the usual sense of the word, because it continues life as a kind of identical twin.

One way to correct the original statement would be: "Complex, multicellular living things die after a period of time."

6. Reread the answer to question 1. The situation for this question is essentially the same. The only difference is that in this question we refer to the direction of the shadow of a pole cast by the sun's light instead of the direction in the sky in which the sun itself appears. These two directions are opposite each other.

A corrected statement would be: "In the United States, when the sun is highest in the sky, the shadow that a telephone pole casts points directly north."

7. To observers in the United States (and others north of latitude 23.5°N) the moon would appear to move slowly toward the right as the earth rotates. But, as was the case for question 1, this is not true for many locations in the Southern Hemisphere. (The word *approximate* is used for the latitude because the moon's orbit is not exactly in the same plane as that of the earth around the sun; it therefore usually appears somewhat higher or lower in the sky than the sun.)

Many people in the Southern Hemisphere have to face the northern region of the sky to see the moon, while people in the United States have to face the southern region. For that reason people in the Southern Hemisphere usually see the moon move to their left, not to their right, as we do.

It is difficult to specify how people near the equator would see the moon because of the plane of its orbit around the earth.

A corrected statement might be: "In the United States, an hour after we have looked at the moon it will appear to have moved to the right of where it was before."

8. First note that no temperature scale Fehrenheit (F) or Celsius (C) is indicated. It is likely that 150° F was meant because 150° C would be a temperature much higher than that of boiling water.

It is all a matter of the length of time for which a person is subjected to the temperature indicated. People can stay in saunas at that temperature for twenty minutes or more. Profuse sweating and cooling of the skin and blood by evaporation of the sweat prevents excessive body temperature and damage to the cells and organs of the body. Longer exposures to such high temperatures strain the heart, cause heart attacks, and could perhaps result in death.

The statement that "nobody can live" at 150° F needs to be modified, perhaps as follows: "No one can live at a temperature of 150° F for more than a relatively short time."

9. Roots of plants grow in a generally downward direction, but they also spread outward. In some plants the roots tend to spread mainly sideward once the roots have grown down into the soil. There are also some forms of plant life, such as algae, that do not have roots.

A qualifying word, such as *generally,* or *mainly,* might be included to make the statement more accurate, perhaps like this: "For plants with roots the main direction of root growth is downward."

10. Some birds, such as penguins and ostriches, have wings but no longer fly, though they probably flew at some point in their evolution. They evolved with the process of "natural selection" under circumstances that made flying less essential, thereby favoring other abilities such as swimming or running. As a result, both of these animals have lost the ability to fly. A qualifying word is needed, such as *most* birds.

A corrected statement might read: "All birds have wings, and most birds can use them for flying."

11. Some fish can move about on land, using their fins as flippers to propel themselves forward. One reason for doing so is to find an improved environment, perhaps another lake. However, such fish cannot survive for long periods of time out of the water.

An improved statement might read: "Fish live in water, but can sometimes move about on land, temporarily out of the water.

12. There are numerous instances of businesses that have installed computers only to find that this reduces their efficiency. A qualifying word

is needed: "The use of computers improves the efficiency of operation of many businesses."

13. "I exist" would seem to be a fact that cannot be challenged. But some philosophers have argued that only our *ideas* have reality. For all we know, our observations and experiences might be the computerized result of some other being's programming. Aside from that unusual philosophical conjecture, the statement "I exist" is as close to an absolutely true fact as one can get.

CHAPTER 3

1. Chapter 7, "Astrology: A Case Study in Defective Reasoning," details the theoretical basis of astrology and the lack of objective evidence for it. The chapter shows that astrology is not essentially different from the ancient beliefs in the magical effects produced by various gods, witches, wizards, elves, and the like.

An illusion that astrology has a factual basis is given by the intricate calculations for the positions of various constellations, the sun, the moon, and the planets in our solar system. After all, these are astronomical facts and therefore "scientific." But they have nothing to do with astrologers' predictions about human personalities and events.

Although astrologers will not admit it, by adopting the ancient system of astrology, with insignificant modifications, they are also adopting the theoretical basis of ancient astrology, namely, magical effects not explainable by objective evidence.

2. Astrologers do not even try to explain how planets and stars might exert their purported effects on people. They hope that scientists will discover it for them.

3. To provide objective evidence for the truth of any astrological prediction about personality and human events, astrologers would have to design carefully controlled experiments. This is a very difficult and costly thing to do for subjective statements like "Today is a favorable time for financial transactions." Some of these difficulties are discussed in chapter 7.

An experiment would have to provide statistical evidence that "today" is a better day for financial transactions than yesterday or most other days. It is also necessary to pin down exactly what is meant by "favorable time for financial transactions." How does one know at the end of the average day whether it was "favorable" or not? This vague term must be demonstrably applicable for people born on the days specified in the horoscope and not for any other persons. If, on the average, the percentage of people who had "favorable" days is the same, regardless of date of birth, what's the point of the prediction?

Astrologers do not undertake such objective experiments. And qualified scientists feel they have better things to do than disprove superstitions based on magical influences. So nobody does it, and astrologers are able to make unchallenged claims that seem convincing to many people.

4. One major common superstition is the widespread belief in "bad luck" or "good luck." Accidents and good fortune are bound to happen to some people. Somebody has to win every lottery. The laws of probability tell us that there are going to be runs of good cards or bad cards for individuals but that these average out over time.

However, when a run of "good luck" occurs for some people, they tend to attribute it to special circumstances and supernatural help that apply only to them. If they had "bad luck" they attribute it to some evil being that has it in for them. In either case they are relying on magical influences.

A related superstition is the belief in "fate," as though a supernatural being predetermines each person's life. Such a view is not much different than belief in magical influences. It is often an excuse for doing nothing to try to change one's circumstances and so-called fate.

Other superstitions of a simpler nature, such as the belief that breaking a mirror brings bad luck, or throwing salt over one's shoulder to ward off evil influences, are remnants of ancient beliefs in magical influences.

5. Burning of gasoline in the engine of a car is the main cause for its motion. When ignited in the cylinders gasoline burns, causing heat, expansion of gases, and high pressure, which, in turn, causes the pistons to move.

Turning the ignition key to start the car causes an electrical circuit to be completed, allows electric current to flow from the battery to an electric motor (the starter) that causes the crankshaft to rotate and puts the engine into automatic operation.

Stepping on the brakes causes a friction material to tighten against a metal disk or cylinder on the wheels. The greatly increased friction causes the wheel, and therefore the car, to lose speed quickly and come to a stop.

There are many other cause-and-effect relationships in the operation of a car.

6. Solid objects, like bread, hold together because their molecules attract each other. When a knife cuts solid food its sharp, wedge-shaped

edge causes the molecules to separate, breaking the bonds that hold them together, producing two pieces of the solid.

Turning on the switch for an electric light "completes the circuit" and thereby allows electric current to flow in the lamp bulb. The current causes the filament of the bulb to be heated to a high temperature and this, in turn, causes the filament to produce light.

Pulling on the door of the refrigerator causes it to open. Pushing the door causes it to close. Magnetic strips around the inside rim of the door cause it to be held tightly when closed to prevent motion of air into or out of the refrigerator.

A similar cause-and-effect analysis can be made for every device in the home.

7. *Smallpox,* a deadly disease caused by a germ, has been eliminated from the earth by vaccinating millions of people. The injected smallpox vaccine causes the production of cells in the body which are able to find and destroy smallpox germs. This results in long-lasting immunity against smallpox.

Typhhoid fever is caused by germs in polluted water. Chlorinating water supplies causes typhoid and other germs to die and thereby prevents diseases that would otherwise be caused by contaminated water.

Acquired Immune Deficiency Symdrome (AIDS) is caused by a virus that must enter the bloodstream to produce the disease. This occurs mainly in the following ways: specific sexual activities, use of dirty injection needles by drug addicts, or transfusion of infected blood.

Knowing the cause of the disease and the various ways the AIDS virus may enter the bloodstream makes it possible to take preventive measures. Many of the major preventive measures are obvious now that we know the cause of AIDS: (a) safer sexual practices, such as abstinence, monogamous relationships, or use of condoms; (b) eliminating the use of contaminated needles by drug addicts; and (c) testing donated blood for the virus.

8. Certainly, the tree has a lot to do with the crash. If it had not been in the way, the car might just have come to a bumpy stop off the road. The tree is not the "primary cause," but a secondary or "contributory cause."

The primary cause of the accident is the drunkenness of the driver, which caused him to be unable to control the car properly, which, in turn, caused him to turn the steering wheel erratically. His poor steering then caused the car to drive off the road and collide with a big, hard-to-move tree (or anything else) that just happened to be in the way.

CHAPTER 4

1. The truck loaded with sand could be moved directly under the girl's window. She can then jump safely onto the sand.

Note that we need to know facts from experience to reason correctly in this case. A shorter fall to the truck is safer than a long fall to the ground. Loose sand absorbs the shock of a fall.

We also need a little imagination and some intuition to put two and two together in a logical way, to understand that moving the truck loaded with sand could cushion the girl's fall. Without this creative ability the problem could not be solved.

2. Study each sequence carefully. Note the relationships between the numbers or letters. Do the numbers increase or decrease, or both? Do they alternate in some way? Try taking the differences between them, or the sums.

(a) The sequence 2, 4, 6, 8, 10 . . . obviously continues with 12, 14, 16. Each number is two more than the one before.

(b) Take the differences between successive numbers. The difference between 1 and 2 is 1, between 2 and 4 is 2, between 4 and 7 is 3, between 7 and 11 is 4. The rule then seems to be: Each successive number is increased by one more than before. Because the last increase (between 7 and 11) was 4, add 5 to 11 to arrive at the next number, which is 16. The sequence is 1, 2, 4, 7, 11, 16, 22 . . .

(c) We would expect c to follow a and b in the alphabet, but it seems to have been skipped. The letters d and e follow, then f is skipped. The sequence continues with g, h, and i is missing; j and k are there. So the rule is: Write two letters of the alphabet, then skip the next.

(d) The numbers go forward in sequence, while the letters that follow each number go backward from z, y, z. So the sequence is

$$1, Z, 2, Y, 3, X, 4, W, 5, V, 6. . . .$$

(e) The pattern is 1, 2, 3 / 1,1, 2,2, 3,3, / 1,1,1, 2,2,2, 3,3,3 / 1,1,1,1, 2,2,2,2, 3,3,3,3, ...

(f) 5, 3, 1 / 6, 4, 2 / 7, 5, 3 / 8, 6, 4. . . .

(g) The number 3 is followed by the third letter of the alphabet, 4 is followed by the fourth letter of the alphabet, and so on. The sequence is: 3, c, 4, d, 5, e, 6, f, 7, g. . . .

(h) Add 2 to 11 for the next number (13), then subtract 3 to get 10; add 4, then subtract 5; add 6, then subtract 7. The sequence is: 11, 13, 10, 14, 9, 15, 8, 16, 7, 17. . . .

(i) c, n, d, r / c, n, d, r / c, n, d, r. . . .

(j) Subtract 2, then add 6. Repeat for each number: 7, 5, 11, 9, 15, 13, 19, 17, 23. . . .

(k) This is a nasty one. First a consonant, then a vowel; consonant, vowel, etc. b, a, r, e, f, i, n, o, t, u, p, e, b, a, z, o . . . . Any consonant or vowel may be chosen.

(l) This is the important Fibomacci series. Each number is the sum of the two that precede it: 1, 1, 2, 3, 5, 8, 13, 21, 34, 55. . . .

(m) Each group of four numbers is repeated in the next group, but with each digit increased by one: 9, 6, 4, 3 / 10, 7, 5, 4 / 11, 8, 6, 5. . . .

(n) Each successive number is the sum of all the previous numbers: 1, 2, 3, 6, 12, 24, 48, 96, 192. . . .

(o) After the letter a, skip no letter. After the letter b, skip one letter. After d, skip two letters, and so on. The sequence is: a, b, d, g, k, p, v. . . .

3. We are informed that all the labels are wrong and must be switched to the correct bags. Therefore bag A, labeled "Apples and Oranges," could not contain both apples and oranges. It must hold either apples or oranges. Because we pulled out an orange, the correct label for bag A is "Oranges." That leaves the labels "Apples" and "Apples and Oranges" for the other two bags.

Bag B, wrongly labelled "Apples," cannot contain only apples. It cannot contain only oranges because bag A has already been identified as containing only oranges. So the only label available for bag B is "Apples and Oranges."

There is one label left: "Apples." So bag C contains apples.

Note the use of *contradiction* to determine which of two alternatives is incorrect. This is a major tool in reasoning. Recall how the answer to the question "Where is Khrushchev?" produced a contradiction during the incident at the Arctic missile base and ruled out dots on the radar screen as meaning "Missiles coming our way from Russia."

4. Mr. Cook can't be the cook, because none of the men have jobs like their names. He is either the tailor or the baker. Because the baker answered Mr. Cook by saying "correct," it follows that Mr. Cook is not the baker. There's only one occupation left for Mr. Cook: tailor.

That leaves the occupations of cook and baker for Mr. Baker and Mr. Taylor. Mr. Baker can't be the baker, so he must be the cook, which means that Mr. Taylor is the baker.

5. Al looked at Beth and Carl. Neither had a black mark. Ms. Brady had said, "At least one of you will have a black mark." Therefore, he deduced that the black mark must be on his own forehead.

6. Al and Carl have been marked, but not Beth. Carl looked at the other two, saw Al had a mark and Beth had none. He then reasoned: "Either I have a black mark or I don't. Suppose I don't. Then Al, looking at Beth and me, would see no black marks. He would then know that he must be the only one with a black mark. But he hasn't said so. Therefore, my assumption that I don't have a black mark is probably wrong. I think I do have one."

So Carl announces that he thinks he has a black mark.

Note that, in this situation, Carl is not absolutely certain of his answer. His reasoning assumes that Al is thinking the same way that he is, and at about the same rate. Carl's decision, therefore, depends on Al's ability to reason properly.

Because the experiment was done in an "advanced high school science class," his assumption is probably correct. If the experiment had been done in a third grade class, for example, it is unlikely that the younger children would have been able to figure out the correct answer.

7. Ms. Brady had put black marks on the foreheads of all three students. Each of the three saw that the other two had black marks. Beth thought to herself, "Suppose I have no black mark. That would be exactly like the previous situation. In that case, it took Carl a short time to figure out that he had no black mark because neither Al nor I had said we had a mark. I'll wait a while longer. If nobody says anything, it is likely that I am wrong in assuming that I have no mark. Then I'll be pretty sure that I do have a black mark."

After a while, Beth announced that she had a black mark. Al and Carl said they also had figured out the problem, but had waited a bit longer than Beth did to announce the answer.

8. The statement that all Cretans are liars was made by a Cretan. So the statement must be a lie if "All Cretans are liars." If so, then Cretans tell the truth. But in that case the statement "All Cretans are liars" is true and we are back where we started. The reasoning becomes an endless cycle of true, false, true, false.

Such a self-contradictory statement is called *paradox*. The paradox arises from misuse of the word *all.* In real life, not all Cretans are liars all the time. Most probably lie some of the time, but only a few lie all the time.

CHAPTER 5

1. The pronoun "them," meaning amebas, is overused. It occurs five times in this short passage. The word *amebas* is used only once. In the second sentence, "them" seems to refer to amebas, but could also refer to "small plants."

Most important, however, is the confusion caused by different ideas being out of proper sequence. There are two main groups of ideas: how amebas are found and cultured, and how to observe them. Read the original passage again. Note how the two groups of ideas are jumbled together. It is best to combine the ideas that belong together, giving each group its own paragraph.

When the ideas are reorganized, the passage can be much clearer as follows:

> Amebas are tiny animals that live on small plants in ponds, often in the mud at the bottom. Scoop up some pond mud and use it to culture amebas in a jar. Allow a week for them to develop before experiments are performed.
>
> To study these tiny creatures, use a microscope with a magnification of about 100.

2(a) "Unique" means "the only one of its kind." How can something be *more* unique if it's the only one of its kind? In addition, the phrase "of all time" is too general and could be construed to imply all of human history. A more accurate statement would be: "Babe Ruth was one of the most outstanding players in baseball history."

(b) "In trouble" is too indefinite. Also, which are diseased, the beetles or the trees? Perhaps there is no disease at all, but the beetles are eating the leaves. A more accurate statement would be: "You can see that the trees here are infested by beetles."

3(a) It is not possible to prove who are the "most warmhearted in the world." Warmheartedness is an abstract quality that cannot be measured. Also, this quality undoubtedly varies widely among the millions of people in any nation. An improved version might be: "Americans are a warmhearted people." Even this statement is open to question. Is it a fact? How does one measure warmheartedness in general?

(b) The views of voters in any district are bound to differ because their interests and attitudes are different. To support *all* the proposals that *everyone* favors is impossible. Candidate Parker is clearly making exaggerated promises in order to get elected.

(c) The statement "All generalities are false" is a generality, too. So, if the statement is true, it follows that the generality it states is false. It is a paradox, self-contradictory, and useless for the purposes of reasoning.

(d) Are we interested in when Eva made the statement or when she will let us know? A better question would be: "Did Eva say when she would let us know?" Or, "When did Eva tell us that she would let us know?"

4. If the subject being debated is "noncontroversial," people will agree about it. Then what's the purpose of the debate?

5. *Plastic glasses:* Containers that hold liquids to drink can be made of a number of materials. Originally those made of glass were called "glasses" to distinguish them from those made of china, ceramic material, or metal. Then hard plastic began to replace some of the uses of glass, so we now have "plastic glasses."

Eyeglasses once were formerly made of glass and therefore are known as "glasses." Today, many "glasses" used to improve eyesight are made of plastic.

Alone together: "Alone" implies one person with nobody else around. The expression makes sense, however, if two people are considered as a couple "alone," with no one else around.

Guest host: A guest is someone who is invited. A host is someone who does the inviting. How can one person be both? It's possible if someone is invited to serve as host to others in the host's absence. The phrase is used primarily on television programs.

Cruel kindness: "Kindness" and "cruelty" have opposite meanings, so the expression contradicts itself. But it is possible for a person to act in a manner that seems kind when in reality it is intended to be the opposite. For example, suppose a drug pusher offers to give a little boy some pills. The boy may think the gift is generous and therefore a "kindness," but the pusher's intention is cruel—to create another drug addict.

Thundering silence: Thunder is loud. A thundering silence would therefore be a loud silence, a contradiction. If silence occurs at a moment when we expect noise, however, the silence stands out in such sharp contrast that it highlights the meaning of silence. For example, if absolutely no applause follows a speech or a performance, those present might notice the silence more than if it were the loud noise of applause.

6. These headlines illustrate special meanings for words in special fields. They become clear when the news story is read.

(a) Three players were tied in the Masters Golf Tournament. Sixty players qualified to continue playing.

(b) A 27-story addition is to be built above an existing structure having nine stories, so it's "Base Plus 27." "Piggyback" refers to the fact that one structure will be built on the other. The site is Madison Avenue in New York City.

(c) "Indy Brat" is the nickname of a racecar driver. He qualified to start in a famous race called the Indianapolis 500.

(d) Curtis Strange, a golfer playing in a tournament, tied his opponent's score at the end of 18 holes of play, the usual end of the game. To break the tie, the golfers continued playing until Mr. Strange beat his opponent's score for a hole, and the game ended immediately in "sudden death" for his opponent.

(e) A baseball team, the Mets, has some new young pitchers. The team depends on their pitching arms to win games. The team had a similar situation the previous year.

(f) Razor Shines, a minor-league baseball player, was finally sent to a major-league team, where he did well.

(g) Chili Davis, a baseball player, has been hitting well despite the handicap of blustery winds at Candlestick Park, where his team plays its home games.

(h) The Birmingham Stallions, a football team, beat the Orlando Renegades by the wide margin of 34 to 10.

(i) Albany, the capital of New York State, is where the state legislature meets. The word *Albany* is often used in New York to mean "state government" or "the state legislature." A tape often marks the end of a race. The headline refers to the fact that the legislative session is reaching its end. Legislators are therefore "straining" to end the session, or reach the tape.

(j) The golfers Fred Couples and Curtis Strange were tied in a tournament.

CHAPTER 6

1. The contradiction in the sentence involves the meaning of words. The commonly accepted definition of "breakfast" is "the first meal of the day." Therefore, a meal that is eaten after lunch can no longer be considered breakfast.

2. The reasoning can be stated as a syllogism:

Premise 1: MacGregor is a Scotsman.

Premise 2. Scotsmen are stingy.

Conclusion: Therefore, MacGregor is stingy.

The conclusion is correctly obtained from the premises. However, Premise 2 is certainly not true for *all* Scotsmen, and probably not true for most of them (or for any other group). At any rate, merely stating the premises does not make them true.

The overgeneralization in premise 2 expresses a prejudice against all the Scottish. The prejudice is also revealed by the use of the word *stingy,* which is generally regarded as a bad quality. Perhaps most Scots are frugal because they don't believe in wasting resources.

3. Johnny thinks he knows that "oil" is a good lubricant for machinery. But different kinds of oil have different properties. Only some kinds can be used for lubrication. Salad oil, although an oil, does not have the properties needed for lubrication. It hardens and gums up mechanisms. That's why it ruined the phonograph.

Johnny's general premise about oil is wrong. He assumes that *all* oils lubricate. Many do not. His mistake stems from a false analogy. The liquid used to lubricate machinery is "oil," but it does not follow that salad oil will do the same job as lubricating oil.

4. Mrs. Bunting has jumped to a conclusion. At best, the evidence might support a "maybe" or "perhaps" kind of statement. Based on the evidence she has, Mrs. Bunting might say, "I do hope this doesn't mean that the Fialco boy will be acting up like the other one."

We might also push this reasoning one step further and ask Mrs. Bunting how she knows that the Putnam boy is nasty. The evidence here may be just as flimsy.

5. Many old refrigerators use more electricity than new ones, making them much costlier to operate over the years. Money saved by not buying a new refrigerator generally means much more money wasted in large electric bills.

The issue can only be determined from dollars-and-cents comparisons of prices of refrigerators and savings in electricity, not through the use of a proverb. An efficient new machine costing $100 more to purchase might save $1,000 in electricity in ten years and would therefore be worth buying now. A proper judgment cannot be made without accurate facts.

6. It is almost impossible to be sure of what people will do in the future. The opinion about Pickering probably was formed by jumping to conclusions and overgeneralizing about events that have not yet occurred. The statement is really only an expression of hope.

The proverb about a "new broom" sweeping clean is a poor analogy. It isn't evidence at all. A new broom may be used to do a better job of sweeping a dusty room, but what does that have to do with the way a new president of a company might behave?

7. This statement is an example of an overgeneralization. The characteristic of smiling and slapping backs may or may not mask an untrustworthy person. Most people probably mean it when they smile. They are just nice, happy, friendly people. The backslapper should be given a chance to demonstrate whether he is putting on a show or really means it.

"I wonder what he's after" implies an opinion that people are only friendly if they have something to gain. This opinion may reflect the ethical values of the person making the statement. Perhaps that person doesn't smile and slap people on the back unless he wants something from them.

8. "Conclusive proof" requires more than circumstantial evidence. If a number of people had seen Tucker commit the holdup, that would be better evidence, and closer to proof. The kind of flimsy, indirect evidence presented here merely arouses suspicion about the possible guilt of the accused. There have been many instances in which such circumstantial evidence resulted in convictions that were later found to be mistaken.

9. Use of the expression "unnecessary government control" indicates circular reasoning. "Unnecessary" means "not needed" and, therefore, by definition, of no use. By circular reasoning, anything said about it thereafter is automatically considered bad, because it is unnecessary.

The statement about "unnecessary government control" is then applied to *any* government control—an overgeneralization. Some degree of government regulation will probably always be necessary in our complex society. The questions really are "What kind?" and "How much?"

The expression "proving for over a hundred years" is an exaggeration. There may be evidence, but hardly proof, to support such a complex statement.

This is not an "either-or" type of situation. Each type of government action should be examined on its own merits.

10. This is an example of circular reasoning. The question is avoided by saying, in effect, "A cow gives milk because a cow is supposed to give milk."

In reality, a cow gives milk to its calves because "hormones," chemical substances produced by its body, stimulate production of milk as food for its newborn calves who would otherwise die. Of course, this is only a partial answer because one can always seek deeper causes with questions like "What causes the hormones to be produced?"

Although this answer is not the whole story, at least it has the virtue of providing some new information that circular reasoning evades.

11. "Too much" implies "not good." So the statement is a form of circular reasoning, which says, in effect, "An amount of freedom that is not good for people is not good for people."

12. The statement that the same policies are followed, if true, is evidence, not proof. A man could completely support the policies of a group and yet not be a member of that group. And is it true that Pemberton follows the ABC party policies "right down the line"? What is the evidence?

The fact that Pemberton seems to do what members of the ABC party do is significant. People might suspect that Pemberton is a member, but that is far from certain.

13. There is a clear contradiction in the statement that "he *never* gives any money to charity, and when he does. . . ." Peck is damned if he does and damed if he doesn't. If he gives money to charity and does it for show, he must have given a lot. Therefore, how can he be a skinflint?

Also, it may not be true that he gives money because he wants more insurance business. This inference is made with little or no evidence.

This may be a case of emotions getting in the way of clear thinking. The person making the statement may just be envious of Peck.

14. This is an emotional rather than a reasoned statement. "I don't care what anyone says" implies that calmer people have advised him not to let his anger get out of hand, but he intends to pay no attention to their advice, even though that advice may be quite sound.

15. "Alternate" years means every other year or every two years. If a mayor is elected every two years for a four-year term, there soon would be two mayors in office. What a mess that would create.

CHAPTER 7

1. Fundamental errors of astrology:

(a) It considers the sun and moon as planets, a mistaken view that is unchanged from that of astrologers of 2,000 years ago.

(b) It assumes that the stars and constellations are fixed in space, a view that comes directly from ancient astrology. We know today that the positions of stars change with time and that the shapes of the constellations are therefore constantly being altered. Shouldn't these changes of position also change their supposed influences? Yet astrologers assume that the powers of the stars are the same as they were thought to be 2,000 years ago.

(c) Because of "precession of the equinoxes," the constellations of the zodiac, upon which astrology is based, have changed positions in the sky substantially since astrology began long ago. This should have changed the supposed influences of the constellations, but astrologers have paid no attention to this.

(d) The eleven calendar days lost in the mid-1700s, because of the acceptance of the Gregorian over the Julian calendar, changed the astrological signs for many people, yet astrologers have completely ignored this fact, and remain locked in the system set up by ancient astrologers.

2. Known forces or effects from stars and planets include: gravity, electrical and magnetic forces, radiation (visible light, ultraviolet, infrared, radio waves, x-rays, gamma rays, and high-speed nuclear particles). Such effects from outer space are very small, do not have any known effect on personality or the future, and reach the earth in a random way. There is no conceivable way by which any of these effects could selectively "know" the astrological signs of five billion individuals on Earth and determine their personalities or futures according to date of birth.

3. Today's astrologers borrowed the methods of making horoscopes from their ancient predecessors, who designed the system in accordance with their beliefs in the magical influences of the gods, with each supposedly controlling a different planet and exerting influence on Earth through them. By adopting this magic-based system of the ancients, today's astrologers

have, in effect, also adopted its basic assumptions about the magical influences of gods.

The claimed effects certainly have a magical quality. Who else but a god could influence every newborn baby to have a specific set of characteristics according to birthday, regardless of place of birth, genes supplied by parents, or social/cultural environment.

4. This is a subject for individual investigation.

5. This question requires an answer based on an actual daily horoscope.

6. Three examples of stretched analogies:

(a) Mars is red and so is blood shed in war. On this basis Mars is supposed to have the characteristics of aggressive males.

(b) Venus is a beautiful planet, so it is supposed to influence humans with respect to beauty, love, and related characteristics.

(c) Jupiter is a slow-moving planet in the sky. Therefore, its influence on humans is supposed to govern such qualities and conditions of life as maturity, comfort, wealth, wisdom, and similar characteristics of successful middle age.

There is no evidence that any of these characteristics actually apply to anyone in real life.

7. In the chart of triplicities the four "elements"—earth, air, fire, and water—are placed in a circle around the twelve astrological signs of the zodiac. If the word *fire* appears next to an astrological sign then a person under that sign is supposed to have a personality that has "fiery" characteristics. If the word *earth* is next to an astrological sign then people born under that sign are supposed to be influenced in a "down-to-earth" manner.

8. The claims made by astrologers for characteristics of people who have different astrological signs are usually so general that making a statistical survey to see if they are really true is extremely difficult. With so many claims pouring out of daily horoscopes, it is for all practical purposes a hopeless task to make an objeactive study.

Most of the claims are so subjective that asking people if they have the characteristics claimed by astrologers would not produce objective data.

The cost of such surveys is prohibitive.

CHAPTER 8

1(a) This is a prejudiced opinion based on a stereotype. Facts are missing or distorted. The statement implies that *all* foreigners are dirty and loudmouthed. Does the speaker know all of them, or most of them, or even more than a few? and does the speaker really know that everybody in town agrees with this view? Are British, Canadian, and Swedish foreigners included in this dislike, or only some very special groups?

Such a prejudice prevents people from getting to know foreigners personally in order to get the facts they need to change their opinions. Is it possible that the speaker would find some foreigners likable?

(b) This statement defines the relationship between dollars and cents, and so is a fact, not an opinion. It can be verified whenever a financial transaction takes place. If we assume that a dollar is worth two hundred cents, we are sure to have an argument every time we try to buy something.

(c) This opinion is an overgeneralization. It would be more reasonable if it did not contain the words *always* and *never*. Is the person receiving the advice rich, well-off, or poor? A wealthy person might be able to afford to risk some money in hopes of making a greater profit with stocks, while a poor person should be more concerned with the safety of the money.

(d) The person who makes this statement has a right to hold that opinion, but should apply it with care. Although the word *all* is not used, it is implied that all cities are crowded and dirty. Many are not. Few cities are completely dirty; most have some clean, pleasant sections. Furthermore, crowds seem lively and exciting to some people. Stores, concerts, museums, hospitals, movie theaters, and other attractive city facilities are more available. Other people prefer the quiet surroundings of the country; so the opinion depends to a great extend on individual values.

(e) Consumer services that rate cars by careful testing rarely single out one car that is worth much more for the money than all the rest. Such a car would have to meet too many different needs for too many different kinds of customers. Cars are usually rated by category, according to size and purpose.

The person making the statement probably means, "I think the Pronto is the best car for me."

(f) Does this opinion conform to the facts or not? It can be verified by checking, but a number of factors should be considered. Are we comparing apples and oranges pound for pound, item for item? Are we comparing big apples with little oranges, or vice versa?

Is this question asked in Florida during the winter, when oranges are plentiful and inexpensive, or in New York state in the fall, when apples are bountiful? Are the prices those of a city supermarket or a farmer's roadside stand?

(g) This is an opinion. Sam Dropleaf may have loaned his car to someone else, or the car may look like Sam's but actually belong to a tourist passing through town.

The statement is also objectionable because the word *must* implies no possibility of doubt. A better statement would be: "That looks like Sam Dropleaf's car."

2(a) Pete's opinion reveals an important defect in his personality. He doesn't like girls to reveal that they are brainy. Is that because he doesn't have a very good image of himself? His statement also shows a deep prejudice against women, based on a stereotype.

He implies that boys *in general* don't want a "brain" around. Can he really decide the question for other boys?

(b) Margie's letter and the columnist's reply make one laugh, but the opinion expressed in the reply may be harmful advice. In the first place, the reply states that "your only solution is. . . ." This rules out other possible solutions, and implies that the columnist is an expert on the subject and really knows what can and cannot be done to help people in such cases.

The flippant advice offered in the column could be harmful if it stopped Margie from seeking the right kind of professional help. Then, too, something may be wrong with Margie. Perhaps she is reacting in an abnormal way to occasional teeth-grinding by her husband. The wife who asks for help is confronted with a problem that is real to her. A reasonable reply might refer her to a doctor or dentist.

(c) Aside from the objectionable name-calling in the word *jerk,* the argument amounts to this: Anyone who doesn't pay a fare is not entitled to occupy a seat on a bus or subway. Therefore, people with young children—who do not pay fares—should hold the children on their laps.

Given its premises, the argument is logical. But the writer reveals a selfish and aggressive character and value system. The writer has no understanding of the difficulties facing a person who must take young children on a subway or bus.

(d) A lot of evidence would be needed to prove this opinion. One can think of contradicting evidence: for example, educational television is supported in part by federal funds. Federal scholarships and loans have made it possible for many young people to attend college. Some studies of Head Start, a federally funded program for preschool children, have shown that youngsters have benefited in later life. The effects of any educational program take years to evaluate.

So the all-or-nothing assertions should be limited. We should be suspicious of phrases like "has to be" and "cannot be improved."

3. An "average" wage is somewhere between the lowest and highest. If everybody was paid the average, there would be no lower or higher wages. Everybody would get the same wage.

The writer is illogical, and probably meant to specify a much higher minimum wage.

4. Are you really sure of your impressions based on the names? Did you get these impressions from personal experience or from what others have told you? Have you ever had the experience of meeting someone you thought you wouldn't like only to discover that your first impression, which was perhaps based on the person's name, was all wrong?

5. Selecting every tenth house on a street would not necessarily be a random sample, although it might serve for some statistical purposes. There might be a pattern to the way houses were constructed that could introduce special selection of a certain type of house or owner.

If the addresses of the houses are recorded with a computer, a list of randomized addresses could be obtained using a list of random numbers.

6. Calling on the telephone only during the daytime introduces a distorting factor because most people who work outside the home would be excluded.

Once a phone number has been selected at random, every effort should be made to reach the person with that phone number: at least several calls should be made at different times, after working hours as well as during the day, and on weekends if necessary.

CHAPTER 9

1. A stereotype is a generalized, unvarying opinion about characteristics thought to be shared by groups of people or categories of things. It is applied to all members of a group as though they are the same.

2. We acquire stereotypes throughout life from the opinions expressed by parents, friends, neighbors, and teachers, as well as from communications media such as television, movies, and newspapers.

Experiences under special circumstances also produce stereotypes. For example, there may be clashes between teenagers from two adjoining neighborhoods with very different cultures or economic and social circumstances. People in each neighborhood then attribute the bad attitudes, values, and actions of small groups of teenagers to *all* young people of similar background.

3. Stereotyped opinions become harmful prejudices if the people holding them are inflexible and unable to adjust ideas to accommodate new facts. Open-minded people readily change their opinions to correspond with new facts. In such cases the former opinions were essentially misconceptions rather than harmful prejudices.

4. It is impossible to know everything about everything in our complex world. We get a smattering of information about many different kinds of people and things. When making judgments, we do the best we can with our inadequate, missing-facts information. These opinions are the roots for the development of stereotypes.

5. Children develop stereotyped opinions from the books (or "comics") they may read. If such reading material portrays men and women in stereotyped roles, with the men always doing traditional "men's work" and women always portrayed as housewives, or just in occupations such as nursing, then boys and girls tend to develop stereotyped views about what men and women do. These stereotyped views then become role models for them.

Today, many authors of children's books are aware of this stereotyping effect and often portray men and women in a variety of roles. A woman may be pictured as a physician, and a man may be shown washing the dishes or cooking. A drawing of a group of children will now include some black or oriental faces, rather than all the youngsters being white.

Similar, but more powerful stereotyping occurs in television programming. For example, old "western" movies about cowboys and Indians, still seen on television, portray Indians as savages. Some more recent movies do present a more sympathetic view of Native Americans and do tend to dispel the negative image.

Blacks, formerly shown on television and in motion pictures only in stereotyped roles, are now usually shown living and acting the way whites do.

6. The answer to this question requires a personal list.

7. The answer to this question requires a personal list.

8. The answer to this question requires a personal list.

9. If a person is expected to have certain characteristics, or perform tasks at a certain level because he is a member of a stereotyped group, then the *expectation* itself is often transmitted to the individual by body language or manner of speaking. The responses by that person may then reinforce the stereotype.

For example, if a person is expected to be abrasive because he is a member of what is considered to be an abrasive national group, then an unfriendly attitude is likely to be transmitted to an individual in that group. The person prejudged to be abrasive is likely to respond in a similar unfriendly way, thereby "proving" abrasiveness for the group and reinforcing the stereotype.

10. An excellent way for people with different backgrounds to change stereotyped opinions of each other is to cooperate for a common, mutually advantageous goal. They get to know each other better as cooperative individuals. The bad stereotype is then contradicted and is thereby weakened.

Schools, television programs, movies, and books can play an important role in changing stereotyped opinions by showing positive images of other groups. Parental influence is also crucial.

11. Discrimination is a harmful act, caused by prejudice and directed against people of different background. These harmful acts may be established and enforced by laws or regulations *(de jure)*, or the result of acts by private institutions, groups, or individuals *(de facto)*.

12. Examples of discrimination by laws, regulations, or institutions:

(a) Zoning laws that require a large minimum acreage to build a home have the effect of excluding middle-class and poor people from living in various communities. This has the secondary effect of transferring the costs and social burdens for poverty, crime, and drugs to less affluent or poor areas that must then raise taxes from a much smaller tax base. This produces schools of poor quality. Since minority groups often have lower average incomes, the zoning laws serve to perpetuate segregation and discrimination.

(b) Laws in South Africa prohibit black people from residing in white areas, or even entering them without identification passes.

(c) In the United States, women were not allowed to vote until 1920.

Examples of discrimination by individuals or groups:

(a) The seller of a house, or a real estate agent, approached by a black couple to buy a house in a white area, gives an excuse not to show the house, or refers the couple to other areas.

(b) A woman who is an outstanding worker in a company is passed over for promotion, and a less competent man is given the post.

(c) A country club admits people only by a vote of the members. All women, people of foreign origin, nonwhites, or nonprotestants are consistently excluded by the prejudiced voting of the members.

13. (a) antilocution, (b) avoidance, (c) discrimination, (d) physical attack, (e) extermination

14. Three examples of prejudice in the United States leading to extermination:

(a) There was a widespread attitude among many whites in the 1800s that "the only good Indian is a dead Indian." In many areas bounties were given for killing Indians. The scalps of Indians were accepted by authorities as proof that an Indian had been killed. Payment of the bounty immediately followed.

(b) The Ku Klux Klan (KKK), a widespread terrorist organization that developed after the Civil War, lynched many blacks, often for trivial reasons. This terror played a major role in depriving blacks of their civil rights in many states of the South.

(c) In some areas of our nation it is dangerous for a black person to walk in a white neighborhood, or a white person to walk in a black neighborhood. Beatings and shootings often end in death.

CHAPTER 10

1(a) Words like *self-seeking, despicable, wasting, corruption, sharks,* and *infest,* appeal to the emotions through name-calling techniques.

(b) The statement is full of glittering generalities—phrases like "for the sake of future generations," "life, liberty, and the pursuit of happiness," and "in the name of our beloved country."

(c) Guilt by association ("seen eating dinner with Hopkins") and the wife-beating question ("How long have you been dealing with this known criminal?").

(d) On the one hand, the statement claims that the highway will cause people to come to town (but not to shop, only to choke the city). On the other hand, it claims that people will no longer stop in the city but will pass right through. These statements are contradictory.

(e) Name-calling and appeals to the emotions are indicated by "pious do-gooders," "slanderous," "mask," "hypocritical," "power-grabbing," "rascals." "Hard-working," and "honest" indicate a plain-folks technique in which the speaker tries to identify himself with the ordinary people in his audience.

2. This account of the game is strongly card-stacked in favor of the Tigers. According to the objective evidence of the box score, the Eagles played a far superior baseball game. They won 11 runs to 4. They had 16 hits to the Tigers' 5. The Tigers made 3 errors; the Eagles, none.

The report describes what the Tigers did but says nothing about the Eagles. If the Tigers had to wait for the game to start, so did the Eagles, who had the additional handicap of going into the game without much warmup, after rushing to get to the game.

Because the star hitter was struck by a pitched ball in the eighth inning (which meant that another man was put on first base), his absence from the game for only the ninth inning could have had little effect on the outcome, which was practically determined by that time.

The shortstop's stumble produced only one run. This had little effect on the final 11-to-4 score.

Note that the Tigers made four runs with only five hits. This is an indication that luck was with them in converting hits into runs.

Excuses are given for the Tigers at every turn: "As a result they got off to a slow start," and "A high wind made matters difficult for the Tigers." Did the wind stop blowing only when the Eagles were involved in plays?

3. An opinion on this question cannot be proved right or wrong. It depends on one's personal experiences and philosophy of life. No matter how many facts are gathered about life in the past, and life now, this question of which is "better" or "worse" cannot be settled to everyone's satisfaction. Inevitably, missing facts make the answer a matter of opinion.

Much depends on what circumstances of life are assumed. Is life better or worse, for rich or poor, city or country, living in peaceful or war-torn areas?

Then, too, it is impossible to know exactly how it felt to be living in the past. History books do not fully transmit the feelings of people who lived long ago. Diaries, autobiographies, and novels written at the time may be better sources but are still incomplete.

However, certain objective considerations indicate progress. For example, infant mortality is far lower and life expectancy has almost doubled. People also have many conveniences and comforts not available in the past, but only if one has the money to pay for them. And one wonders if the resulting pollution of the earth is too high a price to pay for conveniences.

CHAPTER 11

1. This ad flatters the reader. It suggests that anyone who buys Caligulo shirts is "knowledgeable." Are they any more "knowledgeable" than those who buy other brands? And what is an "educated" taste?

2. "From $99,990" means that this is the lowest price. Most of the houses are likely to cost more than that. Some builders have a habit of making certain essentials "optional." If you want the "option," the price of the house goes up considerably. It is wise to take the price of $99,990 with a grain of salt and investigate further.

Would this $99,990 house really have "2 HUGE playrooms plus extra bath"? Not likely. The asterisk (*) indicates that these are options and won't be available at the price given in the ad. What do these extra things cost?

A monthly operating cost of $800 is probably a low figure. Most people borrow mortgage money to buy a house and pay large interest on the money they borrow. Mortgage payments alone are likely to be far more than $800. Did the buyer pay cash, and therefore does not have a mortgage? When the ad says "approximately $800 a month pays all," what does "all" mean? Does it include costs of repairs, which are generally necessary?

There is a mere ten-dollar difference between $99,990 and $100,000. Why is the price listed as $99,990 instead of $100,000? People tend to pay more attention to the first digit of a number. At first glance, "$99,990" gives the impression that the house costs a lot less than $100,000—not just $10 less. For a similar reason, it is standard practice for prices to be set at $1.95 or $2.98 rather than $2 or $3. The consumer should make a habit of converting all such prices into the nearest whole dollar.

Note that "HUGE" appears in big letters for emphasis. In reality, how big are the "HUGE" playrooms?

3. Medical experience has shown that a person in normal health, who eats a balanced diet, needs no extra vitamins. Even if the meals for one day don't contain enough vitamins, the next day's meals usually supply them.

A prolonged vitamin deficiency will show up as a specific health problem. If a person feels well, there is no need to take precautions by consuming vitamins "just in case" something might be wrong. Some people take so many vitamins that illness may result.

If someone does not feel well, taking vitamins instead of visiting a doctor might be harmful. It would make more sense to visit a doctor first if there are signs of ill health, and to let the physician determine if vitamins would be helpful.

4. This mouthwatering ad tugs at the emotions. But certain essential facts are omitted. People who drink too much alcohol will have hangovers the next morning. For large numbers of people alcohol is a habit-forming drug: excessive use can result in hospitalization and often a wrecked family life. Nor is there any assurance that this particular whiskey is any better or worse at aiding relaxation than other brands.

5. This mouthwatering ad attempts to identify the cigarette with likable qualities. It is "friendly" and "satisfying." What's friendly about a product that is one of the major causes of deadly lung and heart disease?

Words like *never* and *always* hardly apply to everyone, all the time. How likely is it that the cigarette tastes "just right" even for most people?

6. "Taste best" is an exaggeration: one person's best taste in cigarettes may be another's worst.

The 7 out of 10 did not say they liked Saharan cigarettes best but merely that there is "just enough menthol." Does this have much to do with determining what is "best"?

There are many missing facts. Were Sahara cigarettes compared with other brands? If so, were the others specially selected for their bad taste? Should we trust the poll in the first place? Perhaps the copy writer made up the results and never took a poll.

Finally, polls taken by cigarette manufactures are often card-stacked because free cigarettes are given to people who are then asked to respond to questions. Most people cooperate in such situations and give favorable reports.

7. This is an example of a pseudoscientific ad. It depends for its effect on a so-called experiment that has no connection with the quality of the soda's flavor and does not prove what is implied. Lemon peels do have oily vapors that burn in a candle flame. But even so, Gingero soda could taste terrible.

All the worthless evidence (which is called "proof") applies only to the fact that lemon peels contain oil, and not at all to the soda. The word *proof* is used to build up an impression of scientific accuracy.

8. Here's another pseudoscientific ad. "Starts faster to ease pain" means little or nothing without information to judge how much faster. If it starts faster, does the pain-killing effect last as long as it does in other medications? Does it cost more? Is it better in any respect other than that of speed at starting pain relief?

9. What does "19¢ less" mean? Less than what? Is it 19 cents less for one blade or a dozen? And who decided that they are the "finest"? Perhaps they are only Zippy's finest.

10. The word *fresh* is misleading. If another company used unspoiled cooked meats that had more protein than PUP'S, that might well be a superior product.

Does PUP'S have more protein per pound, or per dollar? The protein content is compared with "dry" dog food, which would be lighter. It's not clear to what competing product PUP'S is being compared, and what the sentence really means.

"Three times more" is in large print, but "than any dry dog food" is in small print. The ad gives the impression that PUP'S has three times more protein than all other dog foods. But because it also claims to have more protein than "most canned foods," there must be some that have more than PUP'S, and perhaps cost less.

11. Does the ad mean that the whiskey was allowed to age for thirty years, or that the company has been in business and learning to make whiskey for thirty years? Actually, any whiskey that has been sold for that long could make the same claim, and there are many companies that have been in business longer.

12. Would all need for painting be eliminated? Won't windows and doors still have to be done? Would the fuel bill be 30 percent less on every house, or even on most houses? A 30 percent reduction in fuel bills because of the addition of stone walls is most unlikely, particularly when stone is known to conduct heat. This is a phony statistic.

Moreover, if the material is insulation, not stone, use of the name "Pure-Stone" is misleading.

"Cools homes 25 degrees" is another slippery number. Twenty-five degrees cooler than what? Under what conditions? Is it likely that stone walls could keep a house as cool as 70 degrees without air conditioning if it is 95 degrees outside? Perhaps it is 25 degrees cooler in the wintertime—and who would want that?

Beware of card-stacked phrases like "no money down." Too much is left unsaid. What isn't paid immediately generally has to be paid later.

Extra charges and interest costs would pile up. Much more money is usually paid over time if there is "no money down."

The cost is listed as $299.95 for four sections. How big is a section? Because size is not stated, the price means nothing. It is another slippery number.

Note the use of $299.95 instead of $300. By making the price 5 cents lower, the manufacturer hopes to mislead a buyer into thinking the price is $100 lower.

13. "Highest quality at OUR lowest prices" means little. The store with the highest prices in the country could truthfully make the same claim if it lowered its own very high prices by only a cent.

14. This is a pseudoscientific ad that overgeneralizes. There are thousands of doctors in this country. There are even people who claim to be doctors but who are not recognized as such. If two questionable doctors endorsed the medicine, the statement in the ad could be true but would still say nothing about the value of REMIDEX.

Did reputable doctors endorse it enthusiastically, or just by a shrug of the shoulder? Were they paid for their endorsements? Or was the statement simply made up?

15. This is an example of a fantabulous ad. Advertisers and the public have grown so accustomed to wild exaggerations and unprovable claims that it is quite common to see ads for dozens of shows, each of them the "greatest." Language tends to lose its meaning under such circumstances.

Index